# The C&O Canal Companion

A boatman and his children at Georgetown—journey's end.
*Photo courtesy National Park Service*

# The
# C&O CANAL
# Companion

## Mike High

### updated edition

The Johns Hopkins University Press
*Baltimore and London*

This book was originally brought to publication with the
generous assistance of the Laurence Hall Fowler Fund.

The Johns Hopkins University Press
2715 North Charles Street
Baltimore, Maryland 21218-4363
www.press.jhu.edu

Library of Congress Cataloging-in-Publication Data

High, Mike.
    The C & O Canal companion / Mike High.—Updated ed.
        p.   cm.
    Includes bibliographical references.
    ISBN 0-8018-6602-2 (pbk. : alk. paper)
    1. Chesapeake and Ohio Canal (Md. and Washington,
D.C.)—Guidebooks. I. Title: C and O Canal companion. II. Title:
Chesapeake and Ohio Canal companion. III. Title.

F187.C47 H54 2000
917.55´18—dc21                                                  00-059090


A catalog record for this book is available from the British Library.

# Contents

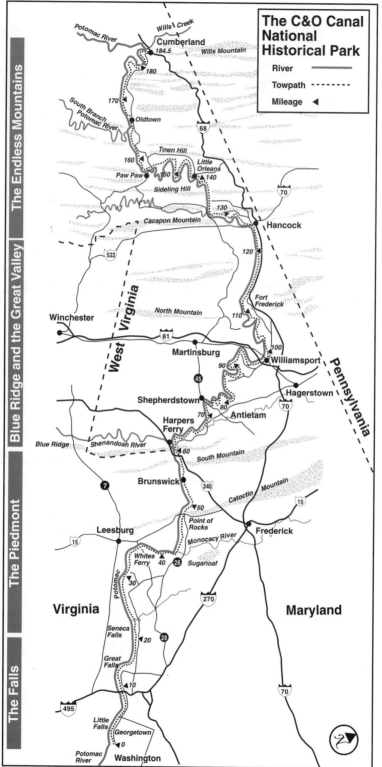

## The C&O Canal National Historical Park

| | |
|---|---|
| River | |
| Towpath | - - - - - |
| Mileage | ◄ |

Potomac River

Wills Creek

Cumberland
184.5

Wills Mountain

180

68

170

South Branch
Potomac River

Oldtown

Town Hill

160

Little
Orleans
▲140

150

Paw Paw

Sideling Hill

70

Cacapon Mountain

130

522

120

Hancock

Fort
Frederick

North Mountain

110

Winchester

81

100

Martinsburg

90

Williamsport

45

Hagerstown

Shepherdstown

80

70

70

Antietam

Harpers
Ferry

Blue Ridge

Shenandoah River

◄60

South Mountain

Brunswick

340

Catoctin Mountain

7

50

15

Point of
Rocks

Frederick

Leesburg

Monocacy River

15

Whites
Ferry ▲ 40

28

Sugarloaf

▼30

270

**Virginia**

**Maryland**

Seneca
Falls ◄ 20

28

Great
Falls

◄10

495

Little
Falls

Georgetown
◄ 0

Potomac
River

**Washington**

**West Virginia**

**Pennsylvania**

Potomac

# Preface

If I had to pick a time when this book began, I suppose it might have been one cold winter evening in 1990. It had been a very difficult year for me physically; I had lost 30 pounds in the space of a few weeks and was experiencing such severe leg pains that I had pretty much given up bicycling altogether. My boss and I drove up to Cumberland on a business trip in early December, and after dinner I wandered out of the hotel to find the terminus of the C&O Canal. I had ridden the canal as far as Antietam Creek, but the 115 miles between that aqueduct and Cumberland, the Queen City, were a mystery to me. I remember looking up at the stars twinkling in the freezing wind and thinking how wonderful it would be to be able to ride all the way up to that bare stretch of towpath coming into town.

As it happened, I was able to make that trip the very next September, and I have made my pilgrimage up the towpath every autumn since. Along the way, I've met dozens of individual cyclists, couples, and small groups who make the towpath ride a regular event. I did not know much about the history of the canal or the region when I took my first trip; few of the riders do. To tell the truth, you don't need to know those things to enjoy what may be the most delightful and varied greenway in America. Whizzing along through the quiet woodlands along the canal is a uniquely cathartic experience, a quite satisfactory experience in itself.

But as time went on, curiosity got the best of me. I began reading about the canal and the neighboring towns, and I realized that there were many more layers of history than I had ever imagined. It was not so much the C&O Canal itself that interested me—railroads had made the canal an anachronism by the day it opened in 1850. No, the canal is just a means to an end, a forested path through two and a half centuries of history.

I was delighted to make the acquaintance of "that vile fellow" Thomas Cresap, who lived on the Potomac frontier and who may have set the stage for the French and Indian War by convincing a cabal of powerful Virginians to form the Ohio Company. And then there was George Washington, whose fascination with the Potomac corridor not only led to the forerunner of the C&O Canal but also determined the placement of the federal city and a national armory. Cresap and Washington saw the river as a commercial network, and their vision was completed in the nineteenth century, as the C&O Canal tied together a string of gristmills, towns, ironworks, foundries, and rifleworks. The labor of building the canal provides yet another layer of history, as Irish and German immigrants toiled and fought with each other and the canal company. Finally comes the Civil War, when columns of soldiers crisscrossed the river and the canal and fought at places like Balls Bluff, Harpers Ferry, Antietam, Oldtown, and Cumberland.

I thought it would be interesting to tie all these stories together in one book. Of course, the book would have mile-by-mile notes on historical sites. But I did not want the reader to lose sight of the larger picture or be overwhelmed by the details. So I wrote separate sections that provide a chronological history of the region and a description of the working canal and the industries of the nineteenth century. These sections are cross-referenced with the mileage notes, so that you can connect specific locations with larger trends. The mileage notes are also internally cross-referenced, so that you can connect, for instance, J. E. B. Stuart's river crossing at McCoys Ferry with his escape across Whites Ford a few days later (*see* miles 110.2 *and* 38.7).

What I've learned from my research is that events along the canal were rarely isolated or random. Just as the canal connected and fostered many different enterprises, the Potomac shaped American history for over a century. It brought together Jefferson and Washington, John Mason and Benjamin Latrobe, J. E. B. Stuart and George McClellan, and even a Cresap or two. It seems an inevitable consequence of the river's design that we now have a national park that lets us travel the same path to the west that they traveled.

# Acknowledgments

In an endeavor as wide-ranging as this, the acknowledgments could easily make a book of its own. Among the many people who shared their time and steered me in the right direction on a number of arcane points, I would especially like to thank Eugene Scheel, Charles Jacobs, and John Frye. Susan Trail, of the National Park Service, was kind enough to make the Cultural Resources Center at park headquarters available to me, and she provided copies of many of the historical photographs for the book. Nancy Seferian, of Greencastle Graphics, was responsible for the arduous task of producing the trail maps from the U.S. Geological Survey maps. Among my fellow travelers, I would especially like to thank cyclists Brian Lekander and Paul Profeta, birdwatcher David Byrne, artist/architects Michael Gavula and Linda Heinrich, and pilot Mark Terry.

Unfortunately, I had not met John Phillips at the time of the first edition, but his detailed knowledge of the Potomac River in the Loudoun County area has been most informative and has caused me to revise the information on Harrisons Island (mile 34.3).

# A Note on Maps and Mileages

The trail maps in the Canal Guide are renderings based on topographical maps prepared by the U.S. Geological Survey, specifically four maps in their 1:100,000 scale series: Washington West, Frederick, Hagerstown, and Cumberland. The rendering of rivers and mountains is not precise enough to use for hiking or river navigation, but it will convey a sense of the terrain that determined the course of the canal.

The mileages were recorded on a cyclometer at $1/100$ths of a mile, rounded to the nearest tenth of a mile. For the most part, I found no more than $1/20$ of a mile variance from milepost to milepost. In those places where it appears that the marker may be misplaced, I have included a note in the text. Because of variations between cyclometers, I recommend that you track the distance from the nearest milepost if you are trying to locate a particular feature along the canal.

Because of the Potomac's winding course, it's not that useful to try to orient oneself by referring to the points of the compass. Instead, I have generally referred to the upstream and downstream directions of the canal and to its river side and berm side. (In American canal lingo, the "berm" is always the side of the canal opposite the towpath—see the *Oxford English Dictionary*'s helpful explication. With a few minor exceptions, the towpath for the C&O always ran along the river side of the canal, so the berm side of the canal was usually the inland side.)

# Historical
# Sketch

## The Potomac Frontier

The story of the Chesapeake and Ohio Canal's efforts to connect the eastern seaboard and the Midwest begins with the very earliest settlement of North America. While it soon became clear that the Potomac River was not a "Northwest Passage" to the Pacific Ocean, later generations hoped to follow it to the rich Ohio Valley, which had been discovered beyond the mountains. In 1748, prominent Virginians invested in the Ohio Company, which set about building a trade route up the Potomac and across the Appalachians to the Forks of the Ohio. This business venture put the British colonials squarely in the path of the French, who were entering the Ohio Valley from Canada. So it was first a very young George Washington and then British General Edward Braddock who followed the Potomac route to the French and Indian War. For all practical purposes, the Ohio Company had dissolved by the end of the border conflict, but the vision of a trade route to the Ohio was still championed by Virginians such as Thomas Jefferson and Washington.

------------------------------------------------------------

### Early Exploration and Settlement

The dream of finding a navigable inland route from the Atlantic dates back to the first permanent English settlement. The Virginia Company's instructions to the colonists who founded Jamestown directed them to search for "rivers that led to the north and west," rivers that might provide an easy passage to the Pacific Ocean. In the summer after that first "starving time," the terrible winter of 1607, John Smith took one of the colony's boats and sailed up into the

Chesapeake Bay. On his return journey, Smith sighted the mouth of the Potomac and brought his ship upriver until he encountered the first falls (Little Falls, miles 3.2–5.7), just above Rock Creek.

The falls effectively limited any westward movement for the remainder of the 1600s. In the meantime, the English colonists gradually extended their hold on the Tidewater region. The king created two major rivals out of the wide swath of land originally granted to the Virginia Company: Maryland in 1633 and Pennsylvania in 1681. These three colonies would fight over boundaries, canals, and railroads right into the twentieth century, and many of the disputes would involve the Potomac River valley.

One of the first expeditions to the west was led by Christoph von Graffenried in 1712. Von Graffenried was a minor Swiss nobleman who had charmed Queen Anne of England enough to receive the title of baron and grants of land in North Carolina and on the Potomac. Queen Anne's generosity was not entirely altruistic; she hoped to rid herself of several thousand German Palatines who were on the dole in camps around London. Unfortunately, Graffenried's first settlement at New Bern, North Carolina, was wiped out by a Tuscarora Indian attack, and only a last-minute change of heart kept the Indians from burning the baron at the stake. He then traveled up the Potomac to find a site for a new settlement, visiting Conoy Island near Point of Rocks (*see* mile 48.2). He was delighted with the fertile river islands, but after an exhilarating canoe ride back down the Potomac rapids, he found that his partners had abandoned him and sailed for Europe.

When settlers finally filtered into the Shenandoah Valley, it was not as part of any planned community or formal land grant. These were not newly arrived immigrants following the Potomac to the west through the Blue Ridge, but rather an influx of Germans and Scotch-Irish traveling down the great valley from eastern Pennsylvania in search of less expensive land. Their scattered valley farms presented a challenge not only to the Iroquois, who used the valley as a warrior's path to the south, but also to the vested interests of the English aristocrats who governed the colony of Virginia.

In fact, no one knew exactly who owned much of the Shenandoah Valley and the mountains beyond. The king had decreed that the Potomac River divided the colonies of Virginia and Maryland; but no one had determined which of the Potomac's branches was its source. A further complication dated back to 1649: Charles II, in exile, had promised several loyal followers the rights to that part of Virginia that lay between the "headwaters" of the Potomac and Rappahannock rivers. The grant had passed through their hands to Lord Fairfax, an absentee proprietor whose agents assiduously collected rent in the "Northern Neck" of Virginia. As more and more wagons began rolling down the Shenandoah Valley, it became imperative that the colony determine who had to pay whom for the right to set up a homestead.

Lord Fairfax and the colony of Virginia sent representatives to survey the Rappahannock and the Potomac in 1736 and again in 1746. The chief difficulty came at the major forks of both rivers, where they had to decide which fork was larger and thus the main course of the river. The representatives disagreed at the forks of the Rappahannock—predictably, Fairfax's men wanted to follow the southerly fork, thus encompassing as much terrain as possible within the bounds of the Fairfax land grant. However, when presented with the same dilemma at the Potomac Forks (see mile 164.8), the commissioners agreed to follow the North Branch of the Potomac to its source.

Of course, it was easy for them to agree, since the representatives for Virginia had no stake in the outcome. The land north of either branch of the Potomac would belong to the colony of Maryland, which was not represented in the surveying party. By taking the North Branch, the commissioners added significant acreage to the Fairfax land. As it turned out, the South Branch was considerably longer than the North Branch, but the results of those early surveys have withstood the tests of time and legal appeal. Maryland's last attempt to claim the land between the North and South Branches was ignored by the Supreme Court in its 1910 ruling on Maryland's western boundary.

## The Ohio Company Expands the Frontier

In March 1748, a small party of men on horseback crossed the Potomac and stopped at a frontier outpost known simply as "Cresap's" (Oldtown, mile 166.7). They were surveying Fairfax's land in western Virginia, and they brought with them a tall, gangly apprentice named George Washington, only 16 years of age. The party was detained at Cresap's for several days on account of bad weather and high water. Their boredom was alleviated one afternoon when a party of Indian warriors materialized and performed a war dance, which the youngster from the Virginia Tidewater found "comical."

An artist's rendering of young George Washington and George Fairfax watching an Indian war dance at nightfall during their stay in Oldtown in March 1748. Washington's diary describes this event as happening earlier in the day. *Illustration courtesy Library of Congress.*

The rains lifted and the Fairfax party continued up the Potomac, crossing back into Virginia at Patterson's Creek (*see* mile 173.5). It was the first of Washington's many visits to Oldtown and Cumberland, but the future significance of the visit was probably lost on Thomas Cresap, the short-tempered Englishman who had settled at this frontier crossroads seven years earlier. Cresap was already involved in an ambitious commercial venture that would soon touch off a world war, a venture that involved Washington's half-brother and many other prominent Virginians. They had banded together to form the Ohio Company, which planned to establish a trade route across the Appalachians and begin settling the Ohio Valley. After two years in the hands of the lieutenant governor and then the Board of Trade back in London, the Ohio Company's petition was finally granted in the summer of 1749.

Cresap had already begun a price-cutting war with the Pennsylvania traders. The next few years were spent in building a storehouse at Wills Creek (Cumberland, mile 184.5) and blazing a narrow packhorse trail across the Appalachians. This humble path was the forerunner of Braddock's Road and the National Road. Cresap and a frontiersman named Christopher Gist also took care to arrange a conference with the Indians on the Ohio, who might well be alarmed at the company's intentions.

But the Indian tribes in the Ohio Valley were hardly the company's greatest worry. The French, having decided to assert their own claims in the region in 1753, sent a military expedition from Canada to claim the crucial Forks of the Ohio (now Pittsburgh). At that time, Virginia's charter was believed to include much of the Ohio River, and Governor Robert Dinwiddie decided to send a warning to the French. George Washington, still a tender 21 years of age, volunteered for the mission. With winter fast approaching, Dinwiddie gave Washington a letter to carry to the commander of the French, and sent him off on a difficult journey through the Appalachians.

## The French and Indian War

Washington passed through Wills Creek in November and set out across the mountains. He traveled all the way to Fort LeBoeuf, near Lake Erie, in search of a Frenchman with sufficient rank to accept the message. His return trip, through snowy forests in the dead of winter, is the stuff of legend. At one point he and Christopher Gist abandoned their starving horses and struck out on foot. They were shot at by an Indian guide and nearly froze to death on the Allegheny River when Washington poled himself off of their hastily built raft.

Washington reported that the French were building a fleet of canoes to continue their journey down to the Forks of the Ohio, and Governor Dinwiddie managed to persuade a reluctant Virginia Assembly to fund a counter-expedition. That summer the young major found himself enlarging the Ohio Company's packhorse trail across the Appalachians for his supply wagons and cannon. The back-breaking work of cutting trees and pulling stumps must have given him many opportunities to reflect on the best way to cross the mountains from the Potomac River to the Ohio Valley—a project that would fascinate him for the rest of his life and would ultimately lead to the construction of the Chesapeake and Ohio Canal.

In the last few days of May, Washington's men ambushed a party of French along the last ridge of the Appalachians, killing the commander and taking the rest prisoner. The first skirmish of the French and Indian War had been won by the British colonials and their Indian allies. The Virginians had almost reached the Ohio Valley, but they withdrew back across Chestnut Ridge and threw together a crude timber fort at Great Meadows that they named Fort Necessity. The French and their Indian allies arrived on July 3 in a steady rain, and Washington was forced to surrender after a brief siege.

Washington returned down the Potomac by way of canoe, and even made a sketch and some observations titled "Notes on the Navigation of the Potomac River above the Great Falls." Significantly, he was still thinking about using the river to reach the lands to the west just a few days after the most terrible setback to his young career.

The Virginia Assembly was not particularly enthusiastic about supporting Governor Dinwiddie's war across the mountains, which was thought to be motivated by his own financial interest in the Ohio Company. But the British government was more than eager to get at the dastardly French, and sent reinforcements in the form of two regiments under the command of General Edward Braddock. Braddock's proud soldiers were chagrined to find themselves engaged in the "infinite labor" of building roads through a primitive wilderness in the spring and summer of 1755. First they enlarged the route through the Virginia mountains (now West Virginia) to Oldtown and then up to Wills Creek, where the Ohio Company's storehouse had become a timber fort. The British officers were not impressed by the structure, but Braddock named it for his commander back in England, the duke of Cumberland.*

Fort Cumberland became the base of operations for the expedition across the Appalachians, as Braddock's men widened the path through the mountains that the Virginia Regiment had cut the previous summer. When they reached the end of the Appalachians, the British began cutting a new trail due north to the French fort on the Forks of the Ohio. Washington had volunteered to accompany the expedition as a member of Braddock's staff, and even though he was sick with dysentery, he now hurried forward to be part of the expected triumph.

By July 8, the British were only 12 miles from Fort Duquesne, and the French defenders were preparing to abandon their position. But that night one of the French officers managed to persuade several hundred of the garrison and their Indian allies to launch a desperation attack

---

*William Augustus, duke of Cumberland, popularly known as "the butcher of Culloden" for the brutal atrocities committed by his troops in the course of suppressing a Jacobite uprising in Scotland. The duke was to dishonor himself in battle on the European continent two years later, leading to his dismissal.

against the invincible British column before it reached the fort. The next day the French and Indians attacked and routed Braddock's men and the Virginia militia just after they had crossed Turtle Creek along the Monongahela River. George Washington miraculously survived, despite having two horses shot out from under him as he tried to rally the troops. Braddock, who had once told Benjamin Franklin that it was impossible that Indian warriors would make much of an impression on his regulars, was carried away in a litter. He died a few days later, along the western ridge of the Appalachians. The rest of the army beat a hasty and disorganized retreat back across the mountains to Cumberland.

The stunning defeat of the vaunted British regulars emboldened the Indian warriors to attack the European settlements along the frontier. These opportunistic raids, known as "the outrages," were brutal and horrifying, but the Indians carefully avoided pitched battles with the frontier militia. The settlers fled in droves that fall, and even Thomas Cresap felt threatened enough to abandon Oldtown and fall back to Conococheague (Williamsport, mile 99.4).

George Washington established his headquarters in Winchester, and set his men to work building a string of forts along the Appalachians in Virginia. (He also claimed some authority over Fort Cumberland, even though it lay on

On July 9, 1755, Indians routed Braddock's men near the Forks of the Ohio (modern-day Pittsburgh). *Sketch courtesy Library of Congress.*

the Maryland side of the river.) Meanwhile, the colony of Maryland built a strong stone fort along the Potomac route to Oldtown and Wills Creek. When completed in 1757, the fort was named Fort Frederick (*see* mile 112.1), after the colony's proprietor, Frederick Calvert.

The line of forts did little to slow the Indian attacks over the next two years. Relief finally came in 1758, when British General John Forbes cut a new road to the Forks of the Ohio and forced the French to retreat. Washington joined this expedition reluctantly, after vigorously protesting Forbes's decision to build an alternate road through Pennsylvania, rather than follow the route through Cumberland that had been developed by Virginia and the Ohio Company. The interests of the Ohio Company were also compromised by the Treaty of Easton, in which colonial representatives convinced many Indians to abandon their support for the French by promising that the British would not settle west of the Appalachians.

Forbes named the captured fort after the British minister of war, and the name survives in more peaceful times as Pittsburgh. Forbes died shortly after his victory, Washington retired from military service, and the outrages around the Potomac quickly died down. With Fort Pitt secured on the Ohio River, the more significant battles took place far to the north. As Quebec fell in 1759 and Montreal in 1760, the colony of New France lost all hope of supply from the Atlantic. The French quest for control of the Ohio River ultimately ended in the loss of Canada under the terms of the Treaty of Paris in 1763.

The troubles along the Potomac frontier were not quite over, though. As the western Indian tribes began to realize that British settlement would no longer be held in check by a French presence, a charismatic chieftain named Pontiac was able to unite the normally fractious tribes in a coordinated series of assaults that overwhelmed many of the smaller forts west of the Ohio. Fort Detroit and Fort Pitt held out, but they were under constant siege. There were reports of scattered Indian attacks along the Potomac, but the true frontier lay much further west now, and Marylanders back in the east were elated to hear that Cresap was still firmly entrenched at Oldtown.

The British were able to relieve Fort Pitt, but they were not able to subdue Pontiac's followers by military force. Instead, they tried diplomacy and waited for the fragile alliance of Indian tribes to weaken. Once again, the British promised that they would not settle the Ohio Valley. In the Royal Proclamation of 1763, the king confirmed the Treaty of Easton by forbidding any settlements west of the Appalachians.

The protracted wars had prevented the Ohio Company from establishing any settlements, but as long as Cresap was around, mischief would be afoot. Cresap negotiated treaties with the Iroquois for the rights to settle around Redstone Creek on the Monongahela, and became involved in a heated dispute with his old rival from Pennsylvania, the trader George Croghan, who claimed that Cresap was selling land that Croghan had obtained from the Indians.

At least Washington had the decorum to wait for the Proclamation Line to be amended in the Treaty of Hard Labour and the Treaty of Fort Stanwix (1768). Once the opportunity arose, however, Washington began acquiring western lands as fast as he could find suitable properties. The veterans of the first Virginia expedition to the Ohio had been promised land in the Ohio Valley, prorated by rank, which, when augmented with other purchases, left Washington with more than 30,000 acres by the end of 1772.

The route to those lands was clearly marked by the Potomac, and Washington corresponded with men such as John Semple and John Ballendine about their schemes to make the river more navigable for commercial purposes. (John Semple, who started the Keep Triest furnace above Harpers Ferry, was one of the first actually to begin digging; *see* mile 66.) John Ballendine's ambitious plan to begin building a canal along the Potomac petered out in the mid-1770s, but it was a venture only slightly ahead of its time (*see* mile 5.6).

At the same time, Washington strove to make his Tidewater properties more self-reliant. This was simply good business, since trade with English merchants was conducted on restrictive terms that were highly unfavorable to colonists. But Washington was also advocating a strict boycott of English goods to protest the taxes that the Parliament was trying to levy on the American colonies to pay for the recent French and Indian War. (It appears that Cresap shared the popular discontent, as he helped organize a Frederick chapter of the Sons of Liberty in 1765 to protest the Stamp Tax.) At the time, armed insurrection was almost unthinkable, but the colonists stoutly believed that only their elected assemblies had the authority to impose such taxes.

When the War of Independence finally came ten years later, it was fought on terrain far from the Potomac River, but the sons of the Potomac were eager participants. Michael Cresap led a company of backwoods sharpshooters on a brisk march to Boston in 1775,* and the militia at Mecklenburg (Shepherdstown) made a similar "Bee-line March" to join the siege. Little is written of their exploits after those early marches, and the Potomac remained a backwater during the war years, devoid of any political or strategic significance. But some of the most famous of America's founding fathers believed that the Potomac was a river corridor brimming with unlimited potential.

---

*Michael Cresap died soon after this famous march, while on an assignment that took him to New York. One of his officers suggested that Cresap was a victim of overindulgence at the many banquets that townspeople had thrown for the passing troops on their march to the north.

## Cresap's Western Outpost at Oldtown

Thomas Cresap had already gained a fearsome reputation as a border ruffian when he came to the western reaches of the Potomac and built a stronghouse at an abandoned village known as Shawnee Oldtown, or "King Opessa's Town." Cresap was born in Skipton, England, in the late 1600s and came to Maryland when in his teens. He spent most of the 1730s staking out Maryland's claim to lands along the Susquehanna River. The Pennsylvanians hotly contested his efforts to settle German immigrants in the disputed area, once bushwhacking him on his own ferry and twice sending posses to arrest him. Cresap and his men repulsed the first posse, shooting and killing one man who tried to force his way into their stronghouse. The second posse laid siege in 1736, but Cresap stood fast, refusing safe passage for his wife and children and damning the "quaking Dogs" who lay outside his window with a string of "horrid Oaths." The posse eventually succeeded in setting fire to the house and driving the defenders out, killing one of them and capturing Cresap as he tried to untie his boat down by the river. The "Maryland Monster" was paraded unrepentant through the streets of Philadelphia, which he loudly pronounced to be "one of the prettiest towns in Maryland." After a year tending to their truculent prisoner, the Pennsylvanians were more than willing to release him, but Cresap would not go until a royal proclamation had been issued that put at least a temporary end to the border squabble. (The border issue wasn't resolved until Mason and Dixon arrived from England in 1764 to perform the most exacting survey ever seen in the colonies.)

After a brief stay along the Conococheague (mile 99.6), Cresap moved to Oldtown in 1741, and was soon immersed in even larger disputes. Oldtown was a convenient stopping place for traders and settlers traveling westward, and it naturally followed that Cresap would become an important force behind the Ohio Company's efforts to open a trade route across the mountains. At the same time, he had to be careful to maintain good relations with the Indian warriors who traveled through the region, often passing south to do battle with the hated Catawbas and Cherokees of the Carolinas. The

Indians, forced away from their preferred "Warriors' Trail" through the lush Shenandoah Valley, expected to be fed when they came to Oldtown and came to refer to Cresap as "Big Spoon." Cresap appealed bitterly to the Maryland Assembly for reimbursement, but it was the price of doing business on the frontier.

The trails that crossed at Oldtown created frequent rivalries and unexpected partnerships. The Cresaps enjoyed the friendship of the Indians in times of peace: Cresap's wife and children had been sheltered by Indians while he was imprisoned in Philadelphia, and Daniel Cresap frequently hunted with Nemacolin, the Indian guide who helped blaze the first trail across the mountains. But Thomas Cresap, Jr. was killed in a sally against the Indians in 1756, and Michael Cresap was accused by none other than Thomas Jefferson of slaughtering Chief Logan's family during the later period of settlement down the Ohio River (1774). (Michael Cresap was probably not involved in this famous atrocity, but he appears to have played a very active role in the brutal war that followed.)

Thomas Cresap's disputes with his countrymen are no less noteworthy. Washington often stayed at "Cresap's" on his westward journeys, but mutual interest in the Ohio Company did not keep the two businessmen from an unpleasant exchange of letters over a disputed property in the Ohio Valley. And Cresap's business with the prominent Virginians of the Ohio Company did not deter him from surveying the South Branch of the Potomac on behalf of the colony of Maryland, which hoped to enlarge its western territory at the expense of the Old Dominion (see mile 164.8).

Cresap died in 1787, well over 90 years old, having married twice and outlived six of his eight children. Though only one of his sons survived him, Cresap was surrounded by a legion of grandchildren at his death. The family name lives on in Cresaptown, upstream from Cumberland, and the Cresap Society continues to hold periodic reunions in Oldtown.

# Opening the Route to the West, 1784–1860

At Thomas Jefferson's urging, George Washington resolved to take on the project of opening the Potomac to navigation and building an overland connection to Ohio. A company was chartered for this purpose, known as the Patowmack Company, with Washington as its president. The company set about removing obstacles from the river and building skirting canals around the falls.

Washington's attention to the Patowmack Company's work was diminished when he was called back to national service as president for eight years (1789–97). However, his presidency led to two other major projects on the Potomac: the armory to be constructed at Harpers Ferry and a capital city to be built near Georgetown, just below the first falls of the Potomac. All of these projects were well under way when he died in 1799.

Washington's efforts to open a Potomac route to the west were furthered by two major projects in the 1800s: the National Road and the Chesapeake and Ohio Canal. While the dream of a continuous canal rising and descending through the rough mountains of the Appalachians turned out to be a castle in the air, the National Road became a major thoroughfare that was used by hundreds of thousands of settlers to travel to the west. And a third transportation route, one that Washington could not have foreseen, was opened as well: the Baltimore and Ohio Railroad, which succeeded in reaching the Ohio River in 1853.

------------------------------------------------------------

## Washington Founds the Patowmack Company

With the Revolutionary War finally concluded, Washington returned to Mount Vernon in 1784 with the avowed intention of retiring from public service. But he still held property across the Appalachians, and he still believed that the Potomac was the best way to the Ohio Valley. As it happened, Thomas Jefferson, who was also keenly interested in developing the Potomac route, had decided that he needed someone to push the idea through the bickering state legislatures in the mid-Atlantic region.

Washington expressed only polite interest in response to a letter from Jefferson in the spring of 1784, but the lure of the Potomac ultimately proved irresistible. Citing the "indispensable necessity" of visiting his western properties, Washington set out in September on a roundabout trip along the river and across the mountains, asking everyone he met about the navigability of the streams and rivers that might bring the waters of the Ohio and the Potomac rivers closer together. He followed the Virginia road through Bath (Berkeley Springs, West Virginia), then crossed over the Potomac to follow Cresap's road through Fifteenmile Creek (Little Orleans, mile 140.9) to his usual stopover at Oldtown (mile 166.7). From there, he passed through Cumberland and over the mountains, where he was given a rather unsympathetic reception by squatters who disputed his claim to the land they were farming.

Despite his personal setback, Washington returned from the west ablaze with enthusiasm. He dashed off letters to Jefferson and the governor of Virginia, proclaiming the Potomac route far superior than the route that New Yorkers were touting to Lake Erie. By Washington's calculation, it was at most 360 miles between Washington and Pittsburgh, though that distance included a 20-mile wagon trip between the Potomac and the Cheat River. Developing this route was more than a sectional interest, he argued, because the Ohio Valley was rapidly filling with foreigners who had little allegiance to the former colonies. These newcomers stood "as if upon a pivot," and "the touch of a feather" would send them into the hands of Spain should they be compelled to ship their produce down the Ohio and then the Mississippi to New Orleans.

As Jefferson had hoped, Washington's involvement (and his personal visit to Annapolis) led to swift approval of the Patowmack Company by the Virginia and Maryland assemblies. In the spring of 1785, Washington also hosted several commissioners from the two states who developed the Mount Vernon Compact providing for joint use of the Potomac River and the Chesapeake Bay. The example of the compact led to calls by James Madison and others for similar meetings to develop interstate cooperation, which ultimately led to the Constitutional Convention two years later.

Washington began his tenure as president of the Patowmack Company by riding with the other directors up to Harpers Ferry in August. The directors planned to clear the river channel for the greater part of the route, but they agreed that skirting canals would be needed around the Potomac rapids at five places: Little Falls, Great Falls, Seneca Falls, Shenandoah Falls (Harpers Ferry), and the House Falls (just above Harpers Ferry). The company advertised for an experienced engineer to supervise the day-to-day operations, but the directors finally settled on James Rumsey of Shepherdstown, an innkeeper turned inventor who had greatly impressed Washington the year before.

After three years of heavy work, Washington's last report to the company directors optimistically projected that the river was on the verge of being cleared for navigation at least as far downriver as Great Falls and Little Falls, where locks would have to be built. There had been no end to distractions in the company's brief history, as Washington had chaired the Constitutional Convention and was widely believed to be the people's choice in the first presidential election. In the meantime, Rumsey soon tired of dealing with indentured workers who ran away at the first opportunity or quarreled with neighboring farmers, and resigned. His replacement was worse and eventually was cashiered. The work proceeded fitfully as the first presidential election was held and Washington had to leave his Potomac home for the inauguration in New York City.

The "ingenious Mr. Rumsey," as painted by Benjamin West. *Courtesy West Virginia Division of Culture and History.*

# Rumsey's Steamboat

Rumsey was born in 1743 in Cecil County in the northeast corner of Maryland. After living in Baltimore, he moved to Bath (modern-day Berkeley Springs) in what was then western Virginia, where he ran a mill, was a merchant, and kept an inn, tinkering the whole time with various mechanical improvements. Rumsey managed to impress Washington with his mechanical bent when the general stopped in Bath during his trip to the west in 1784. Rumsey demonstrated a model of a "pole boat" that could work its way upstream against a current. The idea was a perfect complement to Washington's plans for making the river navigable, and the general later wrote that he had "imbibed" a favorable impression of the erstwhile innkeeper.

When the Patowmack Company could find no experienced engineer to build its canals, Washington suggested that Rumsey be made the superintendent of the project. The year that Rumsey spent with the company (1785–86) proved frustrating, however, and he left to pursue another of his ingenious ideas. This was the steamboat that he was able to demonstrate successfully on the Potomac River in December 1787 (see mile 72.7).

Unfortunately, an inventor from Philadelphia named John Fitch had also demonstrated a steamboat and had already secured exclusive rights to use steam navigation on the waterways of New Jersey, New York, Pennsylvania, and Delaware. (This was the best protection the legislatures could offer an inventor before the creation of the U.S. Patent Office.) Rumsey went to Philadelphia in March 1788, where he impressed several prominent men, including Ben Franklin, who jointly formed the Rumseian Society to support the steamboat project.

In May 1788 Rumsey set sail for England, where he hoped to find the technical resources he needed to perfect his boat. His stay in England was filled with hopes and disappointments, as he supervised the construction of a larger steamboat called the *Columbian Maid*. Creditors were never far from his door, and at one point he had to take work supervising the construction of one of Ireland's canals. But he had several loyal supporters, as well as the continuing interest of Thomas Jefferson, and was able to bring the *Columbian Maid* to the point of completion when he suffered a fatal stroke in December 1792. One of his friends wrote Jefferson that the autopsy had revealed that "overplied with energies of thinking some of the vessals [sic] of the brain were fairly worn out." The *Columbian Maid* was successfully demonstrated on the river Thames a few weeks later.

Ironically, Fitch was also forced to go to Europe to pursue his project, where he too died without realizing his goal. It was left to Robert Fulton to develop a commercially viable steamboat, the *Clermont,* which he demonstrated in 1807. Fitch still receives some mention as a "pioneer of steam navigation," but Rumsey's ingenious accomplishment has for the most part been forgotten. As the residents of Shepherdstown are quick to point out, this is manifestly unfair: Rumsey developed his steamboat quite independently of

Fitch, demonstrated it in the same year, and showed that it could carry passengers and cargo. But there's also an intriguing link between Rumsey and the first commercially successful steamboat—while in England, he was friendly with Benjamin West, who painted his portrait. During those same years, Benjamin West was teaching painting to Robert Fulton, who was an aspiring artist before he turned to engineering. Fulton's paddlewheel boat was quite different from Rumsey's, but it's possible that his interest in steamboats was inspired by his early acquaintance with the Potomac inventor.

Throughout his presidency, Washington kept a watchful if distant eye on the canal project from the temporary capital in Philadelphia. He found time to inspect the difficult work at Little Falls and Great Falls during his occasional "flying visits" back to Mount Vernon. As chief executive, he was also able to lend his gentle suasion to other important projects on the Potomac, such as a bill providing for a federal armory to be established at Shenandoah Falls (Harpers Ferry).

The most gratifying development of all, however, was the political compromise that placed the nation's capital on the Potomac. While there was strong sentiment to designate either Philadelphia or New York as the capital, the northern states agreed to a location on the Potomac, provided that the federal government would assume the existing debts incurred by the states. (Not surprisingly, the northern states had accumulated the lion's share of the debt that would be assumed.) The selection of the specific location along the Potomac was left to the river's most famous resident. Accordingly, when Washington traveled to Elizabeth Town (Hagerstown), Williamsport, and Shepherdstown in October 1790 he was greeted at each stop by burghers touting the advantages of their respective locations. While there was some talk of establishing an inland capital that would be safe from an ocean attack, even the former president of the Patowmack Company must have recognized the difficulties of transportation if the capital were placed above Great Falls. The logical choice was the land adjacent to Georgetown, just below the falls. Once it was announced, Pierre L'Enfant and Washington began laying out plans for the federal city, using Georgetown as their base of operations.

Unfortunately, the Patowmack Company's endeavors did not proceed with the same irresistible force as the work on the capital. The locks at Little Falls were finished in 1795, but were of little use until the much more difficult channel could be finished around Great Falls. After his second term came to an end, Washington was once again

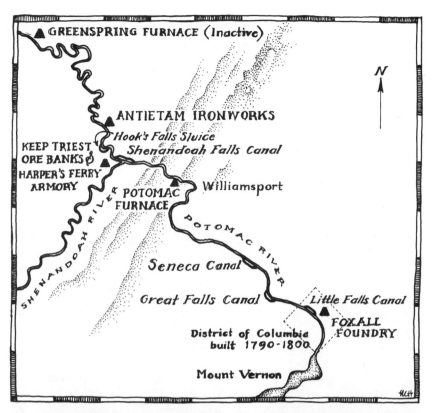

GREENSPRING FURNACE (Inactive)

*N*

ANTIETAM IRONWORKS

*Hook's Falls Sluice*

KEEP TRIEST
ORE BANKS

*Shenandoah Falls Canal*

HARPER'S FERRY
ARMORY

POTOMAC
FURNACE

Williamsport

SHENANDOAH RIVER

POTOMAC RIVER

*Seneca Canal*

*Great Falls Canal*

*Little Falls Canal*

FOXALL
FOUNDRY

District of Columbia
built 1790-1800

Mount Vernon

George Washington's Potomac. By 1802, a scant three years after Washington's death, it looked as if his grand vision for the Potomac was about to be fulfilled. The federal government had relocated to the District of Columbia, and the armory at Harpers Ferry was finally finished. The Patowmack Company's skirting canals and sluices connected ore banks, furnaces, and foundries along the Potomac. *Map by Linda Heinrich.*

able to attend the company's meetings, but when he died in December 1799 the work was almost at a standstill due to lack of funds. Soon afterwards, however, the Virginia and Maryland legislatures appropriated enough money to finish the work at Great Falls. The locks at Great Falls were opened in 1802, and Washington's dream of a navigable Potomac route was finally realized.

## The Patowmack Company in the Era of "Internal Improvements"

Under the leadership of John Mason (son of George Mason), the company collected tolls for the next quarter century but was able to show a profit for only one year. The skirting canals did further some notable enterprises along the river.

Pig iron could be shipped from the Antietam Furnace (mile 69.5) to foundries such as Foxall's near Georgetown (mile 1.5). And "Potomac Marble" was brought down the river from a quarry (mile 38.2) near the Monocacy River to the very doorstep of the U.S. Capitol, using the short-lived Washington City Canal for the last mile of the journey.

John Mason was for many years an influential director of the Patowmack Company and served as its president from 1817 until 1828, when the company's charter was subsumed by the C&O Canal Company. He kept a summer home on what is now Roosevelt Island and also purchased Foxall's Foundry (*see* miles 0 *and* 1.5). *Painting of John Mason (1766–1849) by Charles Bird King, courtesy of Board of Regents, Gunston Hall Plantation.*

Despite these accomplishments, the credits and the debits never quite balanced. Aside from the almost constant repair necessitated by the Potomac's floods, the company spent a great deal of money trying to improve several of the Potomac's tributaries, such as the Monocacy and the Shenandoah. But despite its best efforts, the Potomac's capricious pattern of flood and drought meant that boats could use the river for only a few months of the year. Even at normal levels, the river current was an impediment to transportation. Anything that came downstream had to be poled back up the river. So the river traffic was limited to skiffs, flat-bottomed bateaux, and log rafts that were broken apart and sold for lumber when they reached their destination. It was becoming clear that the only reliable way to carry goods up and down the Potomac route was to use an entirely separate canal as the channel.

The possibility of federal funding for a variety of road and canal projects had been suggested in an 1808 report by the secretary of the treasury, Albert Gallatin. But many politicians of the era were deeply suspicious of any efforts to pay for "internal improvements" out of the national treasury. Even in the early 1800s they realized that regional projects would inevitably lead to pork-barrel politics. However, Thomas Jefferson had assumed the presidency, and he still felt as strongly about the Potomac route as when he had corresponded with Washington twenty years earlier. Jefferson favored a limited federal role in most matters, but he proved very willing to commit funds to the National Road, which roughly followed the route that Washington and Braddock had hewn out through the Appalachian Mountains west of Cumberland.

Begun in Cumberland in 1811, the National Road reached Wheeling six years later, providing a reliable if hilly route through the mountains to the Ohio River. The road was a tremendous success, plied by fleet stagecoaches and huge Conestoga wagons driven by settlers bound for land in the Midwest. East of Cumberland, the wagons and stagecoaches used the improved road that the state of Maryland had built along the upper Potomac Valley, through Hancock and Hagerstown to Baltimore.

Despite its popularity, the National Road had its limitations as a commercial route. Many people realized that the burden of drawing heavy loads up the steep inclines of the Appalachian ridges could be greatly relieved if the cargo could somehow be carried by boat. The competition between the New York route to Lake Erie and the mid-Atlantic route along the Potomac to the Ohio was renewed when the state of New York sought federal funds for a canal following the

Mohawk River west through the Appalachians to Lake Erie. Rebuffed by President Madison's veto in 1817, New York began construction of the Erie Canal using its own funds. Driven by Governor De Witt Clinton's relentless interest, New York succeeded in connecting the Hudson River to Lake Erie (363 miles) by 1825.

Even before the Erie Canal was finished, political leaders in the mid-Atlantic states had become alarmed by the challenge posed by this new trade route. Pennsylvania began work on a trans-Appalachian canal from Philadelphia to Pittsburgh, and a bevy of influential figures in the Washington area met at Leesburg, Virginia, to draw up a resolution in support of a canal along the Potomac River that would cross the mountains and follow westward-flowing rivers down to Pittsburgh. The guiding force behind this "canal convention" was Charles Fenton Mercer, a representative from Virginia, who advocated that the canal begin near Georgetown rather than Baltimore. Mercer was joined by such notables as John Mason, Francis Scott Key, and Albert Gallatin (former secretary of the treasury). Of course, a couple of Washingtons were on hand as well: Bushrod Washington (a Supreme Court justice and nephew to the first president), and George C. Washington (grand-nephew; later to become the canal company's president and a representative from Maryland).

The canal convention was held in November 1823, but it was five years before work would begin on the Chesapeake and Ohio Canal. A survey by the U.S. Board of Engineers priced the C&O project at a staggering $22 million. The shocked canal lobbyists called for a second survey, which reduced the estimate by about a half. Next, the lobbyists descended upon the local legislatures to seek a charter and funding. Virginia, Maryland, the U.S. Congress, and even Pennsylvania assented to the project, and pledged $3.5 million. The lion's share of the money came from the U.S. government and from the District of Columbia (which at that time included Alexandria).

The merchants of Baltimore were disappointed by the choice of Georgetown as the eastern end of the canal, and this may account for Maryland's relatively niggardly offering of $500,000. Baltimoreans turned to a rival enterprise that ambitiously proposed to build a railroad from Baltimore to the Ohio River. This was a risky venture, since the only existing railroads at the time used horse-drawn cars. Steam engines were being developed, but it seemed unlikely at the time that they would ever muster enough power to pull a load up a mountain grade. Nevertheless, Baltimore set the wheels of the Baltimore and Ohio Railroad in motion the same year that the Chesapeake and Ohio canal company began digging upriver from Georgetown. In fact, the groundbreaking ceremonies for both projects were held on July 4, 1828, and the story of these two transportation companies would be curiously intertwined for the next hundred years.

## Building the C&O Canal, 1828–1850

The C&O company ran into trouble from the very beginning. Laborers were scarce, at least suitably cheap ones, so the company brought two shiploads over from England as indentured workers. But the unpleasant sea journey and the working conditions on the canal inspired many of the workers to run out on their indentures. Even when the canal company could seize a runaway, they soon found that the Maryland courts were brimming with sympathy for the misfortunes of the exploited immigrants.

The runaway problem was relatively minor compared to the legal roadblock engineered by the newly formed B&O Railroad. As soon as its surveys established the most favorable route, the B&O sent its agents ahead to buy up the land where its line would reach the Potomac at Point of Rocks. The canal company was horrified to learn that it had been effectively checkmated at this narrow passage between the river and the impassable Catoctin ridge. The company obtained an injunction against the railroad, which returned the favor, and construction from Point of Rocks to Harpers Ferry was delayed for four years while the two companies wrangled in court.

The B&O had some formidable legal help in the persons of Roger Brooke Taney (later to become chief justice of the Supreme Court) and the silver-tongued orator Daniel Webster. Charles Fenton Mercer* spearheaded the canal's legal team, which included one lawyer who was too sick to continue his presentation and another whose preparations were interrupted by bouts of heavy drinking. All things considered, the canal company was extremely fortunate when the courts finally ruled that the Patowmack Company's original charter encompassed the right-of-way for a continuous canal, and that right had been passed on to the C&O Canal. The triumphant canal company was positioned to block the railroad's preferred route permanently, but the

------

*Mercer, who had organized the canal conventions in the 1820s, was now the canal company's first president. Amazingly, he still held a seat on the House's Committee on Roads and Canals, which enabled him to block several attempts by the B&O Railroad to secure federal funding.

Maryland legislature intervened and insisted on a plan of joint construction as far as Harpers Ferry, where the railroad would cross the Potomac and continue its line through western Virginia. Olive branches were extended by both parties, and for the next several years the canal and the railroad cooperated rather amicably.

As if these trials were not enough, a cholera epidemic descended upon the canal during the "sickly season" of 1832. The epidemic had circled halfway around the globe from the Ganges, brought to North America by Irish immigrants who landed in Montreal. The rank and fetid waters of the canal ditch and the work camps were an ideal medium for transmitting the bacteria, which caused violent and horrifying bouts of vomiting and diarrhea. Most victims died of dehydration within a day or two, and their example sent a general panic through the towns of Harpers Ferry and Sharpsburg. By August most of the canal works had been abandoned, not to be taken up again until the next spring.

The delays and catastrophes and constantly escalating costs had brought the canal company to the point of bankruptcy. The company would surely have succumbed at this point if the state of Maryland had not provided a $3 million loan in 1836. (The loan was authorized by the Eight Million Dollar Bill, which also loaned money to the B&O Railroad and several other transportation projects.) The state of Maryland thus committed itself to the completion of the canal, and also took it upon itself to hire and fire company directors with each change of political administration over the next few years.

Unfortunately, the company's travails were just beginning. The $3 million promised by Maryland was contingent on the sale of bonds, and 1836 was the year of a worldwide bank panic. The canal company was late in paying its contractors, and they in turn were unable to pay their men. The hard-drinking Irish immigrants who were the backbone of the work force had already acquired a nasty reputation for settling disputes with clubs and guns. Several Irishmen had died in 1834 in a notable battle near Dam no. 5 (*see* mile 106.2) between workers from County Cork and the "Fardowners" from Longsford.* On New Year's Day 1838, Irish workers at the Paw Paw Tunnel marched up to Oldtown

---

*We will probably never know what started the small war that turned the rival groups into armed camps with posted guards. Canal historians point out that worker violence began when the canal company's funds had begun to dry up. Many of the participants were members of "secret societies" that protected the interests of one group or another in those days before the advent of labor

and demolished several establishments. Later that year, workers at Prathers Neck (mile 108.8) seized some gunpowder from the canal stores and threatened to demolish their own work unless they were paid back wages. In 1839, the Irish working near the tunnel attacked a group of recently arrived German workers, wounding several and killing one man by throwing him into a blazing fire. The local militia responded by tearing up many of the shanty stores and taverns along that part of the line. The company took the Irish attack seriously enough to employ a labor spy to infiltrate the workers' group and collect evidence for the imminent trial. Despite these countermeasures, the ringleaders were let off with light sentences, and the local militia was dunned for damages for the property they had destroyed.

Somehow the canal had pushed its way beyond Hancock, past the first Appalachian ridges, but here the funds petered out completely in 1842. The B&O Railroad had already reached Cumberland and was gathering itself to cross over the mountains to the Ohio Valley. It was clear that the canal was not going to follow the railroad to the Ohio, and there was good reason to believe that it would not even reach Cumberland. In another odd twist to their rivalry, the C&O engaged in a brief relationship with the railroad, which delivered coal from Cumberland to the canal terminus at Dam no. 6 for shipment downstream to Georgetown (*see* mile 134).

Despite the canal's desperate circumstances, much of the work on the last 50 miles had already been completed, including the difficult job of digging the Paw Paw Tunnel. The state of Maryland considered various ways to finish the project, and finally decided to waive its lien on canal revenue to allow the company to borrow more money. The construction from 1848 to 1850 did not adhere to the same standards that had been maintained for the first 134 miles (*see* mile 144), but at least the canal would be able to start earning money.

The Chesapeake and Ohio Canal formally opened on October 10, 1850, in a respectable ceremony replete with speeches, a military band, and cannon salutes. Three boats carried various dignitaries downstream, followed by five

---

unions. Groups fought to eliminate competition from other workers and to keep wages at an acceptable level. The pattern was repeated at canal works throughout the United States and Canada as the construction boom petered out in the 1830s. In the C&O's case, the situation was so threatening that President Andrew Jackson sent federal troops to augment the militia, which is often cited as the first instance of federal intervention in a labor dispute.

boats loaded with coal. The C&O's dignitaries traveled only a few miles before turning back to the scheduled banquet at Cumberland, but the first five boats of coal pressed on, vying for the honor of being the first to arrive in Georgetown. Of course, the company's luck being what it was, two of the boats got stuck near Dam no. 6. Despite fresh teams of mules along the way, it took the other boats a full week to reach Georgetown, with the *Freeman Rowdon* nosing out the *Southampton* on the evening of October 17. Fortunately, the canal operation would go much more smoothly as time went on, with the average trip taking only four to five days.

## Congressman Mercer of Aldie

While the canal's legacy includes such formidable names as Mason and Washington, it's safe to say that there would never have been a C&O Canal without the lesser-known Charles Fenton Mercer. Mercer certainly had the requisite pedigree: his father, uncle, and grandfather all invested in the Ohio Company, and as early as 1763 his uncle was involved in the company's scheme to make the Potomac more navigable.

Charles Fenton Mercer (b. 1778), orphaned at age 15 and never to marry, seemed to find a substitute for family life in public service. He excelled at Princeton, where, as valedictorian, he delivered a stirring address in favor of war with France. But when George Washington nominated him for a commission as lieutenant in 1798, he greatly offended the old general by declining.

Mercer settled down to more peaceful pursuits on land that he had inherited near Leesburg. He built a house that he called Aldie and began operating a mill on the Little River. Commerce led him back to politics, as he campaigned successfully for the Virginia House of Delegates in 1810. Elected to the U.S. House of Representatives in 1817, Mercer enjoyed considerable success in his first ten years in Washington. Despite his generally pessimistic patrician outlook, he was a tireless worker in the political arena, famous for five-hour speeches and voluminous memorials and reports to advocate his favorite causes. Unlike Jefferson's Republicans, Mercer believed in a strong government role to promote commerce and guide the common man.

In 1823 Mercer staged a "canal convention" of influential public figures (including his friends Francis Scott Key and Bushrod Washington) to demonstrate popular support for a bold proposal to construct a canal from Georgetown to Pittsburgh. Mercer was able to steer the project through many obstacles to the triumphant groundbreaking on July 4, 1828. With Andrew Jackson's election that fall, however, Mercer soon found himself swimming against the current. Jackson and his supporters had little inclination to use federal money to pay for a regional commercial venture.

Mercer also found himself frequently voting against the rest of the Virginia delegation. His interest in manufacturing aligned him with northern industrialists rather than the southern planters. In addition, many of his colleagues suspected that he was an abolitionist at heart, because he had founded the American Colonization Society, which aided free blacks in emigrating to a settlement that later became Liberia. (While Mercer was nominally opposed to slavery and had sponsored legislation that declared slave traders to be pirates, his motives in removing free blacks from the country were hardly humanitarian.)

The year 1833 must have been especially bitter for Mercer. First, the leadership of the colonization society passed into the hands of a bloc of northern members. Despite support from many shareholders, Mercer also lost the canal presidency to John Eaton, who was perceived to be a favorite of Andrew Jackson's. Be that as it may, Jackson still was unwilling to fund the canal, and Eaton only lasted a year as company president before being replaced by George C. Washington.

Mercer struggled on in the House of Representatives, winning his district by increasingly narrow margins, until he finally resigned in 1840. One of his last congressional initiatives was a massive proposal for a grand canal that would unite the waters of the Atlantic and Pacific oceans by crossing the isthmus of Panama. He traveled much in his later years, involving himself in a doomed land settlement scheme in Texas that was somewhat reminiscent of the old Ohio Company.

When Mercer died in 1858, the canal was hauling a quarter of a million tons of coal, but the clouds of civil war were beginning to gather on the horizon. His most enduring contributions to regional transportation are two turnpikes from his neighborhood to Alexandria that are still in use today: Leesburg Pike (company director, 1809) and the Little River Turnpike (chartered by Mercer in 1806).

## The C&O Canal in Operation, 1850–1860

The canal's belated arrival in Cumberland, while welcome, was somewhat anticlimactic. The railroad had come eight years earlier, and was already busy at work vaulting the Appalachians to the west. The nation had changed as well, annexing the huge territories of Texas and then California. With each national expansion, the Potomac to Ohio connection was being reduced to a much smaller scale of significance. Unable to reach even the Ohio, the canal would have to content itself with the relatively modest commerce of the Potomac Valley.

While the canal was still being built, the canal company had made a little money carrying produce from the farmlands that lay along its route. But when it finally reached Cumberland it was able to tap a much larger source of income in the rich veins of coal just beyond the town. The canal provided the first direct connection for coal shipments to the port of Georgetown, since the B&O Railroad would not close the gap between Point of Rocks and Washington until it built its Metropolitan Branch after the Civil War. By 1859 the canal was carrying 300,000 tons of coal, and only 20,000 tons of flour, wheat, and corn. Since there were few markets in the sparsely populated mountains, most of the freight was carried in one direction, downstream, with the boats coming back to Cumberland empty. The canal was still far from a viable concern, mired in debt from its construction, and barely able to keep up with repair work occasioned by the all too frequent floods. It certainly could not compare with the Erie Canal, which was carrying 2 million tons of freight a year, and getting additional revenue by carrying immigrant families to the Midwest. The C&O's paltry receipts of $189,000 in 1859 paled in comparison to the B&O Railroad's annual earnings of $3.6 million.

There had been a great flood in 1852, but a succession of floods in 1857 very nearly put the canal out of business. First there was an ice "freshet" in February, and, before the canal company could recover, three more damaging floods in April and May. Its expenditures for maintenance and repair more than doubled that year, reaching $220,000, which far exceeded its revenues. Coupled with the fact that the company was paying more than $140,000 of interest a year on previous loans, the accumulated deficits of the previous decade were staggering.

If they had the time and the broadness of vision to look beyond the financial ledgers at the course of the nation, the directors of the company must have been even more concerned for the canal's prospects. Metaphorically speaking, the largest flood of all was building strength and about to begin crashing down the Potomac, a flood that would separate Maryland from Virginia for more than four full years. And, in a sense, it would all begin on the canal, in the vicinity of Harpers Ferry.

# The Civil War along the Canal and the River

With the onset of the Civil War, the Potomac River became a physical barrier between the North and South. Secessionists burned many of the bridges along the Potomac (Point of Rocks, Berlin, Harpers Ferry, and Shepherdstown). As major supply lines to the capital, the canal and the B&O Railroad became the objects of many Confederate raids.

Since the canal parallels the Potomac River, it witnessed the many river crossings before and after the battles of Antietam and Gettysburg. As a border territory, the Potomac region also gave rise to partisan guerrilla units led by John Singleton Mosby and Elijah V. White (of Whites Ferry) in Loudoun County, and Jesse McNeil and his father in the western mountains around Romney, Paw Paw, and Cumberland.

When the war finally ended after four years of bloody battles, there were many emotional scars to be healed in Cumberland, Hancock, Shepherdstown, and other river communities whose sympathies had been divided almost equally between the Confederacy and the Union.

------------------------------------------------------------

## Locktender and Spy, 1858–1859

In 1858 a well-educated and somewhat garrulous young man named John Cook arrived in Harpers Ferry. Cook earned a living by tutoring and by tending one of the canal locks, but his real purpose was to gather information for an attack on the armory. It was part of a daring abolitionist scheme to capture government rifles and arm slaves for a massive rebellion. The mastermind of the plan, John Brown, arrived with the other conspirators the next summer.

Brown's men captured the armory on the night of October 16, 1859, but were unable to rally support for their rebellion. They were soon surrounded by excited and well-armed contingents of local citizenry, followed shortly by the U.S. Marines under Robert E. Lee and J. E. B. Stuart. On October 18, the Marines battered down the doors to the firehouse held by Brown's men and captured him. Brown had lost two of his sons in the raid, and he himself was hung that December in Charleston. John Cook and three of the other conspirators were executed two weeks after John Brown, making Cook the only lockkeeper on the canal ever hung for treason.

## Bull Run and Balls Bluff, 1861

John Brown's raid greatly exacerbated the tensions between the slave states and the free states. Many southern leaders believed that Abraham Lincoln's election in 1860 would lead to an abolition of slavery. By February 1, 1861, seven states had seceded from the Union. Virginia did not vote to secede until April 17, a few days after the surrender of Fort Sumter. There was strong secessionist sentiment in Maryland, but it was quickly stifled by Lincoln, who could not afford to see the District of Columbia become a Union island.

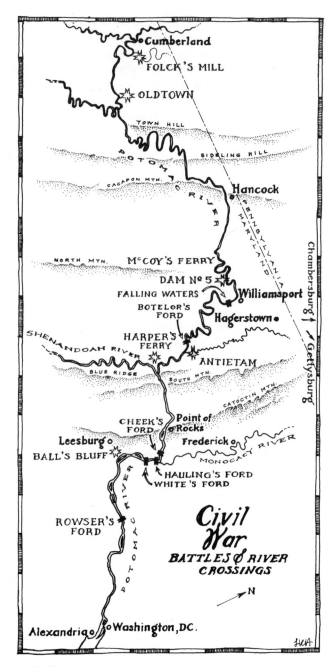

Civil War battles and river crossings. *Map by Linda Heinrich.*

In the early months, no one seemed quite sure how and where the war would be fought. The C&O Canal and the B&O Railroad lay right along the Potomac, within easy reach of Confederate raiders. But Union strategists did surprisingly little to protect these two lifelines to the nation's capital in the first year of the war. Simon Cameron, Lincoln's secretary of war, was a Pennsylvanian with close ties to that state's railroad system. Damage to Maryland's rival transportation systems may have been of little consequence, in his view.

A possibly apocryphal story credits Colonel Thomas J. Jackson, soon to be known as "Stonewall," with striking the first blow. Jackson had assumed command of the Virginians who had seized Harpers Ferry in mid-April. (Union forces destroyed much of the U.S. Armory at that time, to prevent it from falling into Confederate hands.) In May, Jackson demanded that the B&O schedule all of its runs between the hours of eleven in the morning and one in the afternoon so as not to disturb his troops. According to a postwar account written by Confederate General John Imboden, Jackson's men were then able to seize 56 locomotives and 300 cars by cutting the line at Point of Rocks (mile 48.2) and Cherry Run in Virginia (mile 113.9).

Soon Jackson was ordered to retire from Harpers Ferry as the Union army prepared to march south toward the southern capital in Richmond. The first major battle of the war was fought at Bull Run that summer, on July 21, with relatively modest casualties (approximately four hundred men died on each side). But the northern hopes for a quick end to the insurrection were dashed, and Jackson had earned a nickname when another Confederate general pointed out the Virginia Brigade and shouted: "There stands Jackson like a stone wall! Rally behind the Virginians!"

While the new Union commander, General George McClellan, patiently drilled his men, the more radical Republicans were still clamoring for an immediate invasion of the South. It so happened that one of the most bombastic of the Republican "hawks," Senator Ned Baker, also served as a colonel in the Union army. When news came of a Confederate withdrawal in Loudoun County, Colonel Baker and General Charles Stone were ordered to test the defenses around Leesburg. During the night of October 21, seventeen hundred Union soldiers were ferried across the Potomac at Edwards Ferry (mile 30.9) and Conrads Ferry (now Whites Ferry, *see* mile 35.5) in small boats.

Under the senator's rather impetuous direction, the Union forces advanced up the slope on the Virginia side and

In June 1861, Confederate forces under Stonewall Jackson blew up the railroad bridge at Harpers Ferry before evacuating the town. Union troops then built a pontoon bridge across the Potomac. *Illustrations courtesy National Park Service.*

soon found themselves in a precarious position at the edge of Balls Bluff, facing a like number of Confederates ahead of them with the river behind them. The senator was shot dead as he exhorted his troops with quotations from Tennyson. The Union forces soon lost heart and were literally tumbled back down the bluff in a pell-mell race back to the small boats, which they quickly swamped. Many drowned, and many more were picked off by Confederate riflemen as they tried to escape. The Confederates lost 36 killed, while five hundred Union soldiers were captured and another two hundred may have died. The number of dead was never finally fixed, though bodies drifted downstream as far as Great Falls and even Washington, 35 miles away.

The battle had lingering aftereffects because Senator Baker was a personal friend of Lincoln's, and because the Senate formed its Joint Committee on the Conduct of the War to investigate, among other things, the possibility that General Stone had betrayed the army. The Joint Committee operated in a highly irregular manner, imprisoning General Stone on suspicion of treason without charges and with little evidence. The general was eventually released, but his career was ruined. Unfortunately, the Senate committee continued its work throughout the war, adding yet another political encumbrance to the Union war effort.

Senator Edward D. Baker's troops carry his body from the Union line at Balls Bluff, October 21, 1861. *Illustration courtesy Library of Congress.*

## Antietam and J. E. B. Stuart's Second Ride around McClellan, 1862

The war was very close to an end in the spring of 1862, as the Union's Army of the Potomac took a roundabout route, sailing to the eastern peninsula along the York River and briskly advancing past Yorktown and Williamsburg to the outer defenses of Richmond. But the fortunes of war changed dramatically when Robert E. Lee replaced the wounded Confederate commander, Joe Johnston. Lee repulsed McClellan in the daring Seven Days campaign, and then marched north to surprise and rout Union forces under General John Pope in the bloody Second Battle of Bull Run.

The Army of Northern Virginia had suffered heavy losses on the peninsula and against Pope, but Lee decided there was no time to rest. Between September 4 and 7, the Army of Northern Virginia crossed the Potomac at Cheeks Ford (mile 43.6) and Whites Ford (mile 38.7) near Leesburg and skirmished with Union forces at Monocacy and Point of Rocks. On the fifth and the ninth, different units acting under Lee's orders attempted to blow up the Monocacy Aqueduct (mile 42.2) but were unsuccessful. The army rapidly moved north, crossing South Mountain into the protective confines of the Great Valley. Lee split his army, sending a third of his army under Stonewall Jackson's direction to capture Harpers Ferry. General McClellan brought a much larger Union force in cautious pursuit.

On September 17, the two armies met in the bloodiest single day of the war around the town of Sharpsburg and the creek at Antietam, a few miles from the Potomac (*see* mile 69.4). The battle was evenly fought, but ended with Lee's army in a desperate situation. Only the late arrival of General A. P. Hill's forces from the sacking of Harpers Ferry kept the right side of Lee's line from collapsing. However, General McClellan failed to exploit his advantage the next day, and the Confederates began retreating to Virginia that night, crossing at Botelors Ford near Shepherdstown (*see* mile 71.4). On September 20, some Union forces tentatively crossed the ford and mounted the cliffs below Shepherdstown, only to be driven back briskly by Hill's men. McClellan had missed the opportunity to crush the Army of Northern Virginia, which had to take whatever pleasure it could in having avoided a total rout.

The Confederates, however, were not ready to let matters rest. In early October, Lee sent a note to J. E. B. Stuart advising him that "an expedition into Maryland with a

A column of troops crosses at Botelors Ford after the battle of Antietam. The ruins of Botelor's Mill, which furnished cement used to build many of the canal's locks, appears upstream. *Illustration courtesy National Park Service.*

detachment of cavalry, if it can be successfully executed, is at this time desirable." Lee proposed that Stuart ride up to the vicinity of Chambersburg and blow up a railroad bridge along the Conococheague, returning the way he came, unless he was led so far east as to have to cross at Leesburg. The latter prospect must have delighted the flamboyant Stuart, who had ridden entirely around McClellan's army that spring as it advanced up the peninsula toward Richmond. Accordingly, about 1,800 of his men waded across the Potomac near McCoys Ferry (mile 110.2) in the middle of the night of October 10, captured two or three Union pickets, and headed northeast. Once at Chambersburg, Stuart cut the telegraph lines, tore up the train tracks, and burned a small store of weapons and ammunition.

The Union army to Stuart's rear had been thrown into a frenzy by the raid, so he decided not to retrace his steps through the Great Valley. Instead, he continued his merry jaunt south to Whites Ford, again completely circling McClellan's Army of the Potomac as it lay in bivouac around Sandy Hook and Harpers Ferry. As the Confederate column passed Poolesville, one of Stuart's squadrons distracted a force of several thousand Union soldiers under

General George Stoneman, while his men made an easy crossing of the dry canal and the Potomac at Whites Ford. Stuart had lost three stragglers, but otherwise had completed the raid unscathed.

On the north bank of the Potomac, the raid was a final blow to the government's confidence in General McClellan. Lincoln had always been frustrated with McClellan's timidity, and now he used a childhood game called "Three Times Round and Out" as a comparison. Stuart had ridden around McClellan twice, Lincoln said in a semiprivate conversation; once more and his general would be out. By November, Lincoln had decided to cashier McClellan without waiting for another embarrassment. As fate would have it, there would indeed be a third ride around the Union army, but McClellan would not be there and Stuart would come to regret it deeply.

## Gettysburg and the Great River Crossings, 1863

Things continued to go awry for the Union Army of the Potomac. Ambrose Burnside's brief tenure as commander came to an end in the disastrous assault on Fredericksburg in December 1862. The following spring brought a new commander, Joe Hooker, whose initially promising campaign became Lee's most remarkable victory at Chancellorsville in May. However, Lee suffered a grievous loss as well: Stonewall Jackson was mistakenly shot by a Confederate picket and shortly died of pneumonia after an amputation. Nevertheless, Lee decided that it was time for the Army of Northern Virginia to cross the Potomac once again and take the war to the North.

Lee's armies flowed west through the gaps in Virginia's Blue Ridge mountains and entered the familiar corridor of the Shenandoah Valley, marching north. On June 15 and 16, General Richard Ewell's troops crossed the Potomac at Williamsport (mile 99.6), and on June 24, James Longstreet and A. P. Hill's men crossed at Botelors Ford (mile 71.4) near Shepherdstown. When Hooker's Army of the Potomac learned of the Confederate advance, its long train of men and supplies began moving back across the Potomac to Maryland, using pontoon bridges at Edwards Ferry (mile 30.9). Hooker called for Harpers Ferry to be abandoned before its ten-thousand-man garrison was again enveloped by the advancing Confederate Army, but the request was denied by General-in-Chief Henry Halleck, who was loath to see the improved fortifications abandoned so quickly (*see* mile 62.5). A completely frustrated

Hooker offered to resign over the matter, and Halleck quickly replaced him with General George Meade. With this last-minute change in command, the two great armies headed toward Pennsylvania and the three-day battle at Gettysburg that culminated with Pickett's Charge and a crippling blow to Confederate hopes.

Lee's maneuvering just before the battle of Gettysburg was hampered by the absence of Stuart's cavalry, which normally gave him excellent reports on Union troop movements. Stuart had crossed the Potomac at Rowsers Ford (mile 22) on the night of June 27, a day after the Army of the Potomac finished its massive crossing just upstream. From Rowsers Ford, Stuart set out on another of his brazen rides around the Army of the Potomac. Since he had crossed the Potomac about 10 miles south of Hooker, he could claim to have ridden a little better than a semicircle around the Union force to rendezvous with Lee at Gettysburg. However, he spent a valuable week in the process, dragging a captured wagon train behind him. When he finally arrived, in the middle of the battle, he received a stern dressing-down from General Lee instead of his usual hero's welcome.

After the defeat at Gettysburg, the Army of Northern Virginia began a tantalizingly slow retreat which brought them to the Potomac River at Williamsport on July 8. Here they had to wait five anxious days for the floodwaters to subside, while General Meade's army slowly surrounded them. General Meade was in position to attack that Sunday (July 12), but hesitated that day and the next to study further the ring of defenses that Lee's army had dug around the town. When his troops advanced on the Confederate positions on July 14, they found that the earthworks were abandoned, as the entire Army of Northern Virginia had crossed the Potomac overnight. The corps of General A. P. Hill and General Longstreet crossed on a rough pontoon bridge near the aptly named town of Falling Waters, West Virginia (see mile 94.4). The remaining corps, under General Ewell, managed to find a place to ford the river just above Williamsport (see mile 99.6), five miles upstream, and waded across holding their guns and ammunition overhead. The Army of Northern Virginia had again escaped by the skin of its teeth.

Observers in Washington saw another missed opportunity for the Union forces to win a decisive victory over the Army of Northern Virginia. Lincoln drafted a scathing letter to General Meade, in which he pointed out that even after receiving 20,000 reinforcements, Meade "stood and let the flood run down, bridges be built, and the enemy move away at his leisure without attacking him." Lincoln never signed or sent the letter, but the incident continued to irritate him: he said that General Meade's pursuit of the Confederate forces reminded him of an old lady trying to shoo some geese across the road.*

## Jubal Early and the Battles of Oldtown and Folck's Mill, 1864

In mid-March, General Ulysses S. Grant took command of the Union war effort in Virginia and began a relentless advance to Richmond. As the noose tightened around Richmond and Petersburg, federal forces were once again threatening the farmlands of the Shenandoah Valley. Lee sent General Jubal Early west to clear the valley in time for the harvest and draw some of the military attention away from Richmond.

General Early had only 8,000 men, but he soon took the offensive, crossing the Potomac at the familiar ford at Shepherdstown (mile 71.4) on July 5. It soon became clear that he was on his way to Washington, which was lightly defended. After passing through South Mountain, Early met stiff resistance at the B&O railroad bridge over the Monocacy River on July 9 from General Lew Wallace, who fought a losing battle to buy precious time for Union reinforcements to reach the capital. Early's men were able to advance to the outskirts of Washington, but were too few in number to launch a serious assault. They did succeed in creating a minor panic, however, as office workers, invalids, and unarmed troops in transit were rushed to the battlements. After lingering a day, the Confederates retreated back to Virginia, crossing the Potomac at Whites Ford (mile 38.7) on July 14.

Two weeks later, Early sent 3,000 men under Brigadier Generals John McCausland and Bradley Johnson back across the Potomac on another raid. They returned to Stuart's old haunt, Chambersburg, Pennsylvania, on July 30 and burned it to the ground after the town refused to pay a $200,000 ransom. McCausland's men then marched southwest toward Cumberland, pausing at Hancock (mile 124.1) to tender a similar offer to that town, at markedly

---

*Some historians have been kinder about Meade's caution as he approached Williamsport: they point out that, although Meade had 80,000 men and Lee but 50,000, the Confederates had had time to take up a strong defensive position and had brought more ammunition up from Winchester.

General Jubal A. Early's men wreaked havoc on the canal during the summer of 1864. *Illustration courtesy Library of Virginia.*

reduced rates ($30,000). The Confederates could not afford to linger, as Union cavalry under General William Averell were reported to be in close pursuit. The money was not forthcoming, but McCausland spared Hancock after being persuaded by the Marylanders under his command that many of the townspeople were friendly to the Confederacy.

McCausland and Johnson proceeded up the Baltimore Pike toward Cumberland, only to be confronted two miles east of town at Evitts Creek (mile 180.7) by Union forces under General Benjamin Kelley. This was Kelley's great moment, after years of garrison duty and running around responding to reports of skirmishes and sabotage in the hinterlands. Kelley had scraped together a motley assortment of units, including a hundred or so unarmed "stragglers" from the Shenandoah Valley, and positioned them in the woods on the west side of Evitts Creek, looking down on the bridge and a small mill. Kelley's men were well concealed and were able to surprise McCausland's advance party when they crossed the bridge at three in the afternoon on August 1. The Confederates took cover behind the bridge and the mill buildings, but were held off by artillery and rifle fire for the rest of the day, in what has been immortalized as the battle of Folck's Mill. Fearing the pursuit of General Averell's cavalry, McCausland and Johnson withdrew their men that night, using "obscure" roads to retreat 20 miles downstream to Oldtown (mile 166.7).

At dawn the next day, however, the Confederates found the river crossing at Oldtown blocked by 250 men from the 153rd Ohio National Guards. Anticipating a crossing at Oldtown a few days earlier, General Kelley had sent the group down from Cumberland by train, under the command of Colonel Israel Stough. Stough's men had taken up positions on Alum Hill, a narrow hillock between the canal and the river, and had burned the bridges across the canal. Gunfire was exchanged between the soldiers on Alum Hill and the Confederates hiding around the buildings of Oldtown, until some of the latter managed to cross the canal just upstream and outflank Stough and his men by advancing down the towpath side of the canal. Stough retreated across the river, where his men were able to resume their defense using a convenient blockhouse and the support of a B&O train outfitted with several ironclad cars. The Confederates brought up their artillery and put the first shot right through the boiler of the train and the second through a porthole. The third shot scattered the Union troops along the railroad embankment, and after an hour's exchange of gunfire, Stough and 80 of his men still holed up in the blockhouse agreed to surrender.

The Confederate raiders were able to complete the crossing into western Virginia, but Averell's cavalry finally caught them at Moorefield, West Virginia. By late October, the Union was in complete control of the valley, closing "the back door" for the raids into Maryland. All that was left to the war in Virginia was the slow siege of Richmond and Petersburg that lasted into the spring of 1865.

## McNeill's Rangers Kidnap the Union Generals at Cumberland, 1865

The end of the war was now clearly visible, but that did not mean that the Confederates had lost their fighting spirit or their bravado. In the far western corner of Virginia (now West Virginia), a young man named Jesse McNeill harbored a deep resentment against the garrison chief at Cumberland, General Kelley, who had packed McNeill's

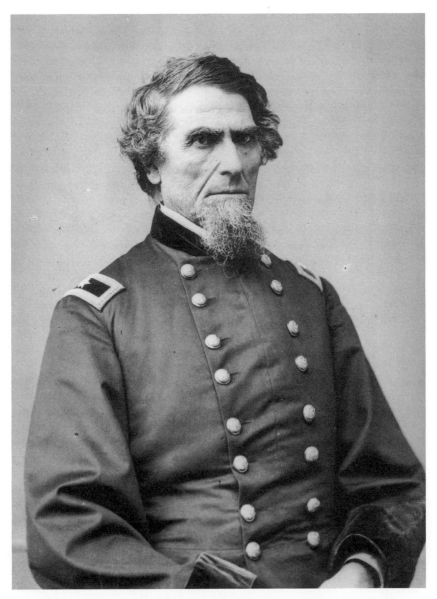

Union General Benjamin F. Kelley, defender of Cumberland and the hero of Folck's Mill. In February 1865, Confederate raiders kidnapped him from his bed in the Barnum Hotel in Cumberland. *Photo courtesy Library of Congress.*

mother and sister off to prison in Ohio as Confederate sympathizers. Kelley had exiled or imprisoned other women, but he was going to find that the McNeill family would be a special problem. Jesse McNeill was a lieutenant and leader of the Partisan Rangers, having fought along with his father, John McNeill. His father had been killed the year before, and Jesse was limping around on one leg, but he had the motive, the means, and especially the willpower to carry out a dramatic revenge.

Sixty-four of the Partisan Rangers rode up from Moorefield to Cumberland, which was defended by 4,000 Union soldiers. Approaching under cover of darkness, they surprised the Union sentinels at the western outskirts of town and persuaded them to reveal the password. They came down Greene Street, past Walnut Bottom, and crossed the chain bridge over Wills Creek around three in the morning. General Kelley was lodged with General Crook at their headquarters in the Barnum Hotel and the adjacent Revere House. The Rangers were able to surprise and disarm the sentries without spreading an alarm, and rousted the generals from bed for a brisk winter's ride south. The operation took all of ten minutes, and was done so quietly that soldiers were left sleeping soundly in rooms next to General Crook's.

Rather than leaving the way they had come, the Rangers made their exit along the canal towpath and were a few miles downstream before they heard a cannon sound the alarm back in town. Crossing the Potomac at Wileys Ford (see mile 182.6), they headed to Moorefield at a breakneck pace, covering the 80 miles by the next evening, which was a good thing, since General George Armstrong Custer's cavalry was hard on their heels. The two generals were escorted to Libby Prison in Richmond, but, under the generous treatment accorded officers, were paroled and back in Cumberland within a month.* Not long afterwards, Lee was forced to abandon Richmond and surrender at Appomattox.

———

*There's a curious postscript to this story, which dramatizes the ambivalent loyalties of those who lived along the Potomac. Exactly six months after the raid, General Crook married the sister of James Dailey, who was a member of the Confederate raiding party led by McNeill. It is likely that Crook was already courting Mary Dailey at the time of the raid, as Cumberland high society continued to offer balls and other social events throughout the war.

# The Decline of the Potomac Valley

The canal enjoyed a brief period of prosperity for about 15 years after the Civil War. But it could not compete with the railroad, even in its specialty, the delivery of coal from Cumberland. In the end, the B&O Railroad purchased the canal and operated it at a loss, just to keep its land from falling into the hands of other railroads.

The B&O and Western Maryland railroads were to have their own troubles, competing with a myriad of other lines, including the enormous Pennsylvania Railroad system. And then the railroads themselves entered an era of decline, as the internal combustion engine and the nation's highway system gave travelers and freight carriers much more flexibility at an affordable price. The B&O line is still in use, but much of the Western Maryland's abandoned track, like the canal, may be converted to recreational trails.

The industry of the valley withered away as water power, which tied the manufacturing plants to the river, was replaced by electricity. The armory at Harpers Ferry was never rebuilt after the Civil War, and the iron industry of the Potomac was no match for the burgeoning steelworks around Pittsburgh. Even the coal industry just west of Cumberland eventually declined and was finally crippled by a massive labor strike in the 1920s.

While the decline of manufacturing and transportation has had a terrible effect on the valley towns, it has also restored the river to a more natural state. Following the canal towpath on foot or on a bicycle, it's hard to regret anything. Just a few miles north of Washington, the Potomac quickly becomes very quiet. The early visions of mills and furnaces and a water route teeming with boats on their way to the Ohio Valley never materialized, but the ebbing of industry has left a natural treasure.

---------------------------------------------------------------

## The Heyday and the Decline of the Canal, 1865–1889

Despite the Confederate raids and the other hardships of war, the canal had survived and eventually even benefited from the shortages and consequent higher prices of the wartime economy. In 1865 the canal took in more money (nearly $360,000) than in any previous year. The company raised wages and actually began paying back some of its loans, although the sudden rush of creditors at the first hint of payment nearly swamped the boat. Urgently needed repairs to the canal were begun. And then, in the 1870s, the unthinkable happened: the canal began making serious money. The numbers for both tons carried and tolls escalated dramatically, with nearly one million tons carried in 1871. This was a fairly respectable number, even when compared to the Erie traffic of 2 million tons in the 1850s.

|      | Tonnage | Tolls   |
|------|---------|---------|
| 1865 | 372,000 | 346,000 |
| 1866 | 383,000 | 356,000 |
| 1867 | 521,000 | 375,000 |
| 1868 | 553,000 | 277,000 |
| 1869 | 724,000 | 368,000 |
| 1870 | 662,000 | 342,000 |
| 1871 | 969,000 | 485,000 |
| 1872 | 924,000 | 460,000 |
| 1873 | 881,000 | 483,000 |
| 1874 | 910,000 | 500,000 |

Source: Walter Sanderlin, *The Great National Project;* numbers rounded to nearest thousand.

More than five hundred boats were plying the canal now, carrying mostly coal, but also some modest amounts of lumber, stone, grain, flour, and even demon whiskey. Giddy with its success, the company even considered extending the canal over the mountains to the Ohio River, as originally planned. Some were now bold enough to argue that the canal would always be able to ship coal more economically than railroads. The company also entertained plans to enlarge all of its locks to accommodate larger boats carrying up to 240 tons, twice the maximum tonnage of the time.

The company settled on some relatively modest improvements. It installed new "drop" gates to speed passage in the congested Seven Locks below Carderock (miles 8–9). It extended the lock walls at a series of locks between Seneca and Harpers Ferry, so that two canal boats could be lifted or lowered at the same time (*see* mile 30.9). It considered ways to let some canal boats out into the Potomac to avoid the backups along the Georgetown wharves. At first the canal company planned another series of locks, but eventually it turned the project over to an independent company that proposed to build an inclined plane to lower boats into the river if it were granted the right to charge tolls. The necessary arrangements were made in 1875 with H. H. Dodge & Company, and the inclined plane was completed in 1877, considerably speeding up operations at the Georgetown terminus (*see* mile 2.3).

But it seemed that no good fortune on the Potomac was meant to last. The 1880s saw steadily declining revenues for the company, as the railroads were able to reduce their prices aggressively for carrying coal to Baltimore's deeper harbor for oceangoing vessels. The canal company was also hurt by periodic strikes and flooding, including a very damaging freshet in 1886.

Finally, on May 30 and June 1, 1889, another devastating flood ripped down the Potomac Valley, bringing canal boats, lockhouses, and sheds tumbling into the river. It was estimated that $1 million would be needed to repair the canal, far in excess of the amount the company could hope to borrow. The canal lay idle that summer and fall, and did not operate at all in 1890. But for an unexpected corporate angel, the operating history of the canal would have ended with the great flood of 1889.

## The B&O Railroad Takes Over the Canal, 1890–1902

The B&O Railroad had not let any grass grow up around its ties in the five decades since it reached Cumberland. While the canal remained mired in the Potomac Valley, the B&O had extended its line to Wheeling by 1853, and had even worked out an arrangement to connect to Pittsburgh in 1872. At the same time, several other railroads were interested in the Potomac route. The B&O already

Railroad eclipses canal: a B&O passenger train speeds along the shared route near Sandy Hook. *Photo courtesy National Park Service.*

had a satisfactory line running through the valley, but it was determined to keep the canal from falling into the hands of its rivals. Consequently, it arranged for loans to repair the canal.

The bankruptcy court agreed not to order the sale of the canal if it continued to function as a profitable enterprise. The B&O arranged to meet the letter if not the spirit of this requirement by organizing the Chesapeake and Ohio Transportation Company, which guaranteed the canal company a profit, provided the company kept the waterway open. The B&O used the Transportation Company to funnel enough money into the canal to pay back the repair loans and keep it operating.

The canal company drastically changed its mode of operation in 1902, when it ended the era of independent boat owners by forming the Canal Towage Company. The boats now carried numbers instead of names, and the company even put the boat runs on a schedule. Practically speaking, the boat owners were probably not that much worse off under the new arrangement—they had struck in previous years to protest overcharging by boatbuilders and the canal company. But there was no doubt that an era of individualism had come to an end: boat captains became company employees and were no longer the masters of their ships.

## The Western Maryland Shares the Route, 1902–1908

As it turned out, the B&O had only temporarily thwarted its competition by buying the canal. In the 1890s, the Western Maryland had worked out a hospitable agreement with the B&O Railroad to connect the two lines at Cherry Run, West Virginia (*see* mile 113.9). The Western Maryland track thus carried some of the B&O's western traffic over to the Reading line in Pennsylvania, bringing it to port cities such as Philadelphia. But by the turn of the century, the Western Maryland was heavily in debt, and the city of Baltimore was looking to unload it.

The Western Maryland's corporate angel turned out to be George Gould, son of the notorious railroad tycoon, Jay Gould. The elder Gould had built a fearsome reputation as a "robber baron" who bought railroads, milked them for a short-term profit, and left them destitute. The younger Gould owned a considerable railroad empire, but he needed a connection to the eastern seaboard.

The city sold the Western Maryland to Gould in 1902, and he immediately began building the line west of Big Pool (mile 112.1) toward Cumberland. The line ran within a few feet of the canal along many narrow stretches of the river valley, and at other times it vaulted the river or ran through ridge tunnels (*see* mile 143.4). The track was completed to Cumberland in 1906. However, Gould's empire was on shaky financial footing, and the Western Maryland went bankrupt in 1908. The ownership changed, but the drive west continued with an extension from Cumberland to Connellsville in Pennsylvania. Further down the road, the Western Maryland would be acquired by John D. Rockefeller, and, in the incestuous and internecine world of railroad acquisitions and regulations, it would eventually be merged with the rival Baltimore and Ohio as a part of the CSX system.

## The Last Flood Suspends Canal Operations, 1924–1938

For its part, the B&O continued to operate the canal until the early 1920s, taking in only about $40,000 to $60,000 a year in tolls, and most assuredly not fulfilling the court's stipulation that it continue to show a profit to hold its charter. In 1924, after a flood of relatively modest proportions, the railroad decided not to go to the expense of further

After the flood of 1924: a canal boat left high and dry near Georgetown (mile 3.7). *Photo courtesy National Park Service.*

repairs. The canal company ceased its boating operation entirely.

If the last years of the canal could be characterized as an artificial life-support system, it was now in a state of suspended animation. The railroad maintained enough of the lower level to supply water to the mills in Georgetown; in fact, the mills would continue to get water from the canal well into the period of federal ownership. But the railroad did not repair the flood damage, and did little to maintain the canal bed and the masonry structures against the inexorable forces of decay.

Fortunately for the railroad, the only entity that seemed to have an aggressive interest in the property was not a rival company but the federal government. In 1926 the engineer commissioner of the District of Columbia, J. Franklin Bell, suggested that the canal be turned into a federal highway. The B&O Railroad was strongly opposed to any project that might impinge on the narrow right-of-way from Point of Rocks to Harpers Ferry.

The Great Depression changed the situation dramatically. President Franklin D. Roosevelt's uncle, Frederic Delano, was the chairman of the National Capital Park and Planning Commission and thought that the canal would make a splendid project for the Civilian Conservation Corps. As it happened, the B&O owed the Reconstruction Finance Corporation $80 million and wanted to borrow another $8.2 million. Under the circumstances, it proved fairly easy to pry the canal loose from the railroad for $2 million in 1938.

The Civilian Conservation Corps set to work on the massive ruin, and succeeded in restoring the first 20 miles to working condition. There was even some talk of rewatering the entire length of the canal, but World War II and another great flood in 1942 washed it all away. The government was having a hard time figuring out exactly what to do with such a peculiar property.

## The Douglas Walk Leads to a National Park, 1945–1971

At the end of World War II, the U.S. Army Corps of Engineers unveiled a proposal it had been developing for eight years. In the interest of flood control, the engineers wanted to build a series of 14 massive dams that would have inundated massive portions of the Potomac Valley—a sort of preemptive strike. The plan included a 119-foot dam just above Great Falls that would have backed up the Potomac almost to Harpers Ferry. Another dam below Harpers Ferry would have flooded the historic part of town and raised the water level all the way up to Shepherdstown. In the process, the Antietam and Monocacy aqueducts and much of the towpath would have vanished underwater.

Against the apocalyptic backdrop of the dam proposal, an alternate plan to turn the canal into a parkway modeled after Skyline Drive began to look much more attractive. Fortunately, the parkway plan moved slowly, and it was still gestating when the *Washington Post* endorsed it in 1954. That's when Supreme Court Justice William O. Douglas penned his famous letter to the editors, inviting them to join him on a walking tour of the towpath. The editors accepted, the Wilderness Society and the Potomac Appalachian Trail Club agreed to make the necessary arrangements, and a fairly sizable entourage started out from North Branch (near Cumberland) on March 20. Only nine of the group (including Douglas but not the *Post* editorialists) hiked the whole way, but the event succeeded in calling public attention to the conservation movement.

Unfortunately, the Douglas hike of 1954 did not lead to any swift resolution. The fight to preserve the natural and historic integrity of the canal was just beginning. Variations on the parkway and dam proposals swirled through hearings and draft bills during the Eisenhower, Kennedy, Johnson, and Nixon administrations. A tentative effort at a parkway was begun, razing lockhouse no. 5 in the process—we now know this as the Clara Barton Parkway. The public power interests favored a system of dams, which, though scaled back from the Corps of Engineers plan, would still have flooded several miles of towpath. Somehow, miraculously, no serious damage was done, and the Chesapeake and Ohio Canal was finally designated a National Historical Park in a law signed by President Nixon on January 8, 1971. It was a small piece of good news that was lost in the front page stories about the Charles Manson trial and the battle reports from Vietnam. In a small irony, the Nixon presidency would begin to unravel 18 months later next to canal mile 0, in a building named for the Tidewater Lock.

Finally installed as the canal's guardian, the Park Service has quietly gone about the work of stabilizing many canal structures and restoring the towpath to a usable condition. At the same time, the Park Service has had the unenviable task of balancing the competing demands of hikers, bikers, horse riders, fishermen, local residents, nature lovers, and historical preservationists. For instance, the widening of the towpath around the cliffs above Dam no. 5 was a great convenience for bicyclists, but incurred the wrath of the preservationists.

The most recent and dramatic challenge to the Park was the two great floods of 1996. The first flood, caused by sudden warming and rainfall in the aftermath of a three-foot snowfall, crested on January 21 and wreaked havoc around the Potomac riverbends and at its falls, particularly at Harpers Ferry and between Great Falls and Little Falls. Hurricane Fran brought a second flood, nearly as devastating as the first, that once again swept through the towns of Harpers Ferry and Point of Rocks. Although it is extremely unusual for the Potomac to rise above towpath level twice in a single year, periodic floods have been a major part of the canal's history. Since the canal became a park, there have been two other notable floods, on June 24, 1972 (Hurricane Agnes) and November 7, 1985 (Hurricane Juan). The 1996 floods, like their predecessors, have occasioned the most remarkable demonstrations of support for the canal and the river, as residents, corporations, and associations have banded together to assist the Park Service in restoring the canal and towpath.

In the end, the C&O Canal may finally outshine its rivals if the connection to the Ohio Valley is made by continuing the trail along the abandoned Western Maryland Railroad through the mountains. Part of this trail already exists through the Ohiopyle National Forest, and an extension is under construction to McKeesport. A further extension from Confluence to Cumberland will make it possible for hikers and bicyclists to travel all the way from Georgetown to Pittsburgh, crossing the Appalachians on a gently graded trail. Considering that much of the Erie Canal's towpath has disappeared along with its mules, the tables have suddenly turned. The C&O Canal may well become the only off-road trail to the west—an unexpected vindication of Jefferson and Washington's faith in the Potomac route.

# Structures along the Canal

Following the canal, you'll see many ruins that are as puzzling to our modern eyes as the toppled remains of Ozymandias. Even in its present state of decay, the simple but elegant stonework for the locks and aqueducts has a much more handsome appearance than the modern highway and railroad bridges that have superseded the canal. But esthetics were a minor consideration for the canal company—a practical purpose lay behind each structure. The deceptively simple canal works give us a window on the water-driven technology of the nineteenth century and the intricate interrelationship of the industries along the Potomac Valley.

The canal itself was a "prism," wider at the water's surface than at the bottom, and large enough to allow two boats to pass each other. Digging and blasting the channel for the canal was hard and dangerous work, and the result was often just referred to as a ditch. The masonry parts were held in higher esteem, and were termed "works of art" in the canal company's documents. These included the locks, culverts, aqueducts, and waste weirs that regulated the flow of water through the canal and turned it into an engine to lift and lower the canal boats.

The stonemasons were the most prominent craftsmen of the canal, painstakingly cutting blocks of stone to as small a tolerance as a half-inch. Unfortunately, this sort of craftsmanship is much too time-consuming and expensive for the modern world. The highway bridges that vault the river and the canal are more sensibly formed of concrete, but this sort of construction did not develop until well after the canal was built. (The ancient Romans used concrete in their glorious aqueducts, but this skill was lost to Europeans in the Middle Ages.) Concrete was not used on the canal until 1906, and is most commonly found as replacement work in waste weirs and lock pockets.

# Locks: The Machinery of Elevation

The most visible piece of engineering along the canal is its locks. There are 74 lift locks in the canal system,* and a smattering of river locks, guard locks, and stop locks, which will be discussed later.

## Levels and Lift Locks

The canal is really an artificial river with almost no current. A canal is relatively simple to construct in the lowlands, but things get a little more complicated when it comes to mountain ridges or even small hills. To deal with irregular terrain, the canal had to be broken into different *levels* of water, and it had to have *locks* to transfer vessels from one level to another. These locks lowered or raised boats by letting water into the lock from the higher level and then discharging it into the lower level. Note that the same transfer of water takes place regardless of which direction the vessel is traveling. Only the order is different: a vessel that enters the lock before it is filled will be raised to the higher level, while a vessel that enters the lock after it is filled will be lowered.

## Lock Gates

Most of the lock gates on the canal are miter gates (sometimes described as swing gates). The design for the miter lock can be traced back to sketches by Leonardo da Vinci. Note that the gates of a miter lock are set at an angle pointing toward the higher level. Thus the natural pressure of water from the upper level will force the gates shut. To balance the levels, the locktender turned iron stems that open the paddles or wickets (small doors at the bottom

---

*The last lift lock was number 75, but the canal company left out one of the locks just below the Paw Paw Tunnel (Lock 65). However, note that the guard locks at Dams no. 4 and 5 were also unnumbered lift locks where canal boats entered the slackwaters, so the system had 76 levels.

of the lock gate) to release water from the upper level. When the water in the lock chamber reached the desired level, reducing the pressure on the gate, the lock gate was opened by pushing the long "balances" that extended from the gate.

A coal boat prepares to head downstream, having just been lowered from the upper level. *Photo courtesy National Park Service.*

## Lock Walls

The lock walls of the canal have endured, even though the gates and other features of the lock may be missing or in poor repair. Unless they rested directly on bedrock, the lock walls were built on a timber foundation. The original stonework varies greatly with the quality of stone that was readily available in different sections of the canal. Stones were brought from Aquia Creek (about 30 miles south of Alexandria) to build the first few locks in Georgetown. The distinctive red sandstone from Seneca was first used in the locks at Little Falls. Further up the canal, the prevalent building stone became limestone, particularly in the Great Valley between Harpers Ferry and Hancock. The lack of good building stone in the upper reaches of the canal was much lamented by the canal company, and can be seen in the smaller, irregular blocks that were cobbled together. In one stretch, "composite locks" were built of rough stone sheathed in wood.

If you look closely at the lock, you'll often see some odd replacement work. The locks just below Great Falls have a

The anatomy of a lock: by using a lock key to open and close the wickets in the lock gates, the lockkeeper could fill or drain the lock, moving canal boats from one level to the next. *Sketch by Michael Gavula.*

layer of brick running under the first layer of stones. In the upper stretch of the canal, where quality stone was scarce, the entire walls of some locks were replaced with concrete.

## Lockhouses

Park visitors may find the surviving lockhouses to be quite charming in the tranquil setting along the towpath, but these one-and-a-half-story buildings were small and spartan homes when you take into account the preference for large families to work the lock. The foundation of the lockhouse was usually of stone, while the house itself was built of wood, brick, or stone. (The lockhouse at North Branch, the last one before Cumberland, is built of logs.)

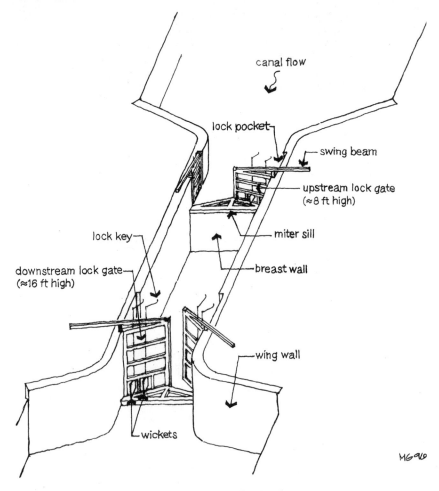

anatomy of a lock

## Bypass Flumes

Above Georgetown, the locks have bypass flumes to allow a continuous flow of water downstream even when the lock is not in use. Some of these locks have very elegant flumes lined in stone, with a picturesque little waterfall over the "tumble" at the end of the flume. Further along the canal, in the portions that are not watered, the flume may be silted up and covered with grass, leaving no sign other than a slight depression running around the berm side of the lock. In other cases, such as the locks at Shepherdstown and Harpers Ferry, the flume runs underground, and makes its appearance through a culvert on the downstream end of the lock.

At many locks a wait house sheltered the lockkeeper during working hours. *Photo courtesy National Park Service.*

## Wait Houses and Other Buildings

Many locks had a little hut next to the lock gates to shelter the lockkeeper in inclement weather. These huts, and the assorted mule barns, tool sheds, and feed sheds clustered around the locks, slowly disintegrated after the canal stopped operating, and the remains were dismantled by the Park Service.

## Drop Gates and Extensions

The canal company altered several locks during the 1870s to accommodate the increased traffic during its boom years. For instance, it installed "drop gates" at the upper end of some of the Seven Locks (*see* miles 8–10). The drop gates were an improvement on da Vinci's design, being quicker and easier to operate. One person could operate the drop gate. First, a lever on the lock wall was pulled to open "butterfly" gates in the floor of the lock; this let water into the lock from the upper level. Then the drop gate was opened by turning the spoked wheel mounted next to the lever. The drop gate was feasible only on the upper end of the lock, because of the greater height required for the downstream gates.

In addition to installing drop gates during the boom years, the canal company extended many locks to accommodate two boats at a time (particularly Locks 25–32).

---

**Where to find locks**

With 74 locks, there's no shortage to choose from. The locks at Georgetown and the locks at Great Falls (mile 14.4), being watered and in use, are the best examples. Riley's Lockhouse (mile 22.7) is open on weekends in season. The Park Service has restored a wait house, lockhouse, and mule barn at Four Locks (mile 108.8), which gives the visitor some idea of the cluster of buildings that used to surround some of the busier locks.

---

# Maintaining the Level

In many ways, the canal was built to replace the Potomac—the canal would provide an improved and completely independent channel of navigation that would not be affected by drought or storms, and had no strong current to deter upstream traffic. But the canal still depended on the river to replace the water that was being passed down through the system of locks. To accomplish this, water from the river was diverted by feeder dams into the canal through guard locks.

### Feeder Dams

Most of the dams were low-lying rubble dams, with the exception of the dams above and below Williamsport. These dams were originally constructed of timber "cribs" that were filled with rock. Unfortunately, they were soon washed out by floods, and were eventually replaced by the present masonry "high-rock" dams. However, if you look closely at the base of the dam, you can still see windrows of stone left by the earlier dams.

The high-rock dams created enormous "slackwaters" that were calm and deep enough for fully loaded canal boats, so the company saved some construction costs by letting the boats out into the river above the dams. Only a narrow towpath had to be built to allow the mules to pull the boats along the riverbank. As the need for electricity expanded, the Potomac Edison Company constructed power plants on the West Virginia side of the Potomac at Dams no. 4 and 5 to take advantage of the substantial "head" of water.

The original plans called for eight dams along the canal, but the company ended up building only six. Dam no. 3 in the canal system merely modified an existing dam at Harpers Ferry that had been built for the Armory Canal on the opposite shore. The seventh dam planned in the system, at Town Creek, was never built. Instead of the seventh dam, the canal company opted to install a steam pump where the Potomac divides into its North and South branches. Later this pump was relocated opposite Patterson Creek, a few miles upstream.

The canal company by no means had a monopoly on river dams. Other dams were built to supply water to mills, and later to the Pittsburgh Plate Glass factory just south of Cumberland. The most significant of these other dams is the one just above Great Falls that diverts water into the Washington Aqueduct (built 1853–76). The U.S. Army Corps of

*The remains of Dam no. 6 provide a unique cutaway view of the common timber crib design that held the loose rubble and stone in place. Photo courtesy National Park Service.*

Engineers maintains the aqueduct dam and is responsible for another water supply dam at Little Falls, just above Dam no. 1.

Most of the smaller dams now lie in ruins, no more than a manmade line of rapids in the river. Dam no. 8 in Cumberland was removed by the Corps of Engineers as part of a flood control project in the 1950s. Maintenance of the high-rock dams (nos. 4 and 5) is a daunting project, which requires the assistance of the Seabees (the U.S. Navy's Construction Battalion).

---

**Where to find feeder dams**

There were seven feeder dams along the canal, most of them low "crib" dams of rock rubble. More spectacular are Dams no. 4 and 5, which are "high-rock dams" launching a cascade of water over a twenty-foot drop (miles 84.6 and 106.6). The scene at Dam no. 5, which is a little more secluded, is one of the highlights along the canal. A good example of a mill dam can be found at the site of Botelor's Mill just below Shepherdstown. Judging from the anglers on hand, the rubble dam also makes a good fishing hole.

---

### Guard Locks

A "guard lock" was added just above each of the seven river dams to draw water from the river and protect the canal from flooding. These locks could also serve as river locks, particularly at Dams no. 4 and 5, where all of the canal traffic was passed into the river. Where the canal was lower than the river to draw water from the dams, the guard lock was also a lift lock to bring boats back and forth from the river level. (Except at dams, the canal company tried to keep the canal at least 16 feet above the normal river level.) Since the guard lock created a break in the towpath side of the canal, mules had to use a crossover bridge, usually a pivoting or raised structure over the lock, to continue along the canal. At Dams no. 4 and 5, where the towpath ran along the riverbank, the mule would also have to cross over the inlet lock above the slackwater to get back on the berm side.

---

**Where to find guard locks**

Each of the seven dams on the Potomac had its own lock to let water in from the river. The guard locks at Little Falls and Seneca are the most interesting, because they are still responsible for the watered portion of the canal. The other guard locks have since been filled or dammed.

---

### Stop Gates

Stop gates were used to divert floodwaters away from the canal and to keep water penned up in the turning basins when lower sections of the canal were drained. Most stop gates look like small locks—stone walls on each canal bank leaving only a narrow passage for boats. On closer inspection, however, you won't find the telltale recesses in these walls for the typical lock gates, only a narrow slot on each side for the wooden planks that were lowered to serve as a temporary dam.

---

**Where to find stop gates**
The most completely preserved is the one at Dam no. 4, which still has the winch house. Another good example is the one at Great Falls (mile 13.8), although the winch house has given way to a footbridge for the Widewater detour. The masonry sides are the only remains of the stop gates near Little Pool, Big Pool, and Cumberland (miles 110.2, 112.1, 114, 120, 183.4).

---

## Waste Weirs

Waste weirs are really just drains built in the wall of the canal, used in times of flooding or when that level of the canal had to be emptied for major repairs. Originally, most of the waste weirs were built of wood, starting with a frame divided by two or three vertical timbers. (Several waste weirs were built of stone, most notably the ones at mile 1.5.) The openings in the weir were covered by cast-iron wickets or horizontal boards. The wickets were turned, or the boards were raised or lowered as needed to let water out of the canal. Unfortunately, the waste weirs have lost much of their charm over the years, as the wooden frames were replaced by concrete in the early part of this century.

Most of the waste weirs are readily identified from the towpath by their concrete side walls, which protrude a few inches above towpath level. Waste weirs are usually found within easy walking distance of a lockhouse, where the keeper could open and shut the weir without having to leave the immediate vicinity of the lock. Except for a few near Hancock, the waste weirs were placed on the river side of the canal, which was the most sensible place to dispose of excess water.

---

**Where to find waste weirs**
The most interesting waste weirs are the ones in the watered portions of the canal, where you can usually see a cascade of water splashing down the stones at the base of the weir. The weirs just opposite the Tavern at Great Falls (mile 14.4) and at Pennyfield Lock (mile 19.6) are particularly good examples.

---

## Spillways

There were other areas along the canal where more unusual measures were taken to maintain the proper water level. In several places, the company built masonry spillways to protect the embankment while excess water poured over the towpath side of the canal. A low spot in the towpath sometimes served the same purpose without the formality of reinforcing stonework. These spillways were known as "mule drinks" because the mules could dip their heads and snatch a little liquid refreshment while still pulling the boat.

---

**Where to find spillways**
The most accessible spillway is just beyond the Key Bridge (mile 1.5); the Park Service has recently restored the spillway just above Dam no. 6 (mile 134.5). The remains of other spillways can be found along Big Pool (mile 113) and below Spring Gap (mile 171.4).

---

# Intersections

While it may be helpful to think of the canal as a watery highway, the analogy has at least one notable limitation: this highway could not have survived an intersection with any of the myriad of tributaries flowing into the Potomac. Either the canal would have been flooded, or it would have quickly drained away into the Potomac. At these intersections, the canal water had to be carried *over* the stream.

### Aqueducts

The most dramatic solution to the problem was the aqueduct, which carried the canal and towpath over the intersecting river. The eleven aqueducts that are officially parts of the C&O Canal are the most visually impressive of the masonry structures in the system. Unfortunately, none of them is watered, denying us the mysterious sight of canal barges gliding through the air above the streambed. (However, it is possible that the Conococheague Aqueduct will be rebuilt as part of the plan for rewatering the canal at Williamsport.)

The aqueducts south of Williamsport are the longest, with the Monocacy Aqueduct (seven arches) often referred to as the masterpiece of the canal system. Unfortunately, the underpinnings of these aqueducts have not fared well, as the riverbed shifts and floods have sent trees and even cars crashing into the piers. The peculiar "Swayback

A canal boat approaches the Conococheague Aqueduct. *Photo courtesy National Park Service.*

Aqueduct" at Catoctin, crippled by design flaws, has almost totally washed away. Even the sight of the elegant aqueduct at Monocacy is now marred by the steel braces that hold it together. Of the lower aqueducts, only the one at Antietam can be said to be in satisfactory condition. Above Williamsport, the aqueducts are smaller, single-arch affairs.

The Park Service often alludes to a "mystery aqueduct," which was originally built as a twin culvert at Broad Run (just above Edwards Ferry). The culverts were damaged by flooding, and in the reconstruction timbers were added to support the canal bed across the run. The structure (now collapsed) never had the masonry arch, but, yes, it probably qualifies as an aqueduct.

If Broad Run has a mystery aqueduct, Georgetown has the thirteenth aqueduct, which is not counted in the C&O Canal system because it was built separately by the city of Alexandria to capture a share of the canal trade. The Alexandria canal ran about 5 miles from the port of Alexandria to a point just above the present-day Key Bridge. Here the city invested a million dollars in building an aqueduct over the river to connect to the C&O Canal just above Georgetown, an enduring piece of work that was completed in 1843. Union forces drained the aqueduct in 1861 and used it as a bridge during the Civil War. Though it was restored to service in the late 1860s, it gradually fell into disuse as canal boats were let out into the Potomac by the inclined plane and at the Georgetown tidelock, where they were pushed by steam tugboats to their destinations downstream. It was again used as a bridge until the Key Bridge was completed in 1924.

---

**Where to find aqueducts**

Two of the most impressive aqueducts are less than 20 miles apart, carrying the canal over the Seneca River (mile 22.7) and the Monocacy (mile 42.2). The triple-arch aqueduct at Antietam is in the best condition (mile 69.4). The last five aqueducts on the canal are more modest single-arch affairs, found in the mountains above Williamsport. → 1971 storm took out one of the three arches

---

### Culverts

Where the intersecting stream was small enough, there was a simpler solution to the problem posed by these tributaries: a small culvert was built to carry the stream under the canal. There are roughly 240 culverts discreetly tucked away under the canal, but they are not easily seen from the towpath. It's well worth getting off the path to see the original culverts, which are elegantly constructed stone arches from 6 to 36 feet wide. The replacement culverts, made of concrete or a corrugated metal tube set in concrete, don't have quite the same charm. Most of the culverts are stone, however, and with more than one culvert for every mile of the canal, there are more than enough masonry culverts to choose from.

Unfortunately, many of the culverts are threatened by increased runoff from parking lots and farms along the tributary streams. The culverts were designed to handle the streamflow of the 1820s, but when the Potomac Valley floods today, many of the culverts can no longer carry all the water safely under the canal bed. Finding an esthetically pleasing and historically acceptable way to supplement the existing culverts is as big an engineering challenge as stabilizing the aqueducts.

---

**Where to find culverts**

Some of the more accessible culverts are found at mile 15.3 (1 mile north of Great Falls Tavern), mile 23.4 (0.9 of a mile north of Seneca Aqueduct), mile 30.9 (just above Edwards Ferry), mile 35.4 (just south of Whites Ferry), mile 100.23 (0.4 of a mile north of Conococheague Aqueduct at Williamsport), and mile 124.4 (0.3 of a mile north of Hancock).

---

### River Locks

River locks were used to allow boats to leave the canal and cross the Potomac. Of course, boats could use the guard locks at the seven dams to enter the river, but the canal company specifically built three river locks to draw trade from the Virginia side of the river. Near Edwards Ferry, it built a lock to admit boats coming down Goose Creek from Leesburg. A separate company was chartered in Virginia to clear obstructions from Goose Creek, but the modest construction efforts that finally began in 1849 were soon rendered useless by the success of the Manassas Gap Railroad. At Harpers Ferry, the C&O built another river lock for boats coming down the Shenandoah River. A separate company had taken over the Patowmack Company's efforts to build skirting canals and locks on the Shenandoah (*see* mile 61: Harpers Ferry). Again, the success of a railroad line (in this case, the Winchester and Potomac) eliminated the cross-river traffic. The third and final river lock was built on the canal where it passed Shepherdstown, and this one appears to have enjoyed some modest success over the years. The trade from these other rivers and towns never really blossomed; it proved easier to connect to railroads than to keep the tributaries of the Potomac navigable. The canal's main business quickly became the coal trade in Cumberland.

---

**Where to find river locks**
Only three locks were designed exclusively for river traffic: the Goose Creek Lock (just below Edwards Ferry), the Shenandoah River Lock (opposite Harpers Ferry), and the Shepherdstown River Lock.

---

### The Inclined Plane

In the prosperous 1870s, the canal was shipping nearly one million tons of coal a year, and the canal boats often had to sit in line for days just above Georgetown waiting to be unloaded. To alleviate the congestion at the lower end of the canal, the canal company considered another way to let some boats out into the Potomac if they didn't need to unload in Georgetown. Inclined planes were already being used at other canals to raise and lower boats quickly where the elevation would otherwise have required a series of locks. However, building such a device was an expensive proposition, and the company was committed to applying its present profits to retiring the interest on its earlier debts. Instead, an arrangement was worked out with a separate group of investors who were willing to put up the capital for the project, provided that they could collect tolls from the boats that used it. Construction began in 1872 and was completed in 1876.

The inclined plane was considered an engineering marvel for its day. To provide a longer and gentler descent, the plane ran at an angle from the canal down to the

Culverts came in a wide variety of shapes and styles. *Photos by C. M. High.*

Potomac River. The plane had three sets of railroad tracks. The middle track carried an enormous caisson, 112 feet long and 17 feet wide, which was designed to carry not only a canal boat filled with more than 100 tons of coal, but enough water to float the boat. The two outside tracks carried cars loaded with rocks that served as counterweights to slow the caisson's descent. When loaded, the caisson weighed about 350–400 tons, and the two sets of counterweights weighed 200 tons apiece. As the caisson descended the middle track, the cars that served as counterweights on each side were drawn up by pulleys. While the counterweights were very closely balanced with the weight of the caisson, additional power was still needed to operate the pulleys. This was provided by a turbine driven by water drawn from the canal.

Aside from avoiding the congestion caused by boats unloading at the Georgetown wharves, the inclined plane lowered boats to the river in one fell swoop, saving the time of passing through the four Georgetown locks. Once in the Potomac, the boats could be towed to downriver destinations such as Alexandria. Inclined planes had been used on canals for nearly a hundred years, but this was the largest yet made and was exhibited as one of America's foremost engineering achievements at the Paris Exposition of 1876.

A ghostly photographic image shows the heavy counterweights (right foreground) and the track for the inclined plane. The caisson that carried the canal boats rests at the top of the embankment, still dripping water. *Photo courtesy National Park Service.*

Of course, nothing in the history of the canal had ever functioned perfectly, and there was a terrible accident in 1877, when the great weight on the pulleys caused the collapse of the supporting masonry, killing three men. After that, the caisson was drained before descending, to reduce the weight. The inclined plane was badly damaged by the flood of 1889. Since canal traffic had dwindled to a third of the tonnage carried in the early 1870s, there was no pressing need to repair it when the canal resumed operation.

---

**Where to find the inclined plane**
The only remains of the inclined plane are a few stones piled by the side of the towpath at mile 2.3 (about 0.8 of a mile below Fletcher's Boathouse), along with a long depression to the river that may be the location of the "race" for the water flowing out of the turbine.

---

# Boat and Mule

When originally organized, the canal company only planned to provide the waterway—it did not intend to operate the boats. The company would make its money on tolls. Company records indicate that there was considerable concern in its early years about the kinds of craft that were floating in its waters. The company charged higher tolls to drive some of the ramshackle boats and rafts off the canal, and forbade the use of iron-tipped poles or other implements that might damage the locks. The light "packet" boats for passenger service, to be drawn by horses, never generated much business; they were much slower than the railroad, and the cramped quarters were only slightly more comfortable than a stagecoach. The canal's business quickly gravitated toward large boats designed to carry as much coal as possible.

The boats were limited by the dimensions of the canal to 14 feet across. Boats were about 90 feet long, limited by the length of most of the locks. There was a mule stable at the bow and a small cabin for the family at the stern, with a cargo hold in between.

The canal was designed to make passage as effortless as possible for the cargo carriers. Its still waters reduced friction to a minimum, and the lock system made it possible to lift the boats upstream using nothing more than the flow of water itself. All the canal boat had to do was overcome inertia, though that was no small matter with a fully loaded boat starting out at Cumberland. The motive force for the boat was usually two teams of two mules each, which was sufficient to keep 120 tons of coal in motion. (To compare this with overland travel, a team of six horses could pull no more than 6 tons of cargo on the National Road.)

The mules could tow a boat at about 4 miles an hour, and the boat crew became adept at switching the team on the path with the mules in the stable during the locking process. Rotating the mules, it was possible to keep going around the clock, but it was more common to tie up at night, making the trip in about four days. Allowing time for loading and unloading, as well as for the return trip, a boat could make about twenty-five to thirty trips a year. Canal operations ceased in winter, though the canal company would keep the canal open a little longer by pulling a loaded boat with a steel prow as an icebreaker. When the canal shut down, the boat families would retire to their winter homes around Cumberland, and the mules would be sent off to the farm. (Just as the transatlantic captains would save every penny by starving their passengers, the boaters would often complain that the farmers had returned their mules in emaciated condition the next spring.)

Considering the remarkable advances in the application of steam power, it may seem surprising that the

Youngsters were often hired as mule drivers, as shown in this scene near Cumberland. *Photo courtesy National Park Service.*

**The C&O Canal Companion**

The boat captain's family usually lived in the rear cabin, and young ladies, too, had a full complement of chores. *Photo courtesy Martin Luther King, Jr., Public Library/ Washingtoniana Collection.*

mule was never replaced by an engine. At least part of the reason was the canal company's fear that the wake of a steamboat would erode the banks of the canal. A handful of steamboats plied the canal, but they were limited to speeds of 4 miles an hour or less. In 1875 the steamboat *Ludlow Patton* was reported to have made the trip from Georgetown to Cumberland in less than 45 hours, presumably traveling around the clock to cover the 184 miles.

**Where to find boats**
The Park Service operates two canal boats from April until the first week of November: the *Georgetown,* at the Georgetown Visitor's Center, and the *Canal Clipper* at Great Falls. A third boat is on display at North Branch, just south of Cumberland.

# Water Industry

The canal had both positive and a negative effects on the existing industry of the Potomac Valley. In many places it cut off access to the ferries and bridges used by farmers, mill owners, and storekeepers. But it also fostered the growth of many enterprises by bringing raw materials such as coal and limestone down the canal, and shipping away cement and iron.

## Ferries

One of the earliest transportation solutions in the Potomac Valley was the ferries across the river. Before the ferries, Indians and the first Europeans simply found a shallow ford and got wet or stuck in the mud. Naturally, ferries quickly followed the very earliest settlers along the Potomac. Peter Stephens began a ferry in the 1730s at the Shenandoah (later operated by Robert Harper and known as Harpers Ferry), and John Hawkins operated one five miles south of there, at present-day Brunswick. By 1755, in the Great Valley beyond the Blue Ridge, there were two well-known ferries near the mouth of the Conococheague (present-day Williamsport) and another at present-day Shepherdstown. At one time, there were reportedly more than a hundred ferries in operation on the Potomac, but the ferries eventually gave way to covered bridges for wagons and finally to modern highway bridges.

---

**Where to find ferries**
The only active ferry is Whites Ferry, at mile 35.5, connecting the area around Poolesville, Maryland, to Leesburg in Virginia.

---

## Bridges

The construction of the canal wreaked havoc upon the many small enterprises that depended upon access to the river. In many cases, individuals brought suit against the company as construction advanced, seeking to recover their losses. To accommodate those who needed to pass over the canal to the river, many bridges were built along the canal. The bridges tended to be expensive, because they had to be built high enough to permit boats to pass under them. The bridge had to have a 17-foot clearance above water level to provide the proper margin of safety for the canal boats returning to Cumberland lightened of their cargo and riding high. The company went to great expense and effort to raise the bridges in Georgetown, and built many other bridges to accommodate wagon traffic, pedestrians, and even a water flume to the Cresap mill at Oldtown. The company also built several road culverts, such as one for the residents of Prathers Neck above Williamsport, a river-bend that was truncated by a canal shortcut.

One clever solution was the pivot bridge, which was constructed at the level of the canal banks, usually along a masonry structure like a lock, but swiveled out of the way to allow boats to pass. Pivot bridges became as common as weeds but were made of wood, which has long since disintegrated.

This photograph taken at the downstream end of Big Pool shows two ways by which local traffic could cross the canal—a pedestrian "high bridge" and a pivot bridge. The pivot bridge was folded against the lock wall and could be swiveled out when needed. *Photo courtesy National Park Service.*

---

**Where to find pivot bridges**
The best example of a pivot bridge is the footbridge in front of Great Falls Tavern, which swivels out of place when the *Canal Clipper* passes through the lock. The bridge at Point of Rocks, formerly a bridge that pivoted on a center pier, is now fixed in place and paved. The remaining pier of a pivot bridge, with a circular pivoting ring in the center, can be found in the canal at mile 9.9, though this bridge was built after the canal company ceased operation to let barges use that stretch of the canal.

---

## Water Wheels, Mills, and Turbines

Water was not just a convenient mode of transportation, it was also a source of power. Before the advent of electricity and power lines, factories and mills were commonly located near rivers and streams, where energy was supplied to their operations through the use of a water wheel. The energy from the water wheel could be transferred through a system of gears to a set of millstones for grinding. The waterwheel could also provide power to rollers and trip hammers, as at the armory rifle works at Harpers Ferry. The ways in which natural materials could be ground, cut, or rolled into useful products was truly astounding. Gristmills produced flour from a variety of grains, cement mills ground limestone into powder, sawmills cut timber or stone to manageable dimensions, rolling mills could produce iron T rails for train tracks, and paper mills ground wood into pulp.

Gristmills and sawmills were the most common enterprises, clustering near the mouths of streams entering into the Potomac. The canal company was aware that its steady supply of water provided a potential additional stream of revenue; however, the original canal charter gave the company water rights only for the purposes of navigation. As the financial problems of the canal company escalated in the 1830s, the various legislatures (Virginia, Maryland, and the U.S. Congress) granted the company the right to sell water to mills and manufacturing plants along its route. However, in deference to the interests of millers in Baltimore, the state of Maryland would not permit the canal to sell water to gristmills until the 1870s.

Waterwheels come in three basic varieties, depending on the height of the available "head" of water. The terminology is fairly straightforward: the water could pour over the top of an *overshot* wheel, it ran under an *undershot* wheel, and a *breast wheel* sat halfway immersed in the stream. The available head of water was an important consideration: the precipitous descent of the Shenandoah at Harpers Ferry drew many industries there, and Caspar Wever counted on a similar 15-foot drop in level of the Potomac to drive the machinery at his planned industrial town at Weverton.

The waterwheel concept was considerably refined by the invention of the turbine, which conducted the water through a pipe, turning the moving "vanes" that lined the inside of the pipe. Turbines were introduced along the Potomac in the latter half of the nineteenth century and proved to be much more efficient than the waterwheel. Turbines did not depend on a head of water for generating power, and they could operate under ice in winter. Turbine technology was only used on the canal to drive the pulleys on the inclined plane near Georgetown, but adjacent enterprises such as the Seneca stonecutting mill eventually converted to the use of turbines.

Turbines proved quite adaptable to the new technology of electricity and were installed in the power plants that were built at Dams no. 4 and 5 toward the end of the canal era. By producing electrical power that could be carried to factories far from the river, the turbine was able to replace not only the waterwheel but the mill as well. The turbine itself has now been replaced by steam-driven generating plants along the Potomac, which use coal and massive quantities of river water to produce electricity.

---

### Where to find mills

The only surviving mill on the canal is McMahon's Mill, at the end of the slackwater detour (mile 88.1). The waterwheel and the exterior of the mill are in good condition, but the mill is not open to the public. Mill ruins are much easier to come by: the stone-cutting sawmill at Seneca is right along the canal basin, and Virginius Island at Harpers Ferry has a myriad of ruins associated with the water industry, including pulp mill ruins. The old gristmill in Shepherdstown boasts a large overshot wheel that took advantage of a sudden drop in the small stream that runs through the center of town. To see the interior of a mill, you may want to visit Pierce Mill (Rock Creek Park), Colvin Run Mill (Route 7 in Fairfax County), or the mill once owned by the C&O Canal Company's first president, Charles Fenton Mercer (Aldie Mill, near Leesburg, Virginia).

---

## Cement Mills

Another prolific industry of the Potomac Valley was the quarrying and milling of limestone. The Great Valley that stretches beyond Harpers Ferry held plentiful supplies of limestone, which had many uses. In its natural state, limestone could be cut and used as a building stone—you'll see it in the blue-gray coloring of the lock walls from Harpers Ferry to Hancock. When heated in a kiln, the limestone could be ground into a powder that was used by farmers as fertilizer and by builders as an ingredient in plaster or cement. Ironworks also used limestone as a flux in their furnaces. The ruins of several limekilns for these various purposes can be found up and down the course of the canal.

Natural cement from limestone was a major ingredient in the canal works, and led to the establishment of several cement mills along the canal route. The expense of importing cement was a major concern when construction began on the Erie Canal. Fortunately, the intrepid canal engineers soon discovered domestic limestone deposits that could be used for hydraulic cement. (Hydraulic cement is so called because it is capable of hardening even underwater —a very useful property when working on canal locks and aqueducts.) Learning from the Erie experience, the C&O Canal Company sought to develop local sources of natural limestone cement.

The primary mill supplying the canal in its early years was the Shepherdstown Cement Mill, also referred to as Botelor's Mill and the Potomac Mill (mile 71.7). In fact, Dr. Henry Botelor contacted the canal company eight months before a single construction contract had been let, offering to supply the canal with cement. Operating at peak efficiency, the mill could theoretically have provided a thousand bushels a day, producing enough cement to build one lock every four days. However, the company had persistent and pernicious problems obtaining enough cement for its works throughout the busiest years of construction. Botelor was also getting complaints from the people buying his flour: he was using the same grindstones for the cement and the flour, so one presumes that the complaints may well have involved chronic constipation.

---

There were three steps involved in producing lime. First, the pieces of limestone were broken down to a manageable size using an "iron cracker." Then these nut-sized pieces of limestone were placed in the kiln in alternating layers with coal of a similar size. The coal and limestone were usually added at the top of the kiln, and the burnt limestone drawn out at the bottom. Finally, the burnt limestone was ground up using millwheels. The resulting powder was measured in bushels and was shipped downstream in sacks or barrels.

---

The company's need for limestone was eventually met by several mills, including the Round Top Mill, which was located right on canal property above Hancock. After the discovery of limestone at Round Top in 1837, the company leased the land and water rights to George Shafer, who had been operating Leopards Cement Mill just upstream. In addition to the Round Top Mill, which began operation in 1838, the canal filled some of its needs by buying from the Cumberland Cement Mill (founded 1836).

There were many other cement mills in the Potomac region during the nineteenth century, including the Antietam Mill opposite Shepherdstown (1883–1906), which used the Shenandoah Valley Railroad as well as the canal to ship its cement. Like most of the natural cement mills along the Potomac, the Antietam Mill was put out of business by the growing preference for slower-setting and stronger Portland cement, which was better suited to industrial and urban construction. (Portland in this case was the Isle of Portland, England, where the new cement was developed).

---

**Where to find kilns**
The ruins of Botelor's Mill lie on the West Virginia side of the Potomac, but the ruins of the mill dam still mark the approximate location (mile 71.4). The chimney and kilns of the Round Top Cement Mill along the cliffs above Hancock are a prominent landmark on the upper portion of the C&O trail (mile 127.4). The ruins of Godey limekilns are visible from the towpath at mile 0.3, and the Shinhan kilns lie next to the canal near Dargan Bend (mile 65.2).

---

## Ironworking: Blast Furnaces, Forges, and Foundries

Spoiled by the ready availability of steel, aluminum, and plastic products, it's hard for us to imagine how much our ancestors depended on iron for essential implements such as pots, knives, and scissors, to say nothing of guns and cannon. The canal structures themselves show both the importance and scarcity of iron: though they were built mainly of stone and timber, you can still find hinges and straps of iron holding the lock gates in place, and iron railings along the aqueducts.

Before the Revolutionary War, some Englishmen wanted to encourage the American colonies to produce pig iron, to reduce the mother country's dependence on Sweden for this raw material. But the Iron Act of 1750 prohibited the manufacture of finished iron products by the colonies—the colonists were supposed to buy these goods from England. Fortunately, our forebears were not so easily discouraged, and by the time war broke out, they had established many ironworks capable of producing muskets and cannon.

There were two important ironworks right along the canal: the Antietam Ironworks (*see* mile 69.5) and the furnace at Green Spring Run (mile 110.4). Just across the river from the canal, there was the Potomac Furnace at Point of Rocks (*see* mile 48.2) and the Keep Triest Furnace on Elk Run (just above Harpers Ferry). The Keep Triest Furnace was

The furnace stack and surrounding buildings at the Antietam Ironworks. *Illustration courtesy National Park Service.*

founded in 1764, but soon ceased operation and leased its iron ore rights to the U.S. Armory and shipped some of its ore up to the Antietam Ironworks. As the railroad and the canal reached the mountains, a major ironworks was begun at Mount Savage (just above Cumberland), and rolled out the early U-shaped rails for the Baltimore and Ohio Railroad in 1844, ending the dependence on rails imported from England.

Ironworking was a heavy industry in its day, requiring substantial capital and expertise. Thus it's not surprising that the same prominent names crop up over and over again in the lists of ironworks owners. Thomas Johnson, the Revolutionary War governor of Maryland, started the Greenspring Furnace, and later operated the Potomac Furnace and the Catoctin Furnace in partnerships with his brothers. (The Catoctin Furnace did not use the Potomac or the canal, but is worth mentioning because it is the only one of these furnaces that has been preserved.) John Semple began the Keep Triest Furnace and another at Antietam, and, like Thomas Johnson, was involved in plans to improve the navigability of the Potomac after the French and Indian War (*see* mile 66). John Brien and John McPherson, who operated the Antietam Ironworks in the early 1800s, also purchased the Catoctin Furnace in 1820.

---

The arches of the blast furnace resemble those of a limekiln, and in some ways the functions are similar. Layers of iron ore, charcoal, and limestone (used as a flux) were dumped into the furnace from above. (The limestone flux kept the molten iron from oxidizing.) The impurities in the molten ore were blown out by a blast of air. The blast came from a bellows driven by a waterwheel. The end product was the molten iron that poured out of the base of the furnace, which was cast in a mold that resembled a row of piglets. Hence the bars that were taken from the blast furnace were called "pig iron."

The pig iron from the blast furnace is the raw material for a foundry or a forge. The iron could be reheated at a *foundry* and cast into anything from cookware to cannons. At a *forge,* reheated iron would be beaten out into wrought iron or bar iron for further working. You can still see some of this wrought-iron work in the gate straps at the canal locks and the railings on some of the aqueducts. The forges eventually gave way to more efficient *rolling mills.*

---

The ruins of the Antietam Ironworks are close enough to the canal to merit an explanation of how the iron-working industry created an intricate network of relation-ships along the Potomac. The best location for a furnace was close to timber (for charcoal), iron ore and limestone deposits, and a head of water for the waterwheel. The mouth of Antietam Creek had all these elements, and it had the advantage of water transportation. Iron ore could easily be brought to the furnace from the rich ore banks just above Harpers Ferry (*see* miles 62.4 *and* 66). The pig iron that the furnace produced could then be boated through the Patowmack Company's skirting canals and later the Chesapeake and Ohio Canal to foundries such as Foxall's and Duvall's in Georgetown (miles 0.4 and 1.5). The Antietam Ironworks also supplied iron to the industries of Harpers Ferry, shipping it down the canal and across the river at the Armory Dam. When blast furnaces started to use coal instead of charcoal later in the 1800s, the canal was also there to supply coal from Cumberland.

To businessmen like John Mason of the Patowmack Company, the location of the Antietam Ironworks along the Potomac must have seemed a great stroke of luck. After years of watching pig iron pass through the Patowmack Company locks at Great Falls and Little Falls, Mason bought Foxall's foundry in 1815. Mason's luck got even better in 1828, when the C&O Canal began its construction right through the foundry property. The canal was destined to bring many tons of pig iron down from Antietam without depending on the unpredictable river levels of the Potomac.

Ultimately, though, ironworking was a technology doomed to obsolescence. The advent of steelworks and their concentration around Pittsburgh led to the decline and fall of this once proud Potomac industry. The rapidly expanding network of railroads made it possible for distant factories to supply the Potomac region with superior and less expensive products. Ironically, George Washington's vision of trans-Appalachian commerce ended up benefiting the Ohio country much more than his beloved Potomac.

**Where to find ironworks**
A brief detour at mile 69.5 brings you to the site of the Antietam Ironworks along Antietam Creek. Unfortunately, the only remains of the industrial village are several limekilns that once produced lime that was used as fertilizer. However, another major furnace of the period, the Catoctin Furnace, is maintained as part of the Cunningham Falls State Park, and offers occasional demonstrations of ironworking. It's about fifteen minutes north of Frederick, Maryland, on Route 15.

# Visiting the Canal

## Activities and Itineraries

The canal and the river offer such a wide range of recreational activities that it's hard to imagine something that you do outdoors that can't be combined with a trip to the C&O. The following pages suggest ways to see the canal on foot, by bike, or by canoe, as well as some more exotic possibilities. Some tips for enjoying the canal:

• Get a subscription to the *Kiosk* newsletter, which includes a schedule of the Park's history and nature walks. On the World Wide Web, you can get more information at www.canal.com.

• Remember that spring and summer weekends are especially crowded, particularly from Georgetown to Great Falls. The canal is well shaded from May to October, but you'll want to bring insect repellent in the summer and wear long pants if you're going off the trail for a better look at culverts and other structures.

• Don't ignore the winter season. The canal is somewhat sheltered from the wind, and when the leaves are down you can get a much better feel for the topography of the area, particularly in the mountain regions.

When you decide what kind of trip you'd like to take, use the "Resources" section at the end of this book to find hotels, campsites, and stores along the way.

The footbridge to Olmsted Island at Great Falls has been a popular attraction for many years. *Photo courtesy National Park Service.*

## Day or Weekend Trips

If you like the outdoors in small doses, you may want to visit the canal while staying at some of the towns along the way. Whether you plan to take day hikes or short bicycle rides, you can use the bed and breakfasts and motels at Harpers Ferry, Shepherdstown, Paw Paw, or Cumberland as staging areas for your visits to different parts of the canal. If you're willing to stay a little further from the river, Berkeley Springs (9 miles from Hancock) and the hotel at Town Hill (on Scenic Route 40) are good base camps for the upper reaches of the canal. The following pages suggest some different ways to work your way up the canal to Cumberland. Refer to the "Guide" section for more details on what to look for.

### Seneca Aqueduct

An excellent alternative to Great Falls, the portion of the canal around Seneca River and the Seneca Falls has nearly as many interesting features, albeit on a smaller scale. The red stone aqueduct across Seneca River is the closest and most accessible aqueduct for Washingtonians. The aqueduct is built as one piece with Rileys Lock, an arrangement found nowhere else on the canal. On weekends,

Girl Scouts in period dress lead tours of the lockkeeper's house.

A brief walk upstream and around the berm side of the turning basin brings you to the ruins of the old stone-cutting mill that provided more of the strikingly red sandstone for the Smithsonian castle. A half-mile downstream you'll find Violettes Lock and an Inlet Lock, at one time the site of Dam no. 2 and Rowsers Ford. In fact, Seneca would be my favorite stopping place on the canal if it wasn't for the constant roar of the jetskis on weekend afternoons.

### Edwards Ferry/Whites Ferry/Monocacy

This pleasant 12-mile stretch across the Potomac from Leesburg has an assortment of historic and architectural features, all within a two-hour bike ride (round trip) or a day's hike. Edwards Ferry is a nice stopping point because its small parking lot is off the beaten track, where River Road turns into a single lane winding through dark hollows. Here you'll find such curiosities as the remains of Jarboe's store and the "mystery aqueduct," as well as the Goose Creek River Lock. It's also a good place to launch your canoe or kayak for a tour of Harrisons Island.

Whites Ferry is more convenient than Edwards Ferry, but its parking area is starting to resemble the hustle and bustle at Great Falls on weekends. Of course, no visit to the area is complete without taking the ferry over to Virginia, where you can pay a visit to the Balls Bluff Battlefield. Should you wander to the north of Whites Ferry, you'll pass scenic Locks 26 and 27 on your way to the barely stabilized Monocacy Aqueduct, which was once the jewel of the canal system. If you want to start upstream and work your way down, the aqueduct has its own parking lot at the end of Mouth of Monocacy Road.

### Shepherdstown

Not as famous as Harpers Ferry, but far more charming, Shepherdstown is a wonderful place to spend a day or a weekend. Your walking tour of the town should include a stroll around the gristmill (the giant overshot wheel is visible from Princess Street) and a visit to the working replica of Rumsey's steamboat.

Across the Potomac, where Rumsey tested his boat, the canal passes Ferry Hill Plantation at Lock 38. Walking downstream, you'll find the Shepherdstown River Lock (0.5 mile), Packhorse Ford (1.3 miles), and, if you're really ambitious, Antietam Aqueduct (3 miles). Moving further inland on the Maryland side, it's only three miles to the historic battlefield of Antietam, now an extensive national park.

### Williamsport/Four Locks

This is a delightful and little-known stretch of the canal, encompassing the Cushwa Loading Basin and the Conococheague Aqueduct at the lower end, and the vista at Dam no. 5 and the little community of Four Locks roughly 10 miles upstream. Unfortunately, accommodations in Williamsport are limited, but you may want to spend the night with the llamas at the Ground Squirrel Holler Bed and Breakfast near Taylors Landing, a 15-minute drive away.

### Hancock/Round Top

Whether you stay in town, or in nearby Berkeley Springs (on the other side of the river in West Virginia), there are a number of notable canal features within close proximity. Just below the town lies the Tonoloway Aqueduct, and just above the town a broad and splendid masonry culvert lets Little Tonoloway Creek slip under the canal bed. Two miles upstream, you'll find the ruins and the cliffside kilns of the Round Top Cement Mill. From Hancock, it's a quick ride up to Little Orleans (15 miles) or down to Fort Frederick (13 miles). The further you travel upstream, of course, the quieter and more peaceful the surroundings, as the canal and the river pass through the Green Ridge State Forest.

### Paw Paw

A unique landmark on the canal, the Paw Paw Tunnel is difficult to get to, but well worth the visit. If you can find your way to the parking lot off Route 51, take a walk south to the tunnel entrance (0.5 mile). A flashlight would be handy, because the tunnel runs 0.6 mile and is quite dark. Beyond the tunnel you'll find a long gorge cut through loose shale, a most romantic scene on an overcast day. Another mile downstream from the tunnel will take you past Locks 66, 64$^2$/$_3$, 63$^1$/$_3$, and 62, as well as the odd remains of a waste weir and a beaver dam. If you're feeling spry, you may want to try the ridge trail instead of the tunnel on the way back.

The Paw Paw bends, downstream from the town of Paw Paw, make a splendid autumn canoe trip. You'll enjoy a unique view of the mountain ridges and the twisting bends that the canal company avoided when it built the tunnel. Check with the Little Orleans Campground or Bill's Boats for canoe rental and advice.

### North Branch/Cumberland

To see the frontier outpost and the canal's end, take Amtrak's Capitol Limited, which follows the old B&O railroad track to Cumberland (and on to Pittsburgh and Chicago). After a walking tour of the town and the former site of Fort Cumberland, take the scenic train ride up to Frostburg and back.

To explore the canal in a more natural state, you'll want to get south of the town. You can rent a bicycle at the Walnut Bottom Bed and Breakfast and take an hour's ride down to Spring Gap. On the way you'll pass the locks and the canal boat replica at North Branch, pass through the Narrows, and see the remains of the steam pump near Pattersons Creek. The truly ambitious may want to cycle another 8 miles down to Oldtown to visit the ducks and pass by the Cresap house (a historic landmark dating to 1763; open to the public only on select days).

If you're traveling by train or car, an overnight or weekend stay in Cumberland can easily be combined with a trip across the mountains (*see* "Extensions," later in this section, for a description of historic landmarks west of Cumberland.)

## Bicycle Trips

My favorite way to see the canal, as you may have guessed, is on a bicycle. Freed from the distractions of cars and road maps, you can travel anywhere from 40 to 60 miles a day in a progressively deepening reverie, cleansing your psyche of all the frustrations of urban living. The 184 miles of towpath provide many options for the cycling enthusiast. You can drive your car to one of the smaller locks and take a morning or afternoon for a brisk round trip, or you could bicycle to an overnight stop and come back the next day (for instance, from Harpers Ferry to Shepherdstown, touring the Antietam Battlefield on one of the days). Or you can choose the whole enchilada, an experience that many riders have decided to make an annual ritual.

One thing you'll notice on the canal is that it doesn't really matter whether you're heading upriver or downriver because the canal towpath is essentially level, except for the 8-foot rise at each lock. (On average, you'll pass a lock every 2 to 3 miles, though they tend to be clustered around the falls.) I've tried it both ways, and I have a strong preference for leaving Georgetown and working my way west to the mountains. Traveling upstream, you follow the rough chronology of early settlement (1700–1750) and the progressive stages of canal construction a century later (1828–50). Oddly enough, as you move forward through the chronology of events, you gradually move backwards in time, leaving the settled valleys for the mountain forests of Appalachia. By the third and fourth day, civilization is far behind, and the frontier beckons in the winding river-bends of Paw Paw and the outposts at Little Orleans and Oldtown.

The decision to travel upriver or downriver is important in terms of how you plan to start your trip. If you live in the Washington area and want to start in Cumberland, you have to convince someone to drop you off in Cumberland. This can be difficult, since it's a three-hour drive just to get there. An alternative is to take the pedals off your bike, box it, and take it down to the bus station as luggage. The bus will put you in Cumberland around noon, so plan on a short first day, overnighting near Paw Paw. On the other hand, if you're going to start in Georgetown and finish in Cumberland, you still have to get someone to pick you up—you may be able to convince some friends to spend the weekend at the inn and rendezvous with you.

The next choice that you have to make is whether you want to camp or stay at hotels along the way. Either way, you'll need panniers on your bike for a change of clothes and other necessities. To camp, you'll also need to buy, borrow, or rent a small tent or sleeping bag. The more aggressive riders cover the trail in three days, but that's a demanding pace on an unpaved surface, and leaves you with no time or energy for detours or savoring the vistas and interesting sidelights of the trail. Four to five days is a more reasonable time frame. Use the chart of towns and campsites in the "Resources" section to plan your overnight stops at appropriate stages along the way.

The usual recommendation is to use a mountain or hybrid bike with tires at least 1.25 inches in diameter. However, I've ridden the canal with people on touring bikes, and Steve Roberts gives an interesting account of his trip down the canal on a computer-rigged recumbent bicycle in his book *Computing Across America*. As an alternative, you might consider renting a mountain bike in Georgetown.

Once under way, you'll find that there are surprisingly few bike shops near the trail, so be sure to bring a patch kit and a spare inner tube to be safe. The best shop outside of Georgetown and Cumberland is Potomac Push-bikes in Williamsport. (Keep in mind that they close early on Saturday and are not open on Sunday.) Brunswick and Hancock have some basic department store bike parts,

A pride of
cyclists pose by
the Cabin John
Aqueduct at
about the turn of
the century.
*Photo courtesy
Library of
Congress.*

and that's about it unless you can find a handy mechanic at a garage.

If you feel like you need a little help with the logistics or just some moral support, you may want to contact one of the companies that lead bicycle tours on the canal (*see* "Resources"). The Potomac Pedalers also hold frequent rides along the towpath.

## Canoeing and Kayaking the Canal and River

Canoeing and kayaking in the canal itself is naturally limited to those parts of the canal that have water: Georgetown to Seneca, Big Pool at Fort Frederick, Little Pool near Hancock, and the watered stretch between Town Creek and Oldtown. The longest stretch, the 20 miles from Georgetown to Seneca, is extremely popular with canoeists and kayakers, but you'll want to avoid the clumps of locks at miles 8.4–9.5 (Seven Locks) and miles 13.6–14.4 (Six Locks). A clever trick is to take a canoe or kayak to Violettes Lock, put it in the Potomac, paddle across the river downstream and go through the old Seneca Canal along the Virginia shore—then cross back to the Maryland side and paddle back up the canal to avoid the current.

Canoeing the river can be very easy, until you hit one of the many rapids that made the canal seem like a good idea. From Chain Bridge down to Little Falls are Class V rapids (significant hazard to life). The stretch of rapids around Harpers Ferry (Dam no. 3 to the Route 340 bridge) are considered hazardous Class III rapids. Only kamikaze paddlers have taken the plunge down Great Falls, which are Class VI rapids (risk of life). If you are an expert paddler with a death wish, be advised that before attempting to shoot Great Falls, you must register with the Maryland Department of Natural Resources/Boating Administration at (410) 974-2916.

## River Levels for Boating

|  | Point of Rocks | Shepherdstown | Hancock | Paw Paw |
|---|---|---|---|---|
| Dangerous | Above 5 feet | Above 5 feet | Above 5 feet | Above 7 feet |
| Caution | 2 to 5 feet | 2.7 to 5 feet | 3.5 to 5 feet | 5 to 7 feet |
| Normal | 0.7 to 1.5 feet | 1.7 to 2.4 feet | 2.5 to 3.5 feet | 3 to 5 feet |

*Source:* Maryland Natural Resources Police

Aside from the falls, most of the river is pleasant and slow-moving. If you know what you're doing, there's no more time-honored way to follow the Potomac River. The Indians were the first to use the river for transportation, and George Washington was shooting "the Spout" at Harpers Ferry at the tender age of 21, on his way back from the French and Indian War. One of the earliest European travelers in this region, Baron von Graffenried, left an evocative account of his return journey down the river from Conoy Island (*see* mile 48.2). He was most impressed by the skill of his Indian guides, who sang in unison as they steered through the dangerous rapids at Great Falls while the baron prudently watched from the riverbank.

If your singing voice isn't that good, you may want to seek the assistance of one of the many outfitters that lead canoeing and rafting expeditions on the Potomac (*see* "Resources"). In addition to renting equipment, the outfitter will usually provide dropoff and pickup services, so that you don't have to worry about getting back upstream. Keep in mind that 15–20 miles can be a full day in a canoe, even if you're just going downstream. Upriver, there are several dams that require a portage (notably Dam no. 4 at mile 85 and Dam no. 5 at mile 105), and the water is often so shallow in the Paw Paw bends and other stretches that you'll scrape bottom more than a few times.

If you want to take some longer canoe trips on the river, it helps to break the river into sections that avoid the falls and the dams. For convenience, I've divided the river into three sections: Piedmont (between the rapids at Harpers

Ferry and Seneca Falls), the Great Valley (between the high-rock dams and the rapids at Harpers Ferry), and the Mountains (between the dams at Cumberland and the high-rock dams). The table below gives the best put-in and take-out points in each stretch of the river.

| Piedmont | | Great Valley | | Mountains | |
| --- | --- | --- | --- | --- | --- |
| Brunswick | 55 | Dam no. 4 | 84.6 | Spring Gap | 173.3 |
| Point of Rocks | 48.4 | Taylors Landing | 81 | Oldtown | 166.7 |
| Nolands Ferry | 44.6 | Snyders Landing | 76.8 | Paw Paw | 156.2 |
| Monocacy | 42.2 | Shepherdstown | 72.7 | Little Orleans | 140.9 |
| Whites Ferry | 35.5 | Antietam Creek | 69.6 | Hancock | 124.4 |
| Edwards Ferry | 30.9 | Dargan Bend | 64.9 | McCoys Ferry | 110.2 |
| Seneca | 22.7 | | | Four Locks | 108.8 |

There are no boat ramps between Great Falls and Little Falls, but if you put in near the Angler's Inn parking lot on MacArthur Boulevard, it's a rough six-mile paddle down to Little Falls. Take your canoe out of the Potomac just below Sycamore Island and use the canal to paddle down to the Lock 6 parking lot.

Since time immemorial, drought and flood conditions have also played random havoc with the river's navigability. The *Washington Post* regularly lists the current water level in its "Weather" section. The National Weather Service also provides river levels for the entire Potomac on its answering machine at (703) 260-0305. For the Potomac below Monocacy, 3–4 feet is considered a fairly good level; anything over 5 feet is dangerous, and under 3 feet may be too shallow in many spots.

## Hiking the Towpath

Long-distance hikers have an enviable equanimity, keeping a pace that's more appropriate to the canal era than to a modern world hurried along by television sound-bites, interstate highways, and jet travel. For the more sociable sort, the C&O Canal Association offers occasional group hikes, including occasional hikes to commemorate the anniversary of the original 1954 hike inspired by Justice William O. Douglas. For comparison's sake, the association hike covers the canal in 14 days, with most days ranging from 12 to 16 miles. A more aggressive pace for a smaller group would take about 8 to 9 days.

For the most part, campsites are scattered conveniently along the towpath, every 4 to 8 miles. There are two notable exceptions. The first unrestricted-use campsite on the towpath is at Swains Lock, which is 17 miles from the start of the canal in Georgetown. However, you can camp at mile 11 if you obtain a pass for the Marsden Tract campsite (contact the park ranger at Great Falls). Another significant gap is the 12-mile stretch from the Bald Eagle Island Campsite (mile 50.3) to the Huckleberry Hill Campsite (mile 62.9).

The campsites have portable toilets and water pumps. The Park Service checks the quality of the water regularly, and will remove the pump handles if the water is unfit for drinking. (The pump handles are also removed in winter.) A chart indicating the location of campsites and stores is included in the "Resources" section.

## Other Things to Do on the Canal

### Birdwatching

The islands and wildlife sanctuaries along the canal and river bring many birdwatchers to the towpath. Many birdwatching areas lie within 30 miles of Georgetown, such as Fletcher's Boathouse (mile 3.2), the Dierssen Waterfowl Sanctuary (mile 20), and the McKee-Besher Wildlife Management Area (mile 27.2). One long-time Potomac birdwatcher, David Byrne, describes some of the sights along the canal as it nears Washington:

Dabbling ducks—particularly mallards and black ducks—gravitate to the lower canal in late autumn and winter. More than five hundred mallards were counted on one November tour between Fletcher's Boathouse and Seven Locks. The still water and plentiful vegetation provide a perfect habitat for the dabblers.

Winter also brings ducks and geese to the river itself; rafts of lesser scaup, Canada geese, and the various mergansers frequent the river as it narrows toward the fall-line. Other waterfowl—grebe and coots, particularly—are in evidence throughout the winter months.

Flickers, hairy, downy, and red-bellied woodpeckers are a common sight in the drowned deadwood between the river and the canal. Also, the huge and spectacularly red-crested pileated woodpecker has made a resurgence in this area in recent years. Brown and bare patches of brambles provide both shelter and a contrasting backdrop for the scarlet northern cardinal and its slightly duller mate.

Prehistoric-looking great blue herons—a rare sight a generation ago in this area—stand motionless at river's edge, awaiting prey.

During the spring and fall, heavily wooded areas along the towpath are magnets for warblers and a myriad of other migrating songbirds.

Removal of DDT and other pesticides from the food chain has saved once-endangered raptors—bald eagles are once again nesting along the tidal Potomac. Ospreys and redtailed hawks are a common sight.

It is the ecological diversity of the lower towpath (along with the decreased pollution) that accounts for the variety and number of birds. River, canal, marsh, swampland, and timbered areas provide both casual and serious birdwatchers a constant opportunity to observe and learn.

For more information about participating in bird-watching, you may want to contact the Audubon Naturalist Society (301) 652-9188. You may also find it helpful to consult Claudia Wilds's book, *Finding Birds in the National Capital Area*. Wilds not only discusses the lower stretch of the canal, but describes good sites all the way up to the dirt roads of the Green Ridge State Forest and the canal terminus in Cumberland.

### Fishing

Anglers and other "afishionadoes" are regular visitors to the park, wading out into the river at places like Whites Ford and Botelors dam to reel in bass, crappie, and tiger musky (stocked). The Dickerson Conservation Area (Whites Ford) is especially popular because of the warm water produced by the power plant just upstream. The spawning season in April brings shad, herring, and many fishermen to the Chain Bridge area just below Little Falls. (The U.S. Army Corps of Engineers is considering a fish ladder around the Little Falls Dam to help the fish upstream on their spawning runs, an idea that was once even attempted along the forbidding gorge at Great Falls.)

You can also fish in the canal itself; the watered portions of the canal have catfish, carp, sunfish, pickerel, and occasional bass. In addition to the stretch from Georgetown to Seneca, the watered stretches of the canal include Big Pool and Little Pool below Hancock and an area below Oldtown that has been rewatered by local organizations expressly for fishing.

The Potomac River falls under Maryland jurisdiction, so you must get a state fishing license to fish in the canal or the river above Little Falls.

## Hunting

Hunting is strictly forbidden in the park, so the deer, groundhogs, and wild turkeys that you see along the canal are safe from human predators. However, hunting is one of the most popular recreations on the properties that border the canal, especially beyond Hancock. So don't be surprised to find yourself surrounded by an excited pack of beagles at Little Orleans, or to be engaged in a discussion of black-powder hunting on the firing range at Fort Frederick. Note that hunters are allowed to cross the park if their guns are unloaded and cased.

## Horseback Riding

As a bicyclist, I probably should not be encouraging this, but there are a number of stables that use the towpath as a riding trail. (Not that I don't like horses—it's just their residue that's a nuisance.) Horses are allowed on the towpath upstream from Swains Lock but are prohibited in the congested areas below there. The Park Service can't seem to make up its mind on whether bikes or horses have the right-of-way on the towpath. Some park publications say that the horses must stop to let bicyclists pass, but the park also distributes leaflets saying the opposite.

## Rock Climbing

Rock climbing is very popular at Carderock and along the Great Falls gorge, not too far from the canal. Much further along, the towering cliffs on the other side of the dry canal bed also tempt many climbing groups. For instance, the cliffs just below Killiansburg Cave (mile 73.2) are a popular training site. It's also possible to do a little **caving** in the Great Valley, where the limestone cliffs are pockmarked with caves. However, you should not explore the caves alone or without a knowledgeable guide.

## Skiing and Skating

During winter storms, some skiers turn the towpath into a cross-country trail, and even though the Park Service has posted warning signs, many skaters take to the ice in the watered portions of the canal. If you want to take to the ice, remember that the temperature has to have been well below freezing for several days for it to become sufficiently thick—a condition that is relatively rare in this temperate clime. However, it does happen on occasion. In the winter of 1994, when the daytime high temperatures barely reached the teens, the dog and I had the pleasure of walking across Widewater to the islands along the far shore.

### Riding the Train

You can get an interesting perspective on the canal and the Potomac Valley by using something other than a car to head west. For instance, you could take the train to a weekend getaway in Harpers Ferry or Cumberland. The Capitol Limited connects Washington, Pittsburgh, and Chicago, using the historic B&O route from Harpers Ferry to Cumberland. This very scenic route hugs the West Virginia riverbank from McCoys Ferry until it approaches Cumberland. Amtrak offers a "Route Guide" in brochure form that details some of the historic locations along the railroad line. Unfortunately, the train travels only once a day in each direction, and it does not take bicycles at this time (though this policy may be reconsidered).

### Flying

An even more dramatic view is the river valley seen from a small plane. This requires a strong stomach, because of the turbulence that lingers over the mountains, but it is a truly unforgettable experience. Renting a plane can be relatively inexpensive; contact one of the smaller local airports for more information. (For better visibility, ask for an airplane with an overhead wing.)

## Extensions: Completing the Route to Pittsburgh

While the Chesapeake and Ohio Canal never made it to the Ohio River, plans are under way to use the old Western Maryland Railroad line to connect the towpath trail all the way to Pittsburgh. This would be a bicyclist's dream, creating an off-road corridor for six to seven days of uninterrupted pedaling along the Potomac and over the Appalachian chain to the very Forks of Ohio. If George Washington were alive today, I have no doubt he'd have traded in his matchcoat for Spandex.

As of this writing, there is no extension to the towpath beyond Cumberland. But that does not mean you have to stop at Wills Creek. From mid-April to early December, you can take a 32-mile ride on the **Western Maryland Scenic Railroad,** from the train station at the end of the canal out to Frostburg and back (800-TRAIN-50). Or you can get in your car and find the **National Pike** a few miles west of town, in the form of Route 40. The National Pike is humble by today's standards, a two-lane mountain road that approximates the route of Braddock's Road and Nemacolin's Trail across the remaining 60 miles of the Appalachian Mountains. The terrain is often spectacular, including crossings of the Casselman and Youghiogheny rivers, and passage across the major ridges of Savage Mountain, Negro Mountain, Laurel Hill, and Chestnut Ridge. A drive over these mountains in summer will give you an invaluable perspective on the herculean labors of the soldiers who built the first road for Washington and Braddock. A drive on a snowy winter's day will likely send your heart to your teeth and make you wonder what combination of poverty and persecution could have driven settlers to this harsh frontier.

If you look closely along Route 40, you can still see an occasional small white obelisk used to mark the miles to Wheeling. And about 50 miles west of Cumberland, you'll come to the site of **Fort Necessity,** now a small National Park. The Visitor's Center overlooks the broad meadow that Washington injudiciously chose for his charming encounter with the French, with a reconstruction of the small circular stockade that his men built to protect their supplies. A few miles further along the pike are **Jumonville Glen,** where Washington ambushed a French scouting party, and the site of **Braddock's Grave,** where the unfortunate general is believed to have been buried during the retreat from the massacre near Fort Duquesne.

As if this weren't enough history, you can drive 8 miles east of Fort Necessity, to the **Ohiopyle State Forest,** and find the Youghiogheny River, just as George Washington did two hundred years ago. While his men were clearing that first road over the mountains in 1754, Washington briefly considered a shorter water route down the Youghiogheny River, but abandoned the plan when he came to the impassable Ohiopyle Falls. The park includes rental facilities for canoeing or rafting on the river, as well as guided river tours. Also note that Frank Lloyd Wright's famous **Fallingwater** house is adjacent to the park.

Of particular interest to C&O towpath enthusiasts is the hiker-biker trail following a railroad right-of-way along the river. The trail presently runs 28 miles from Connellsville to Confluence. Plans call for the trail to be extended north another 43 miles to McKeesport, which would bring it to the very doorstep of Pittsburgh. Unfortunately, the southern connection to the C&O Canal is still only in the planning stages. The proposed southern trail will be known as the Allegheny Heritage Trail and will complete the 60 miles from Confluence to Cumberland. In the meantime, if you want to hike or bike the northern extension across the mountains to Pittsburgh, you'll have to drive to Ohiopyle. For more information about the park, bike rentals, or accommodations at Ohiopyle, contact either Laurel Highlands, Inc. at (412) 238-5661 or Ohiopyle State Park at (412) 329-8591.

## Extensions: Washington and Alexandria

Precious little remains of the two local canals that connected to the C&O. At mile 1.1 of the towpath, you'll find a small park alongside the ruins of the *Alexandria Aqueduct.* Close to the Virginia shore, a single pier of the aqueduct is still visible just upriver from the Key Bridge. The only other sign of the canal is a modern facsimile of a lock and an interpretive display along the waterfront at the Canal Center Plaza in Alexandria. (Follow the George Washington Parkway to Washington Street in Alexandria and take Montgomery Street east to Canal Center Plaza.)

The *Washington City Canal,* which was built before the C&O Canal, conducted boats along what is now Constitution Avenue, turned south just before reaching the Capitol, and then split into two different channels leading to the Anacostia River. The canal was used to bring stone to the U.S. Capitol for construction, some coming from Aquia Creek downriver, and some of the Potomac Marble coming from the quarry near Dickerson (*see* mile 38.2). In addition, the canal connected the traffic coming down the Potomac River with the deepwater port facility at Anacostia. Unfortunately, the canal kept silting up, and turned out to be more of a nuisance than an asset to the C&O Canal Company. A solitary lockhouse still stands at the intersection of Constitution Avenue and 17th Street, almost in the shadow of the Washington Monument.

The C&O Canal towpath trail connects to the bicycle trail along Rock Creek Parkway, which is another part of the remarkable web of paved off-road recreational trails that radiate from the city. You can take the *Rock Creek Trail* nearly 25 miles north to Lake Needwood (adjacent to Rockville). If you head south on the Rock Creek Trail and cross at Memorial Bridge, you have even more choices. On the Virginia side, you can head downriver past National Airport and through Alexandria, all the way to *Mount Vernon.* If you head upriver, you'll pass Roosevelt Island and come to an elevated concrete bridge that carries the trail over the George Washington Parkway. Crossing a couple of intersections in Rosslyn, you can connect to the bike trail along Route 66, which will connect in due time to the *Washington and Old Dominion Trail (W&OD).* The W&OD Railroad trail runs 45 miles, from Shirlington along Interstate 395 in Arlington, through Falls Church, Vienna, Herndon, and Leesburg, and finally ending in Purcellville. It's possible to use both the W&OD and the canal to make an interesting round trip from Georgetown, crossing at Whites Ferry and using Route 15 to connect to Leesburg. To make this a two-day trip, you can stay at the Days Inn at Leesburg, or at one of the bed and breakfasts in the very scenic stretch of rolling farmland between Leesburg and Purcellville.

## Other Canals in the Mid-Atlantic Region

Once you've visited the C&O Canal, you might be interested in comparing it with some of the other canals in the mid-Atlantic region. A good starting place is just across the Potomac.

**Patowmack Canal (Great Falls).** One of the five skirting canals built by Washington's Patowmack Company, the Patowmack Canal offers a spectacular view of the Great Falls area, with the remains of the canal passage that was blasted through the towering rocks on the Virginia side. Take Old Georgetown Pike (193) north from the Washington Beltway (495) and turn right at signs for the Great Falls Park.

**Patowmack Canal (Seneca).** Another Patowmack Company skirting canal, Seneca Canal is north of Great Falls Park on the Virginia side of the Potomac. The barely recognizable remains of the canal are on state parkland; however, the park area has not been developed for public use. It is legal to visit the area, taking care not to trespass on the private property in the vicinity. Take Old Georgetown Pike (193) north from the Washington Beltway (495), passing signs for Great Falls Park and Riverbend Park. Turn right on Seneca Road and follow it until you reach a gate across the road. Park along the shoulder and enter the parkland by following one of the trails immediately to your right (east). Turn north at the earliest opportunity and follow the trail to the river (a little over a half mile).

Fortunately, parts of many historic canals have been preserved as public parks or converted into recreational trails. Here are some of the canals in the mid-Atlantic states, listed in alphabetical order.

**Chesapeake and Delaware Canal.** This 13-mile canal near Chesapeake City, Maryland, still serves as a shortcut between the bays of Chesapeake and Delaware, and is a part of the Intercoastal Waterway. An unpaved path along the canal is suitable for bicycling. Contact the Inn at the Canal for reservations and information at (410) 885-5995.

**Delaware and Raritan Canal State Park.** Approximately 70 miles of this trail is deemed suitable for bicycling. From Philadelphia, take Interstate 95 North; immediately after crossing the Delaware River into New Jersey, take the exit for Route 29. Contact the park at (908) 873-3050.

**Dismal Swamp Canal.** One of the earliest canals, the Dismal Swamp project was blessed by George Washington and begun in 1787. The canal survives only as a "ditch," but the region around it has some interest, as it is a part of the Great Dismal Swamp National Wildlife Refuge in south-eastern Virginia. Unpaved roads, particularly the Washington Ditch Road, are suitable for hiking and biking. Contact the refuge manager at (804) 986-3705 on weekdays for more information.

**Lehigh Canal.** Located along the Lehigh River at its juncture with the Delaware River, the Lehigh Canal has a museum and a restored locktender's house; it also offers rides in a canal boat. Follow Interstate 78 to the town of Easton, Pennsylvania. Call (215) 250-6700 for more information.

**Towpath Bike National Recreation Trail.** An 8-mile trail that adjoins the Lehigh Canal trail. The trail itself is a converted railroad right-of-way. Contact the township of Easton at (215) 253-7191.

**Union Canal.** Near Reading in southeastern Pennsylvania, the Union Canal, completed in 1827, was nearly 80 miles long and joined the Schuylkill and Susquehanna Rivers through an impressive system of locks, aqueducts, and a tunnel. Presently this trail is only 4.5 miles in length; plans call for it eventually to connect to the trails around Blue Marsh Lake. Contact Berks County Parks and Recreation Department at (215) 372-8939.

Even further afield, of course, lies the grandaddy of all American canals, the Erie Canal. Still going strong after 170-plus years, the canal now carries motorized vessels during the boating season. There are several trails running along different stretches of the old and the modern Erie canals. The best path runs along the original (now abandoned) Erie Canal, from Dewitt (near Syracuse) to Rome. Call the New York tourism number, (800) I-LOVE-NY, for a map. If you're in Syracuse, the Erie Canal Museum is worth a visit (318 Erie Boulevard; 315-471-0593), as is the Erie Canal Village near Rome.

If you still have canal fever after visiting these North American canals, you may want to ask a travel agent for information about touring the European waterways. England, Ireland, and France all have extensive working canal systems. It's relatively easy to tour with a group or charter your own boat and travel the Canal du Midi, much as Thomas Jefferson did in 1787. And if that's not enough, you can always visit the great interocean canals at Panama and Suez.

# Canal Guide

# The Falls

The first 23 miles carry us past the falls of the Potomac: Little Falls, Great Falls, and Seneca Falls. It is no accident that the canal starts along the fall line: larger boats could sail upriver only as far as the Indian village of Tohoga along Rock Creek (later Georgetown), which was the head of navigation on the Potomac. This is where John Smith stopped when he first explored the Potomac River in 1608.

The falls are picturesque but not a significant impediment to a nation that travels by automobile. In an earlier era that depended on boat and wagon for commerce, the fall line was as significant an obstacle as the Appalachian Mountains that loomed further inland. The fall line was the reason the nation's capital was built here rather than at an established town further up the Potomac.

As might be expected, the change in elevation at the falls is more dramatic than in any other stretch of the canal. Overall, the first 23 miles have nearly a third of the canal's 74 locks, which raise the water level by 200 feet (the elevation at Cumberland is 604 feet). While the scenery along the canal near Little Falls is relatively serene, the towpath from Carderock to Great Falls offers spectacular vistas of the narrow river gorge. The highlight of this section is undoubtedly Great Falls National Park, with its scenic views, restored tavern and locks, and nature trails.

------------------------------------------------------------

The official beginning of the canal is indicated by a concrete marker at the **tidewater lock** immediately downriver from Thompson's Boat Center, at the intersection of Virginia Avenue and Rock Creek Parkway. The tidewater lock is in a terrible state of decay, almost broken in half and filled up by silt and other debris.

When the canal was in operation, Rock Creek was dammed at this point to create a large turning basin for the canal boats below the first lift lock. Canal boats could use the tidewater lock to enter the Potomac, and in later years were pushed by tugboat downriver to deliver their cargo of coal to Alexandria or Indian Head.

Before the canal era, the Mason family of Northern Virginia operated a ferry at the mouth of Rock Creek. The Masons were involved in almost as many Potomac River projects as the Washingtons. George Mason is famous for his role in the Constitutional Convention, but he was

---

also the last trustee of the old Ohio Company. In the mid-1700s, George Mason obtained a patent for the island opposite Rock Creek (now known as **Roosevelt Island**) from Lord Baltimore. When he died in 1792, the island passed to his son, John Mason. At that time, it was known as Anastolan Island or Mason's Island (though George Mason referred to it as "Barbadoes" in his will). John Mason turned the island into a carefully culti-vated garden estate, using it as a summer home until 1830. During those years, John Mason assumed George Washington's role as the guiding force behind the Patow-mack Company and purchased Foxall's Foundry *(see mile 1.5)*.

There is no towpath just yet, so you'll have to continue around the Thompson Boat Center and take a right turn on the bridge over Rock Creek. Then take a left turn (just beyond the parking lot) to follow the paved Rock Creek bicycle path upstream. This area was submerged in the canal years, and known as "The Mole"; now it is paved over and crossed by several elevated roadways.

Humble beginnings: the tidewater lock at mile 0 in canal days. Note the dam across Rock Creek on the other side of the lock. Today the Watergate complex would loom in the background of this scene. *Photo courtesy National Park Service.*

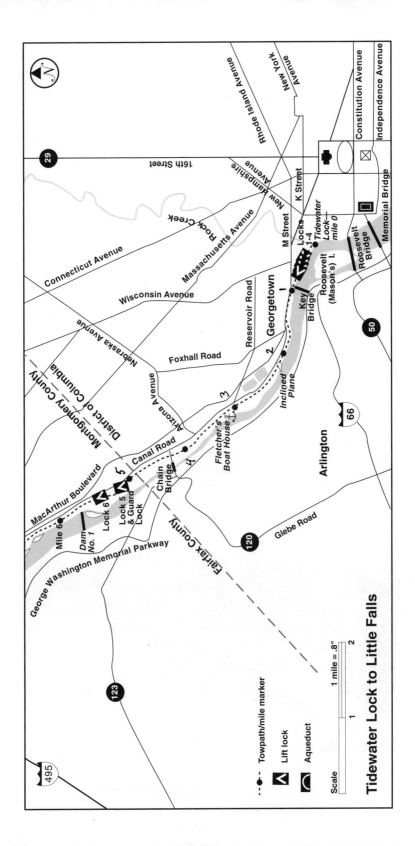

# Tidewater Lock to Little Falls

Scale

1 mile = .8"

| | | | |
Scale: 1 — 2

**Legend:**
- Towpath/mile marker
- Lift lock
- Aqueduct

Mason's Island (now Roosevelt Island) lay just across the Potomac from the tidewater lock. It was no longer used by the Mason family when this Civil War photograph was taken. *Photo courtesy National Archives.*

The Mole at Rock Creek, just above the dam and the tidewater lock. Note the exposed pipes curving under the Pennsylvania Avenue Bridge—this was part of the Washington Aqueduct system, which still brings water all the way from Great Falls to the McMillan Reservoir near Catholic University. *Photo courtesy Library of Congress.*

A sign marks the ruins of the *Godey Limekilns* **MILE**
(1833–1908) on the other side of Rock Creek Parkway. The **0.3**
limestone was brought by canal boats from the quarries
of the Great Valley (between the Blue Ridge and the
Appalachians), and was burned down and ground into
a powder that was used to make plaster, some of which
was shipped back upstream. Much further upstream,
near Shepherdstown and Hancock, the canal will pass
by limestone kilns and cement mills that supplied the
cement for the canal's locks, aqueducts, and culverts (*see*
miles 71.7 *and* 127.4).

Take a left on the brick path leading into Georgetown,
just before you reach the Pennsylvania Avenue Bridge.
The modern towpath begins along the berm side of the
canal. Originally, the towpath ran along the river side
of the Rock Creek basin, with the mules crossing over
at 29th (Green) Street to avoid the wharves along that
side. The towpath continued on that side from 29th
Street through Georgetown, crossing back to the river side
just beyond the old mills. The banks of the canal are lined
with stone as it passes through Georgetown.

*National Historical Marker for the C&O Canal.*
The power plant on the other side of the canal is the
West Heating Plant operated by the U.S. General Services
Administration. The steam produced by the plant is carried by a maze of underground tunnels to government
buildings throughout the city of Washington. This is the
first of several relatively modern facilities along the
canal that originally depended on coal, brought by
rail, and water, in this case drawn from Rock Creek (*see*
miles 40.6 *and* 99.1).

*Lock 1.* The first four locks are clustered together in quick
succession at the beginning of the canal. The original
stone for the first four locks was freestone brought
upstream by boat from Aquia Creek in Virginia, but
much of it has been replaced by a patchwork of brick and

other stone. Stone from Aquia was used in many buildings, including the U.S. Capitol, during the early construction of the city of Washington.

The path continues on the other side of 29th Street (formerly Green Street) to **Lock 2.** The Green Street Bridge was one of several stone bridges in Georgetown that were rebuilt in the 1860s as higher iron bridges to provide more clearance for unloaded canal boats going back upstream; after the canal era, the bridge was lowered again.

**M I L E**
**0.4**

The path crosses 30th Street. The building on the other side of the canal on 30th Street was originally **Duvall's Foundry,** which opened in 1856 and closed after the Civil War. The location of the foundry suggests that it depended on canal boats to bring its raw material—coal from Cumberland and perhaps pig iron from Antietam —for its castings. Duvall's Foundry was not as prominent or long-lived as Foxall's, but in 1874 it fitted the canal's first steamboat, the *Ludlow Patton,* with a boiler, rudder, and propeller. The foundry building was later converted into a veterinary hospital that tended canal mules (*see* Foxall's Foundry, mile 1.5 *and* Antietam Ironworks, mile 69.5).

**Lock 3.** A bust of William O. Douglas (erected by the National Park Service, May 17, 1977) commemorates the Supreme Court justice who led the fight to keep the canal from being turned into a scenic roadway. The *Georgetown* canal boat docks here between its scheduled excursions upstream. The **Georgetown Visitor's Center,** which is closed on Mondays and Tuesdays, carries an assortment of books and sells tickets for the boat ride (*see* "Resources").

**Thomas Jefferson Street and Lock 4.** Delis along the path here provide a quick opportunity to pick up a sandwich for the road—food and drink are scarce when you leave Georgetown.

The path crosses 31st Street. The small brick house on the northwest corner of the intersection (1061 31st Street) was a supply and boarding house for the C&O company. On the other side of 31st Street, the brick path turns into sandy gravel. Note the plaque on the historic brick building on the corner, with an evocative quotation from Justice Douglas.

**MILE 0.5**

An 1890 survey of the waterfront shows that the property on the other side of the canal was occupied by the **Moore and Waters Guano Works.** The guano works were part of the nineteenth-century fascination with exotic and relatively expensive foreign fertilizers. Canal records show early shipments of "guano, bone dust, and poudrett" to points between the falls and the Blue Ridge: Edwards Ferry (mile 30.9), Monocacy (mile 42.2), and Sandy Hook (mile 59.5). In the early years of the canal, the guano probably came from Peru, which had a stranglehold on the international guano market. In the 1850s, Congress passed the Guano Islands Act, which gave U.S. citizens the right to claim "islands, keys, and rocks" in the Pacific and Caribbean for the purpose of guano mining. Most of the Caribbean guano was shipped to firms in Baltimore, which could proudly lay claim to being the guano capital of the United States. (As an alternative to expensive imported fertilizer, many farmers preferred to use lime from the Great Valley for fertilizer; *see* miles 65.2 *and* 69.5.)

## Georgetown, District of Columbia

It's difficult to believe, but this patrician enclave just beyond Rock Creek was once a grimy port city, up to its elbows in Potomac industry and transportation. Georgetown grew up at the "head of navigation" on the Potomac River, where cargo was exchanged between oceangoing ships and wagons or smaller boats.

Early explorers such as John Smith and the fur trader Henry Fleet reported a small Indian village called Tohoga on this hill above Rock Creek. The first land grants in this area were made around 1700 by Lord Baltimore, since land to the north of the Potomac was part of the colony of Maryland. The town of George, named after King George II of England, was officially authorized by the Maryland Assembly in 1751.

Commercially, the Port of Georgetown began as a shipping center for tobacco (the trade tapered off in the 1830s). In 1790 it took on a second role as a residential neighborhood on the outskirts of the planned city of Columbia, later named Washington. President Washington met in Suter's Tavern with local proprietors to obtain land for the capital in 1791, and Pierre L'Enfant used the tavern as his studio for laying out the new city. Washington had long been in the habit of riding up from Mount Vernon and taking the ferry over to Georgetown to attend meetings of the Patowmack Company. Although the temporary capital was in Philadelphia, the first president still found time to stop in Georgetown and take a look at the canal works at the falls. In later years, it was his custom to dine at the Union Tavern at Washington and Bridge Streets (30th and M); he often stayed overnight at the home of Thomas Peters (near the waterfront between 26th and 27th Streets). When the government relocated to the unfinished federal city at the turn of the century, the members of Congress took up residence in Georgetown, a bumpy carriage ride away from the new Capitol.

The construction of the C&O Canal had a profound effect on the waterfront of Georgetown. Wharves were built to handle the coal, stone, timber, and other cargo from the canal boats. Mills sprang up to take advantage of the water conducted into town by the canal, in particular the paper mill and gristmills that were clustered on the river side of the canal beyond Wisconsin Avenue (see mile 0.7).

Despite these industries, events conspired against the town's commercial potential. As a port, Georgetown had difficulty competing with Baltimore; its harbor was too shallow and required dredging just to stay open. Baltimore's links to the west also proved more convenient, from the National Road to the Baltimore and Ohio Railroad. In this century, few people remember that canal wharves and mills once stood at the foot of Wisconsin Avenue.

### AMENITIES

The Georgetown Visitor's Center is a modest little office on the canal between 30th Street and Thomas Jefferson Street, mainly serving as a meeting point for walking tours and for canal boat rides. Rides are offered Wednesday through Sunday, from early April to early November, and last about an hour and a half. Fares range from $3.50–$5. Call the Ranger Station at (202) 653-5190. Georgetown has a little of everything along M Street and Wisconsin Avenue. The shops at the Foundry and along the towpath are good for sandwiches; for unassembled foodstuffs, visit the Food Mart on M Street. Cycling necessities can be procured at Big Wheel Bikes or the Bicycle Exchange (M Street). Several hotels are convenient to the canal, but they tend to be expensive and not particularly bike-friendly. Street parking is difficult to find—plan on using a parking garage.

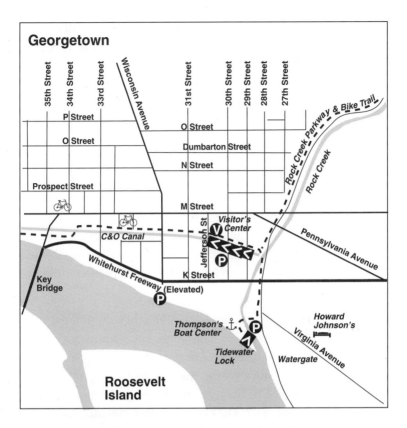

# Georgetown

35th Street
34th Street
33rd Street
Wisconsin Avenue
31st Street
30th Street
29th Street
28th Street
27th Street

Rock Creek Parkway & Bike Trail

Rock Creek

P Street
O Street

O Street
Dumbarton Street
N Street

Prospect Street

M Street

Visitor's Center

C&O Canal
Jefferson St
Pennsylvania Avenue

Whitehurst Freeway
K Street

Key Bridge

Whitehurst Freeway (Elevated)

Thompson's Boat Center
Tidewater Lock
Watergate
Howard Johnson's
Virginia Avenue

Roosevelt Island

A stone bridge carries Wisconsin Avenue over the canal. A weathered plaque on the downstream side gives a completion date of 1831. Canal construction had already begun in the fall of 1828, so this bridge gave ample clearance for boats. A high stone wall runs along the berm side of the canal.

**MILE**
**0.6**

Steps in the stone wall lead up to the Georgetown Park shopping complex. A steel walkway overhead connects the complex with the river side of the canal. The land on both sides of the canal belonged to the *Capitol Traction Company.* The company operated street-cars in the District of the Columbia, at first drawn by horses, later powered by electricity. The building on the river side of the canal began as a warehouse to store feed for the streetcar horses; it later became a generating plant

---

when the streetcars were converted to electricity. The Georgetown Park complex is a recent construction; the lot on which it stands was used by the Traction Company as a bus stable and repair shop. The company's carbarn, with its distinctive clock tower, still looms near the canal on M Street at the Key Bridge (mile 1.0).

Another walkway leads to the Capitol Traction Company building on the other side of the canal, adjacent to a smaller footbridge.

Set back from this footbridge, on the river side of the canal, is an old brick building that housed one of several gristmills along this stretch of the canal. Note the water intake for the mill, just upstream from the footbridge.

The canal company charter originally limited it to charging tolls for navigation. But as time went on, the charter was amended to allow it to sell water for milling operations. Over the years, as many as eight flour mills operated in Georgetown, as well as a cotton mill and a paper mill. The canal not only provided the water-power for the milling operations, but its boats brought the grist and the timber. The mills continued using canal water long after the canal was closed for transportation purposes in 1922. In fact, the Wilkins-Rogers Milling Company was paying the National Park Service for canal water into the 1960s.

Steel and concrete footbridge over canal (no canal access).

**MILE 0.9**

Steel footbridge. *Cross here to the towpath on the other side of the canal—the path on the berm side will end shortly.* The steps above the footbridge lead to a small park commemorating **Francis Scott Key,** the Georgetown lawyer who is most famous for writing the words to the "Star-Spangled Banner." Key happened to be in Baltimore during the assault on Fort McHenry in 1814, but he was a longtime Georgetown resident who lived just a few hundred feet upstream from here. Key was a political ally of canal president Charles Fenton Mercer, and participated in the first "canal convention" to rally support for the C&O project in 1823. Ironically, he moved from here in the 1830s because of the "turbulence" of canal construction.

The **Francis Scott Key Bridge** crosses overhead (completed January 1923), followed by two off-ramps from the Whitehurst Freeway. Despite the best efforts of the Columbia Historical Society, the house where Key lived and practiced law was razed to make room for the freeway entrance. Steps lead up to the freeway and down to K Street. The abutments are adorned with graffitti by local underground celebrity "Cool Disco Dan," among others.

A small park with benches and iron fence stands beside the last remaining stone arch of the **Alexandria Aqueduct.** Sighting along the dry canal bed, you can see the remaining pier of the old aqueduct near the Virginia side of the river beside the Key Bridge. The aqueduct connected the C&O Canal to a long-since-vanished canal along the Virginia banks of the Potomac, leading all the way to the port city of Alexandria. The aqueduct was also used as a bridge during the Civil War and from 1888 to 1923, and was dismantled in 1933.

The city of Georgetown was not enamored of the aqueduct, which carried business to the rival city of Alexandria. Francis Scott Key, the same lyricist and lawyer who had supported the C&O Canal project, led the court battle against the Alexandria Aqueduct. The case was eventually decided by the Supreme Court, which ruled against Key's argument that the construction of the aqueduct should be halted because it was impeding the free navigation of the Potomac.

The green "shingle-style" boathouse along the river below, bracketed by distinctive octagonal turrets, was built in 1890 for the Washington Canoe Club.

**MILE**
**1.1**

A canal boat turns into the channel of the massive and solidly constructed Alexandria Aqueduct. Note the Georgetown tollhouse just to the left of the aqueduct. *Photo courtesy Smithsonian Institution.*

The remains of the old Alexandria Aqueduct point toward the Virginia shore, with the Key Bridge in the background. *Photo by C. M. High.*

A line of boats tied up, waiting to be unloaded at Georgetown. The truss of the Alexandria Aqueduct (converted to a road bridge) is visible just downstream. The distinctive tower of the Capitol Traction Company's carbarn still stands today. *Photo courtesy Library of Congress.*

Steps lead down the canal embankment to K Street and the **Capital Crescent Trail,** which follows an old B&O Railroad spur along Little Falls Park to Bethesda, Maryland. The spur delivered coal to the government heating plant on Rock Creek (*see* mile 0.3); the Park Service acquired the land for this trail after the plant had started getting its coal by truck.

**MILE 1.5**

The steps also lead to a former road culvert, which has been converted into a pedestrian tunnel underneath the canal. The tunnel leads to a path through **Glover Park** along Foxhall Road. Glover Park extends 3 miles through Northwest Washington and is maintained by the National Park Service.

Though you won't find a stream running through here anymore, this was once the location of **Foundry Branch,** which supplied waterpower to a foundry on the river at this spot. The foundry was built by **Henry**

***Foxall*** in 1801, purportedly at the suggestion of Thomas Jefferson, who thought the nation's fledgling capital should have a place to produce arms. The foundry used pig iron that was brought down through the Patowmack Company's locks from the furnaces of the Great Valley (*see* Antietam Ironworks, mile 69.5).

The foundry was especially active during the War of 1812. The pig iron from the upriver furnaces was melted down and used to cast cannon barrels. Some of these cannon were carted all the way across the Appalachians, just in time for Commodore Oliver H. Perry to turn them against a squadron of British warships on Lake Erie on September 13, 1813. Perry's terse battle report signaled American control of these inland waterways: "We have met the enemy and they are ours."

In 1815 Foxall sold his foundry to John Mason, who was also the president of the very same Patowmack Company that made possible the delivery of raw materials to the foundry. When the C&O Canal was built right above the foundry buildings, it provided a ready supply of water to the facility. Mason operated the foundry until his death in 1849, after which it passed through a succession of owners before falling into disuse toward the end of the century.

Just beyond the footpath, the towpath crosses a spillway and a pair of waste weirs. The best view of this unusual pair of waste weirs is from the path below. These waste weirs are built of stone and brick rather than the much more common replacement concrete. Waste weirs were opened or shut by turning "stems" that protruded through the top of the weir, but here the heavy flow of water out of this stretch of the canal creates a continuous waterfall below.

***Three Sisters Islands*** in the Potomac River—a favorite stopping place for canoeists or other boaters coming from Thompson's or Fletcher's boathouses (miles 0 and 3.2).

The rubble remains of the *inclined plane,* with an interpretive display. The inclined plane was built in 1876 to speed up canal traffic near the busy wharves of Georgetown by lowering boats directly into the Potomac River (avoiding the delays at the four locks leading to the Rock Creek basin). The inclined plane was extremely useful during the canal's boom years, but it was never repaired after the destructive flood of 1889, because canal traffic had dwindled dramatically by that time. If you look carefully, you can see the remains of an old stop lock in the canal prism just downstream.

**MILE**
**2.3**

*Fletcher's Boathouse,* between the canal and the river, rents canoes and flatboats and offers seasonal concessions and fishing supplies.

**MILE**
**3.2**

After the floods of 1996, the Park Service built a sturdier bridge over to the parking lot and the *Abner Cloud House,* one of the oldest buildings along the canal. Cloud built the house in 1801 and used the basement to store grain and flour from his mill, just a few hundred feet upstream, which used water from the original Patowmack Company skirting canal (*see* Mile 5.6).

Just beyond the footbridge you'll find good examples of a road culvert and a waste weir. This waste weir is more typical than the one at mile 1.5. The weir opening is framed in wood and closed off by planks that could be lifted out of the way to let more water out. Follow the channel leading from the weir down to "Lock Harbor" on the river to see some rubble ruins— likely the remains of the lift locks for the old skirting canal. They were replaced by three stone locks in 1817.

An old B&O railroad bridge crosses above the towpath and Canal Road—a double-span steel truss bridge of the nineteenth-century pin-connected, Whipple trapezoidal design. This is one of the few structures along the canal that actually benefited from the floods of 1996. Now open for cyclists and foot traffic, it carries the Capital Crescent Trail inland for 7 miles to Bethesda.

**MILE**
**3.7**

**MILE 3.9** A long wooden walkway carries the towpath over a modern concrete spillway.

**MILE 4.2** A pedestrian ramp leads up to the latest incarnation of *Chain Bridge,* which marks the head of navigation on the Potomac. The passage cut by Pimmit Run on the Virginia side made this an important crossing point for traffic to Leesburg. A Virginia tobacco inspection warehouse appeared in 1742, followed by a gristmill, brewery, distillery, cooper, and blacksmith shops.

The first bridge over Little Falls opened to traffic on July 3, 1797. On the 19th of that same month George Washington used it for the first time and is said to have complained that the toll was so high that he should have chosen the ferry to Georgetown. The first and second wooden-covered bridges fell victim to floods. The first chain suspension bridge was built in 1808 but was destroyed by a flood in 1810. Several more chain bridges were erected, but by the Civil War they had been replaced by a truss bridge. The low-slung modern version was built after the catastrophic flood of 1936. Finished in 1939, it bears little resemblance to its predecessors, though it sits on piers that date back to the 1870s.

During the first months of the Civil War, the Chain Bridge dramatized the divided state of the nation, with Union sentinels stationed on one end and Confederate sentinels on the Virginia side. One peaceful summer night in 1861, Private William Scott fell asleep at his post on the District side and was sentenced to be shot. Hearing of his case, President Lincoln pardoned the "sleeping sentinel"—one of the most famous instances of Lincoln's mercy, celebrated in a popular poem that depicted Lincoln arriving in person as Private Scott faced the firing squad. Scott's reprieve was short-lived; he died bravely the following spring. Meanwhile, the Union army secured the opposite shore of the Potomac and built Fort Marcy and Fort Ethan Allen to guard the approach to the bridge.

The Chain Bridge in two of its incarnations: as a chain suspension bridge in the early 1800s and as a wooden truss bridge under heavy Union guard during the Civil War. *Illustration courtesy Smithsonian Institution; photo courtesy Library of Congress.*

**MILE 4.5°** The hydroelectric station now unused on the berm side of the canal was built by the U.S. Army Corps of Engineers to take advantage of surplus water from the Dalecarlia Reservoir. From the towpath follow the concrete-surfaced road down to the boulder-strewn floodplain. At the end of the path, a concrete platform offers a view of Little Falls—the rapids that likely ended John Smith's exploration up the Potomac in 1608. The army built the platform in the 1970s as part of an auxiliary system to fill the reservoir in the event of drought.

**MILE 4.7** Leaving the District of Columbia; entering **Montgomery County,** Maryland, which was established in 1776. At the outset of the War of Independence, the Maryland Constitutional Convention decided to create two new counties out of the upper and lower divisions of Frederick County. Montgomery County was named for Richard Montgomery, a revolutionary general who had fought for the British in the French and Indian War, settled in New York, and died in 1775 leading an assault on Quebec (*see* miles 42 *and* 57.8).

**MILE 5** *Lock 5 and guard lock.* Much of the lock has been replaced with red sandstone after flood damage. The original gray or tan-colored sandstone came from Aquia Creek and from a quarry within one mile of the lock. The concrete apron between the two locks reinforces an old dike that protected the area against flooding. The guard lock, adjacent to the lift lock, leads to an inlet channel from Dam no. 1 upstream.

The wooden bridge across the lock leads to a gravel parking lot and a spiral concrete pedestrian bridge that connects to Ridge Road in the lovely little community of Brookmont on the cliffs above.

**MILE 5.2** A dirt road leads down to the guard lock. There are several short trails in this area that make for a pleasant walk.

**MILE 5.4** *Lock 6 ("Magazine Lock" or "Willards Lock").* Again, much replacement work in the lock walls. The

## Washington's Canal

From Fletcher's Boathouse to Little Falls, the C&O Canal followed the channel of the old skirting canal originally built by George Washington's Patowmack Company. Washington founded the Patowmack Company in 1784 to make the Potomac River navigable far enough upstream to reach the wagon trails across the Appalachians that led to the tributaries of the Ohio River. The Patowmack Company spent much effort removing obstructions from the river itself, and only built short skirting canals to avoid the major rapids at Little Falls, at Great Falls and Seneca Falls on the Virginia side of the river, and opposite Harpers Ferry on the Maryland side. The company also considered Cow Ring Sluice at Hooks Falls to be a part of its improvements (*see* miles 3.2, 14.4, 22, 60.2, *and* 66).

The locks at Little Falls (known affectionately as "George" and "Martha") were opened in 1795, but were not of much use until the much more difficult construction was completed at Great Falls in 1802. The early canal system was too much affected by the river's floods and droughts to provide reliable service. Eventually the Patowmack Company's charter was subsumed by the Chesapeake and Ohio Canal, which began construction in 1828 of a canal that was planned to reach all the way to Pittsburgh (*see* mile 5.6).

nicely preserved stone lockhouse is one of the few that is still inhabited. The parking lot is accessible from the Clara Barton parkway.

A dirt path leads to a kayak run in the river channel formed by High Island. Some of the best kayakers in the United States take advantage of the temperate weather to train here year-round (*also see* mile 40.6). This point marks the upper end of Patowmack Company's skirting canal around Little Falls. Here also President John Quincy Adams broke the first ground for the C&O Canal on July 4, 1828. At the time, the company only planned to extend the Little Falls canal upstream, letting boats enter and exit the canal just below the falls. However, the businessmen of Georgetown prevailed upon the canal company a few months later to extend the canal from Little Falls down through their port city.

**MILE 5.6**

*Little Falls Dam (Dam no. 1).* Two dams are here: the curving lower dam that funnels water into the

**MILE 5.7**

kayak run, and an upper dam that runs straight across the river to Little Falls Pumping Station. The lower dam is where the first of the seven feeder dams were built to water the canal. The rubble remains of the canal dam were grouted and capped with concrete in 1944 and 1949. Dam no. 1 waters the shortest stretch of the canal, but the mills in Georgetown used a significant amount of water from the canal to drive their water wheels and turbines.

The army built the upper dam in 1959 to supply water to the city of Washington. Depending on the river level, Little Falls provides 15 to 30 percent of the city's water supply, with the rest coming from the dam at Great Falls.

**MILE 5.8** The towpath passes under a concrete bridge for the *Little Falls Pumping Station,* which draws water from the upper dam.

**MILE 6.2** Large warning sign for boaters approaching the dam. If you are canoeing, you can take out above here and use the canal to get to Lock 6. The peculiar iron trough in the canal evidently serves as a drain, although the National Park Service is not quite sure who put it there.

**MILE 6.4** A pedestrian bridge over the canal provides access from MacArthur Boulevard. (If you're coming by car, park across from the Sycamore Store.) The boat landing on the river is used by the rope-guided ferry for *Sycamore Island.* The island is owned by the Montgomery Sycamore Island Club, an association of 155 families that dates back to 1885. The dues are quite affordable, catering to a solidly middle-class membership, but the waiting list moves only slightly faster than the one for Redskins season tickets.

**MILE 7** *Lock 7* was built of granite from a nearby quarry, with Aquia freestone for the coping. Here you can see the first of the newer "drop gates," at the upper end of the lock. The old miter gates were replaced by drop gates at several locks in this stretch to speed up traffic during

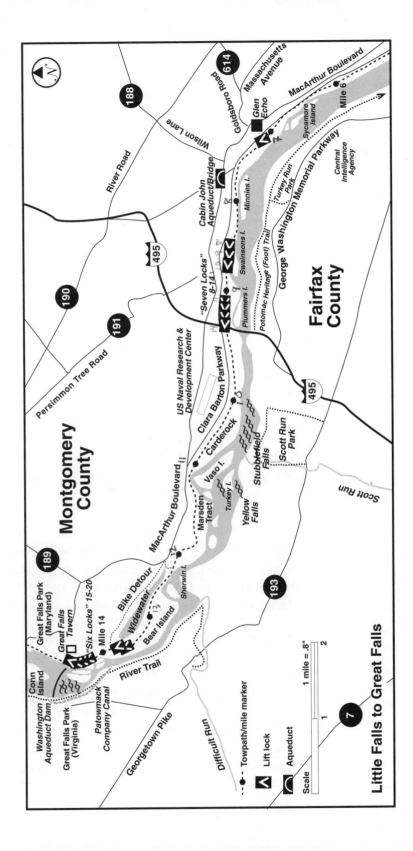

# Little Falls to Great Falls

**Montgomery County**

**Fairfax County**

MacArthur Boulevard
Mile 6
Sycamore Island
Central Intelligence Agency
George Washington Memorial Parkway
Turkey Run Park
Minnies I.
Swainsons I.
Plummers I.
Potomac Heritage (Foot) Trail
Scott Run Park
Scott Run
Stubblefield Falls
Carderock
Clara Barton Parkway
Yellow Falls
Vaso I.
Turkey I.
US Naval Research & Development Center
Marsden Tract
Sherwin I.

Massachusetts Avenue
Goldsboro Road
614
Glen Echo
188
Wilson Lane
River Road
Cabin John Aqueduct/Bridge
495
190
191
"Seven Locks" 8-14
Persimmon Tree Road
MacArthur Boulevard
495

189
Great Falls Park (Maryland)
Great Falls Tavern
"Six Locks" 15-20
Mile 14
Bike Detour
Widewater
Bear Island
River Trail
193
Conn Island
Washington Aqueduct Dam
Great Falls Park (Virginia)
Patowmack Company Canal
Difficult Run
Georgetown Pike

Scale

● Towpath/mile marker
◄ Lift lock
◖ Aqueduct

1 mile = .8"

0    1    2

7

the canal's boom years (1870s). A nicely preserved lockhouse of whitewashed stone stands on the berm side and can be reached from a parking lot on the Clara Barton Parkway (inbound only).

**MILE 7.6** The towpath crosses a modern concrete-lined culvert for Cabin John Creek and passes a wooden bridge replaced after the 1996 floods. The path on the other side of the bridge leads under Canal Road and up wooden steps on a steep hillside to a parking lot on MacArthur Boulevard at its intersection with Wilson Lane. Take a right on the MacArthur Boulevard bike path to get to the *Clara Barton House* and *Glen Echo Park* (0.5 mile), both maintained by the National Park Service.

If the leaves are down, you may want to take a short detour on this path to look at the *Cabin John Bridge,* a dramatic stone arch that carries MacArthur Boulevard over the creek and valley. Originally built as part of the Washington Aqueduct system, it still supplies water from Great Falls to the Dalecarlia Reservoir. The bridge's 297-foot span had the distinction of being the largest masonry arch in the world for many years. The granite and sandstone used to construct the arch were carried by boat on the C&O Canal. While the sandstone came a relatively short distance from Seneca, some of the granite was carried by ship all the way from Massachusetts to Georgetown. A dam and a lock were built on Cabin John Creek to allow the boats to leave the canal and bring the stone directly to the construction site.

Construction began in 1857 and was completed during the Civil War, which accounts for its original name, the "Union Arch." When the bridge was begun, the names of President Franklin Pierce and his secretary of war were inscribed on the west abutment. The secretary of war at the time was Jefferson Davis, but his name was expunged after he became president of the Confederate States of America. In 1908 President

The great arch of the Cabin John Aqueduct during construction. *Photo courtesy Smithsonian Institution.*

Theodore Roosevelt was apprised of this anomaly and ordered that Davis's name be restored.

**MILE**
**8.2**

Passing Minnie Island on the Potomac, an 8.5-acre island donated in 1994 to the Potomac Conservancy. Contact the Conservancy to find out how to visit the island (*see* "Resources").

**MILE**
**8.4**

***Lock 8.*** This is the first of the "Seven Locks" that are crowded into the next mile. It was built of red sandstone boated down from Seneca—probably on the Potomac River, as the canal was not yet opened above here. Much of the sandstone has been replaced over the years. The whitewashed stone lockhouse is vacant but in good condition. The path just beyond the lockhouse leads up the hill to a parking lot on the Clara Barton Parkway (accessible to inbound traffic only).

→ Now houses the Potomac Conservancy's River Center

The U.S. Geological Survey has placed a marker in the lock wall along the lower berm side indicating an elevation of 68 feet—this corresponds roughly to eight locks with an average rise of 8 feet each.

**MILE 8.7**

**Lock 9,** largely built of granite from the quarry near Lock 7, with a coping of Aquia freestone, and some sandstone.

**MILE 8.8**

**Lock 10,** built entirely of granite, half from the quarry near Lock 7, and half brought by wagon from a quarry four miles inland. Markers next to the lock describe wildflowers along the canal and the drop gate system.

The parking lot off of the inbound parkway makes this a popular takeout point for kayaks and canoes. It's easy to miss, though—steer into the channel formed by Swainsons Island to find the sometimes muddy landing. The lockhouse is now a Park Service residence.

**MILE 9**

**Lock 11.** The approach to this lock from downstream is one of the most scenic on the canal—the bypass flume has stone walls and a nice "tumble" at the end. A lockhouse stands on the river side of the towpath, along with benches and displays describing the drop gate lock and the life of the lockkeeper and his family. The lock was built in 1833 of red sandstone boated down from Seneca.

Just beyond the lockhouse, you'll find one of the original mile markers, shaped like a tombstone and inscribed "9 miles to W.C." (Washington City).

**MILE 9.3**

**Lock 12,** largely built of granite that was brought by wagon from the quarry near Lock 7, with some sandstone. Again, note the drop gate at the upstream end.

**MILE 9.4**

The modern highway bridge for the **Beltway (Interstate 495)** crosses over the canal.

**Lock 13.** It's easy to overlook this lock because it's obscured by the shadows of the bridge. The lock walls are mostly granite from the same quarry that was used for Lock 10, while the stone for the coping and quoins was brought from Seneca. The stonework for the bypass flume is in exceptionally good condition.

**Lock 14.** This is the last of the "Seven Locks." The walls were built of granite, half from the same quarry that was used for Lock 10 and half boated down from a quarry 5 miles away. A U.S. Geological Survey marker here indicates the elevation as 117 feet above sea level, which corresponds to the 14 locks to this point, averaging an 8-foot rise apiece.

Sign next to the towpath for **Billy Goat Trail,** Section C, East End. This is the beginning of a 1.7-mile loop along the river, rejoining the towpath at mile 10.9. This trail is not suitable for a relaxed stroll, but if you have a good pair of hiking boots, it will lead through some of the recesses and hidden wonders of Great Falls Park.

The pier in the middle of the canal was once part of a pivot bridge. The knoll left by the road embankment offers a view of the remains of the circular pivot mechanism. The bridge was built in 1941 to provide access to a Civilian Conservation Corps camp. The canal company had long since ceased operations, but a pivot bridge was still needed because the National Park Service was operating barges in the canal in this area.

The road culvert underneath the canal provides access to the parking lot at Carderock.

Sign for Billy Goat Trail, Section C. This end of the trail leads to cliffs that rock climbers have dubbed "Matt's Splat" and the "Guillotine."

Splendid view of the river gorge at **Carderock,** with Vaso Island on the opposite side of this channel. The cliffs just downstream are a favorite haunt for rock climbers.

This bend in the canal is still very susceptible to flood damage, as evidenced by the repair work along the steep embankment.

**MILE 11.4**

Sign for *Marsden Tract Day Use Area.* This campsite is the closest one to Georgetown, but you must obtain a permit from the ranger station at Great Falls to use it. The campsite has toilets and picnic tables, but no water pumps.

The wooden footbridge over the canal leads to the intersection of MacArthur Boulevard and Brickyard Road.

**MILE 12.3**

This wood and steel bridge with concrete abutments was one of the few pleasant consequences of the floods of 1996, replacing the old earthen dam that supported foot traffic down from the parking lots off of MacArthur Boulevard (opposite Angler's Inn). The *Widewater Bicycle Detour* begins here. If you're on a bike but don't want to take the detour, note that you will have to carry it over a rocky stretch about a mile farther upstream. Passage is easier if you take the detour, though you will have to carry your bike over the steps at the pedestrian bridge upstream.

On weekends, you'll see a flotilla of kayaks and canoes being carried across the bridge and down to the river. Experienced paddlers can either play in the rapids in the riverbend just upstream or take a mild whitewater excursion down to the takeout at Lock 10 or below Sycamore Island (heed the warning signs for the Little Falls Dam and transfer your boat to the canal to paddle down to Lock 6).

**MILE 12.6**

Widewater begins, a natural channel that was adapted for the canal's purposes. Unfortunately, the embankment at the south end of Widewater is vulnerable to floodwaters rushing down the canal from Great Falls and has been known to give way on a few occasions. The stone drain in the middle of the channel is a modern addition to control the prevalent flooding along this stretch of the canal.

**MILE 13**

A concrete bridge carries the towpath past an inlet with its own waste weir to let water out at the far end. This is one of the two inlets along Widewater that take the brunt of the floodwaters seeking the natural channel

Cyclists crossing wet rocks where the towpath is interrupted at Great Falls. To avoid this hazard, take the Berm Road detour from mile 12.3 to mile 13.8. *Photo by D. Michaels.*

back to the Potomac River. Before the canal company built an embankment and towpath to contain the water here, the land between Widewater and the Potomac became an island when the river level rose (shown as Bear Island on maps).

The second inlet, with a stone wall to contain flooding at the far end. Bikes have to be carried across stepping stones for about twenty feet and then carried or rolled for the next tenth of a mile. (An alternative is to take the Widewater Detour at mile 12.3.)

**MILE 13.4**

A wooden walkway leads up to Lock 15.

**MILE 13.5**

**Lock 15.** This is the first of the Six Locks, which carry the canal up 50 feet and past Great Falls. These locks were built of red sandstone boated down from Seneca. However, note the band of replacement concrete under the first row of stones. The timbered cribs on the far side of the lock are a good example of the type of construction that was used on several of the canal dams.

**MILE 13.6**

**Lock 16,** with much brick replacement work along the lock walls. A whitewashed lockhouse stands on the berm side of the canal.

**MILE 13.7**

*Stop gate* with a high wooden pedestrian bridge that connects to the Widewater Detour. The bridge replaces the old winch house; the winch was used to lower planks that blocked the flow of water down the canal during floods. The water was diverted toward the river by the embankment next to the stop gate. This reduced the flood damage downstream in the Widewater area.

The Billy Goat Trail makes another appearance at this juncture.

**M I L E**

**3.9**
A wooden fence along the towpath guards visitors from the sheer drop to the river below. The canal embankment is reinforced by a wall of stone. From this juncture you have a panoramic view of the cliffs and broken stone as the river gorge wends its way around the Rocky Islands below.

**M I L E**
**14**
Note that there is no mile marker 14—mile 14 begins just upstream from the fence.

**M I L E**

**4.1**
*Lock 17.* Constructed mainly of red sandstone, with some replacement concrete.

A footpath leads to **Olmsted Island** and Great Falls Overlook, where you can view the falls from an oblique angle. The view is even better from Great Falls Park in Virginia, on the other side of the river.

**M I L E**
**4.2**
*Lock 18,* its walls showing a patchwork replacement of concrete and brick. The ruins of a lockhouse stand on the other side of the canal.

On the hillside along the berm side of the canal, you'll see an abandoned waste weir that was part of the Washington Aqueduct. Unfortunately, the waste weir discharged water into the canal when the water level rose, which was the last thing the canal needed during a flood.

**M I L E**

**4.3**
*Lock 19.* Patchwork replacement of concrete and brick.

**Lock 20.** The last and most familiar of the Six Locks, Lock 20 stands next to the famous **Great Falls Tavern,** which was both a lockhouse and a hotel for visitors to the falls. The dark stone building next to the tavern houses the intake works for the Washington Aqueduct.

**MILE 14.4**

On the river side of the towpath, there is a concrete platform with a railing above the **Washington Aqueduct** intake for the water supply of the District of Columbia (built 1853–64). Looking out over the river, you can see the dam that diverts water into the aqueduct. On the far shore, you can make out the entrance to Washington's skirting canal at Great Falls, just above the aqueduct dam (*see also* mile 5).

## Washington Aqueduct

The Washington Aqueduct was yet another public works project that dramatized the importance of the Potomac River. Like the canal and the Harpers Ferry armory, the plan to tap the river's water supply can be traced to George Washington. In 1798, with the capital under construction, Washington suggested that "the water of the Potomac may, and will be brought from Great Falls into the Federal City, which would, in future, afford an ample supply of this object."

For the first half-century of its existence, however, the federal city relied on nearby streams and springs for its water supply. When Congress finally commissioned a study of the water supply in 1852, it was probably not as concerned about drinking water as controlling fires such as the one that had destroyed much of the Jefferson collection in the U.S. Capitol the previous year.

Lieutenant Montgomery C. Meigs of the U.S. Army Corps of Engineers conducted the study for the project and was named its chief engineer. Meigs was later removed from the project, and the Civil War caused some delays, but the 12-mile-long aqueduct began carrying water to the Georgetown reservoir in 1864. The aqueduct runs underground most of the way, so its works are largely invisible to the public except for the spectacular arch at Cabin John (*see* mile 7.6). While the aqueduct system has been expanded through the years, the original works still carry raw water to the Georgetown Reservoir and the newer Dalecarlia Reservoir, where it is filtered and treated for consumption by District residents.

# Great Falls, Maryland

Great Falls is probably the most popular and diverse park in the Washington area, judging from the long lines of cars and throngs of visitors on warm weather weekends. To avoid the crowds, plan your visit to the park during the off-season, on overcast days, or weekdays. The park has a $4 entrance fee, but if your financial resources are limited, you can always follow the canal into the park (there are no tollbooths along the towpath).

As the name suggests, the Great Falls were the most significant impediment to navigation on the Potomac River. A boatman's nightmare, the falls have always been a spectacular sight for the carefree tourist arriving by car or carriage. The best way to see the area is to put on some hiking boots and follow the Billy Goat Trail, which runs through the rocks and woods between the canal and the river. The fractured chasms and schisms that make up these rock gorges and islands in the Potomac provide a landscape of fantasies for geologists, naturalists, and laymen.

The canal company recognized the potential tourist trade at the very outset of construction (1828) and made plans to add a hotel to the lockhouse near the falls overlook. The Great Falls Tavern was completed over the next four years, and served as a hotel as well as a tavern for guests who took the carriage ride out from the city to enjoy the view. In its early years, it was referred to as the "Crommelin Hotel" after a Dutch investor who had helped the canal company out of one of its early financial pinches.

The canal is still watered at Great Falls, with the locks and weirs in good working condition, so it is an excellent place to see how the canal operated. As at Georgetown, you can even take a trip in a canal boat. The canal was not the only waterworks at Great Falls; you'll also find the intake for the Washington Aqueduct next to the tavern.

There's even the chance to do a little prospecting—the boulders in this area are largely veined with quartz, but the same conditions that produced the quartz veins also produced some veins of gold. A Union private, stationed here at the beginning of the Civil War, found a few rocks with some promising flecks in them. He bought farmland in the area, and after the war came back to begin a mining venture. Three major mineshafts were sunk in the vicinity of Great Falls: the Ford Mine, the Watson Mine, and the Maryland Mine. While some significant finds were made, the amount of gold that could be recovered often did not justify the costs of extraction. Interest in the mines petered out in the twentieth century, with the Maryland Mine closing for good just before World War II.

### AMENITIES

Rides on the *Canal Clipper* are offered Wednesday through Sunday, from early April to early November, and last about an hour and a half. Fares range from $3.50 to $5. Call the Ranger Station at (301) 299-3613. The Visitor's Center in the old tavern is a good source of literature on the C&O Canal. Restrooms and a seasonal concessions stand can be found in the neighboring builidings.

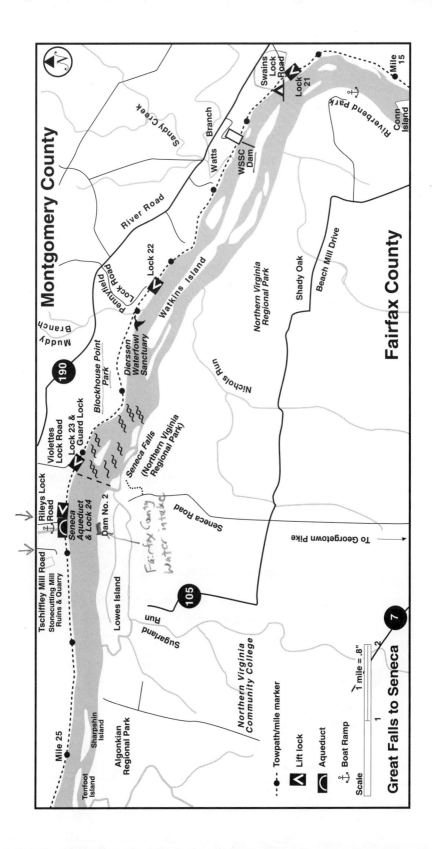

# Great Falls to Seneca

## Montgomery County

- Mile 25
- Tenfoot Island
- Sharpshin Island
- Algonkian Regional Park
- Muddy Branch
- 190
- Tschiffley Mill Road
- Stonecutting Mill Ruins & Quarry
- Rileys Lock Road
- Violettes Lock Road
- Seneca Aqueduct & Lock 24
- Lock 23 & Guard Lock
- Dam No. 2
- Lowes Island
- Seneca Falls (Northern Virginia Regional Park)
- Blockhouse Point Park
- Fairfax County Water intake
- Dierssen Waterfowl Sanctuary
- Pennyfield Lock Road
- Lock 22
- Watkins Island
- River Road
- Sandy Creek
- Watts Branch
- WSSC Dam
- Swains Lock Road
- Lock 21
- Riverbend Park
- Conn Island
- Mile 15

## Fairfax County

- Sugarland Run
- 105
- Northern Virginia Community College
- Seneca Road
- To Georgetown Pike
- Nichols Run
- Northern Virginia Regional Park
- Shady Oak
- Beach Mill Drive
- 7

### Legend

- ---- Towpath/mile marker
- Lift lock
- Aqueduct
- Boat Ramp

Scale    1 mile = .8"

**MILE 15.9** This small brick building houses a small pumping station that provides 5–8 million gallons of water a day for the city of Rockville. (The rest of Montgomery County is served by the much larger plant at mile 17.5.)

**MILE 16.7** *Swains Lock (no. 21),* built of red sandstone from Seneca. The lockhouse is still occupied by the Swain family, which operates a seasonal refreshment stand and rents boats. The campsite just beyond the lock has picnic tables and toilets. There's no water pump, but running water is available from the faucet near the parking lot. This is the closest place to Georgetown for camping, unless you get a permit for the Marsden Tract Campsite. Also note that no horseback riding is permitted on the towpath below Swains Lock.

*Closed in 2008*

**MILE 17.5** This modern concrete filtration plant serves a purpose similar to that of the much older Washington Aqueduct at Great Falls (*see* mile 14.4). The plant was built in 1961 by the Washington Suburban Sanitary Commission and is currently capable of drawing 280 million gallons of water a day.

When the commission was first established in 1918, it was concerned with the water supply for 32,000 residents in a narrow band around the District of Columbia. Now the commission's Potomac and Patuxtent River plants provide water through a 4,300-mile network of underground pipes to 55 storage tanks and 1.3 million residents of Montgomery and Prince Georges County.

The plant includes a river overlook area for the public, with several informative plaques about the Potomac River and valley.

**MILE 18.5** Watkins Island and smaller islands are visible in the Potomac.

**MILE 19.6** *Lock 22 (Pennyfield Lock).* The lock walls are of red sandstone from Seneca. The whitewashed lockhouse is built of shale, except for the door and window sills and lintels, which are of sandstone. According to Thomas

Hahn, this was a favorite fishing spot of President Grover Cleveland, who used to stay at the Pennyfields' house on the berm side of the canal.

The fenced trail on the other side of the lock leads to a large parking lot at the end of Pennyfield Road, which connects to River Road.

Just beyond the lockhouse is a good working example of a typical board-and-concrete waste weir.

Sign for the ***Dierssen Waterfowl Sanctuary,*** a 30-acre marshy tract of land that is maintained by the Maryland Department of Natural Resources. A footpath leads down to the river floodplain and around the pond. This is a good birding area, but be sure to bring long pants in summer.

First cliffs of ***Blockhouse Point,*** the site of a Union outpost during the Civil War. The inland area beyond the cliffs is Blockhouse Point State Park, which can be reached from River Road. This is one of the most distinctive scenes along the canal, where the rocky forested cliffs are reflected in the still water of the canal, just a few precious feet of earth from the rough rapids of the Potomac.

For paddlers who have just shot the rapids of the Seneca skirting canal along the Virginia side of the river, this is a good spot to carry your canoe or kayak from the river to the C&O Canal. (Check to make sure that the canal is watered below Violettes Lock when you put in at mile 22.)

The second set of cliffs along Blockhouse Point.

The double lock here, of red sandstone from Seneca, combines ***Violettes Lock*** (no. 23) and the guard lock for ***Dam no. 2.*** Dam no. 2 was a low rubble dam that is no longer visible. It was put into service in November 1830, watering the canal down to Little Falls and allowing the proud company directors to bring dignitaries and newspaper editors up from Georgetown on the canal packet *Charles Fenton Mercer*.

The dirt path just below the river lock leads down to the Potomac, at the approximate location of **Rowsers Ford.** Just above the lift lock, a dirt path leads down to the river and an excellent place to launch your canoe or kayak above the Seneca rapids. If you paddle to the Virginia side of the river, you can shoot some mild whitewater through one of the original skirting canals excavated under the direction of George Washington (*see* mile 5).

## Rowsers Ford

This ford, which took advantage of the low water just below Dam no. 2, was an important river crossing during the Civil War. The infamous Confederate guerilla John Mosby used Rowsers Ford on his raid up to Seneca. But by far the most dramatic crossing was made by J. E. B. Stuart just before the Gettysburg campaign, in the summer of 1863.

The main body of Lee's army had moved up the Shenandoah Valley and crossed the Potomac at Shepherdstown and Williamsport (mile 71.4 and mile 99.4) in the middle of June. The Union Army had just crossed at Edwards Ferry (mile 30.9), not very far from here, on June 25 and 26, in pursuit. On the very next day, June 27, J. E. B. Stuart's cavalry came down to the banks of the Potomac from Dranesville to Rowsers Ford. The water was unusually high, too high for artillery and ambulances, but Stuart decided to cross anyway. The men unloaded boxes of ammunition and carried them across by hand. The guns and caissons were dragged across the river, thoroughly submerged. There was no moon to light the way and no clear sign of where to enter and leave the river, so the long line of horsemen had to stay in close contact. Driven by the river current, the line of riders would drift imperceptibly downstream, until someone would come out from the Maryland shore to put them right again.

Once on the far bank, the soldiers captured a canal boat and turned it perpendicular to the current, fashioning a bridge. In fact, they were able to seize a series of canal boats, and were planning to set them on fire until the boat captains' entreaties persuaded them to have mercy on small businessmen. Instead, Stuart's men turned the boats lengthwise and drained the water from that level, leaving the boats sitting as obstructions in the canal prism.

Stuart's men rode on from the ford, capturing a train of 125 wagons as he paused in Rockville. When he finally arrived in Gettysburg, it was not to a hero's welcome but to a very frustrated General Robert E. Lee, who had been without his usual cavalry reports in the critical days just before the battle.

A canal boat enters the Seneca Aqueduct and Rileys Lock, heading downstream. *Photo courtesy National Park Service.*

The canal company had expansive plans for a manufacturing town at this location, using the waterpower from the canal and Dam no. 2. The community was to be called Rushville, in honor of Richard Rush, the former secretary of the treasury who had managed to obtain an emergency loan from Dutch investors in 1829. (The Dutch were to be similarly honored by a community at Great Falls named Crommelin, but neither project developed on the scale envisioned by the canal company.)

For three years, Dam no. 2 was the head of navigation on the C&O Canal. In fact, the stretch from here to Little Falls was the first part of the canal to be opened—the lower portion of the canal into Georgetown was not completed and watered until 1831. The guard lock for the dam was also a lift lock to be used by boats, so the canal was able to draw some business from the Virginia side of the river.

Much of the canal had been built as far as Point of Rocks (mile 48.2), but it could not be completed all the way to the next feeder dam at Harpers Ferry until the court battle with the B&O Railroad over the right-of-way was resolved. The railroad and the canal company agreed on a plan of joint construction in May of 1833, and by late October 1833 the canal company had speedily finished the fourteen mile stretch from Point of Rocks to the Harpers Ferry dam (mile 62.4).

Dam no. 2, like the dam at Little Falls, suffered severe damage over the years from flooding. The 1866 Annual Report stated that both dams were "dilapidated and ineffective for a full supply of water when the river is low." By 1873 a canal engineer had concluded, "now there is hardly a trace of either dam left . . . They have been replaced by dykes of stone and brush."

**Rileys Lock** (no. 24) and **Seneca Aqueduct,** built of the distinctive red sandstone from the quarry on the other side of Seneca Creek. This is the only place along the canal where an aqueduct and a lock were built as a single structure. The aqueduct opened in 1833, a full five years after the ground breaking for the canal. The upstream arch was washed out by a local flood in 1971. The lockhouse is open for tours in the spring, summer, and fall, conducted by Girl Scouts in period dress. (The *Kiosk* newsletter includes a schedule of lockhouse tours; *see* "Resources.")

**Seneca Creek** appears as "Sinegar Creek" on early maps of the region. The creek may have taken its name from the Seneca Indians, one of the Five Nations of the Iroquois, who made their home in the western reaches of what is now the state of New York. The Iroquois often followed the river valleys, such as the Monocacy, the Shenandoah, and the Conococheague, on their annual southern raids. However, it is more likely that the name, which means "stony creek," was simply a description.

# The Piedmont and the Sugar Lands

Above the fall line, the Potomac peacefully courses through the rolling Piedmont farmland dubbed "the sugar lands" by the first Europeans to visit the area. No doubt they were thinking of sugar maples, but visions of sugar must have been dancing in their heads, because the sight of the prominent crested ridge near the Monocacy River suggested nothing to them so much as a loaf of sugar (Pain du Sucre).

From Poolesville to Darnestown, this is popular bicycling terrain, and at many a rise you can spot the landmark of Sugarloaf looming in the distance. If you look to the southwest of Sugarloaf, you can also usually spot the towering smokestack of the Dickerson Power Plant (taller than the Washington Monument), which marks the towpath and the Potomac River just a mile downriver from the Monocacy Aqueduct. The power plant also marks the general vicinity of Whites Ford, a river crossing that was often used by Confederate soldiers during the Civil War.

The trail along the Monocacy River was one of the preferred routes of the Iroquois warriors traveling south from their villages in western New York. Later the Monocacy trail brought many German settlers from Pennsylvania, drawn by the rich farmlands and lower rents.

For an interesting perspective on the region, drive, hike, or bike to the overlooks near the top of Sugarloaf Mountain. From the top of Sugarloaf, you can see 10 miles to the northwest, where the river flows through a notch in the Catoctin ridge known as Point of Rocks.

------------------------------------------------------------------

The towpath turns a distinctive shade of red here, leached from the famous red sandstone of Seneca. The canal widens into a turning basin for boats, a reminder of the early years when Seneca enjoyed a brief heyday as the farthest point on the canal.

MILE
22.8

Use the dirt embankment across the canal to take a brief detour around the berm side of the basin to the ruins of the *Seneca Stonecutting Mill* (0.2 mile), which is a part of Seneca State Park. If you follow the path along the basin a little further, you'll find the sandstone quarry that supplied much of the stone for the locks in the lower canal, and later supplied the stonecutting mill.

The mill was constructed in 1837, too late to cut any of the sandstone that was used in the canal locks below Harpers Ferry. However, it was used to cut the sandstone for the Smithsonian Castle building (1847–49) and the Cabin John Bridge (1857–63), and it cut stone from other quarries to be used in the U.S. Capitol and the Washington Monument. The mill drew water for its operation from the canal (runoff was deposited in Seneca Creek) and used the stone quarried farther down this path. The channel for the water ran right through the building, first powering a waterwheel and later a turbine. The saw had a toothless blade and cut stone at the then astonishing rate of an inch an hour.

Look closely and you'll find a small circular U.S. Geological Survey marker in the middle of the towpath—204 feet above sea level, which roughly accounts for the 24 locks from tidewater just below Georgetown to this point. (Each lock raises the level approximately 8 feet.)

***Horse Pen Branch Campsite.*** This is the first of the true "hiker-biker" campsites, properly secluded from casual automobile access. However, if you're hiking and need a stopping place closer to Georgetown, keep in mind that you can camp at Swains Lock (mile 16.7) or Marsden Tract (mile 11.4—permit required). The campsite is named for the stream that crosses under the canal another 0.7 of a mile further along.

Parking lot for the ***McKee-Besher Wildlife Management Area*** (Maddux Island), accessible from Sycamore Landing Road. Much larger than the area at Dierssen (mile 20), McKee-Besher encompasses 300 acres of woods and fields in Montgomery County and can be reached either from the canal or River Road. Hunting is permitted in some areas, and field trials are held in the spring and fall.

A large turf farm lies on the other side of the canal. This is the first sign of the rich farmlands of the Piedmont Valley that stretch to the foot of Catoctin Mountain (mile 48.2). The runoff from farms and developed areas greatly exceeds the streamflow of the canal days. One of the major problems facing the Park Service is how to

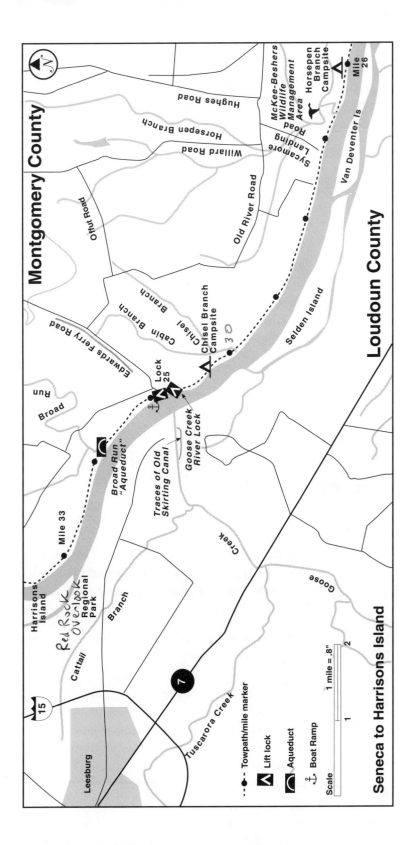

Montgomery County

Loudoun County

Leesburg

15

7

Harrisons
Island

Mile 33

Red Rock
Overlook

Regional
Park

Broad Run
"Aqueduct"

Broad
Run

Lock
25

Edwards Ferry Road

Cabin Branch

Chisel
Branch

Chisel Branch
Campsite

Goose Creek
River Lock

Traces of Old
Skirting Canal

Branch

Cattail

Tuscarora Creek

Goose

Creek

Selden Island

30

Old River Road

Offut Road

Willard Road

Horsepen Branch

Hughes Road

McKee-Beshers
Wildlife
Management
Area

Sycamore
Landing
Road

Van Deventer Is

Horsepen
Branch
Campsite

Mile
26

Seneca to Harrisons Island

Scale

1 mile = .8"

1        2

Towpath/mile marker

Lift lock

Aqueduct

Boat Ramp

increase the capacity of the culverts running under the canal bed without detracting from the historic setting.

**MILE 30.5**

***Chisel Branch Campsite.*** This campsite is named for the stream that crosses under the canal about 0.5 of a mile further back.

**MILE 30.7**

The towpath is carried by wooden planking over an opening in the wall of the canal, connecting to the channel for the ***Goose Creek River Lock.*** The remains of the river lock, still in very good condition, can be found a few hundred feet away. The purpose of this lock was to admit boats that had entered the Potomac from Goose Creek, on the Virginia side of the river. Charles Fenton Mercer, the Virginia congressman who spearheaded the canal effort and became the canal company's first president, owned a mill in Aldie that might have benefited from the cross-river traffic, but this trade never lived up to expectations. Although the Virginia Assembly authorized funds in 1838 to make Goose Creek navigable, work was not begun until 11 years later and was eventually suspended because of the success of the Manassas Gap Railroad.

**MILE 30.9**

The ruins of ***Jarboe's Store*** still stand next to the towpath at Edwards Ferry. This brick shell is a reminder of the many stores, sheds, and warehouses that crowded around some of the upstream locks, providing a place of exchange between the canal boats and the surrounding countryside. Most of these buildings were wooden structures that were abandoned and later dismantled when the canal became a park.

***Edwards Ferry*** and Edwards Ferry Road. A small parking lot and a boat ramp mark the site of Edwards Ferry, which has long since ceased operations. In October 1861, Union troops crossed the river from here by boat, in a supporting action to the crossing from Conrads (Whites) Ferry to ***Balls Bluff*** upstream (*see* mile 35.5). A friend of Lincoln's, U.S. Senator Ned Baker, led the Union troops and was killed in the battle.

After the battle of Chancellorsville, the Union army built a pontoon bridge across the river here, anticipating that they might have to cross the Potomac from Leesburg to follow the Confederate army north. This great crossing came to pass on June 25 and 26, 1863, after it was learned that Lee was moving up the Shenandoah Valley to invade Maryland and Pennsylvania. Two weeks later the armies would meet at Gettysburg (*see also* Rowsers Ford *and* Packhorse Ford, miles 22 and 71.4).

**Lock 25.** The tell-tale reddish tint of the lock walls indicates that they were built of red sandstone boated up from Seneca. The brick lockhouse is still in good condition.

Note the low earthen dam extending from the downstream end of the lock, and the loose stone on the sides of the canal. These remains are signs of the boom years of the 1870s, when the canal company lengthened Locks 25–32 to accommodate two canal boats at a time. The extended walls were rather hastily built of loose stone held together by timber cribs; when the timber rotted away, the stones tumbled into the canal bed.

The exposed remains of the Broad Run culvert, or aqueduct, whichever you prefer. The Park Service refers to this as the **Mystery Aqueduct** because it was not planned as one of the 11 aqueducts between Georgetown and Cumberland. This was first constructed as a double culvert for Broad Run, but later was converted to a sort of an aqueduct, with the canal bed supported by a wooden trunk rather than the typical masonry arches.

**Turtle Run Campsite.** Named for one of the intermittently flowing streams in the vicinity, this campsite has a good view of **Harrisons Island.** The island may have been home to the Piscataway Indians, a tribe of "friendly" Conoy Indians who had enjoyed generally amicable relations with the first settlers in St. Mary's County on the Chesapeake Bay. The colonists viewed the peaceful Piscataway as a useful buffer against the more warlike northern Iroquois tribes who came from the Susquehanna Valley. As the English settlements expanded in the late 1600s, however, the Piscataway tired of being called to account for every attack or dispute between settlers and Indians. They moved several times before arriving here, first to a village at the mouth of Rock Creek, and then to the Bull Run Mountains in Virginia.

Alarmed at the sudden disappearance of this friendly tribe, the colony of Virginia sent a pair of "ambassadors," Giles Vandercastle and Burr Harrison, to find the emperor of the Piscataway. After several days of riding they found a group of Piscataway, including no more than 80 or 90 bowmen, living in "cabins" around an unfinished fort: "They live on an Island in the middle of the Patowmack River . . . about a mile long or something better, and about a quarter of a mile Wide in the Broaddis place . . . the banks are about 12 foot high and very hard to ascend." This description fits Harrisons Island and Conoy Island in this stretch of the Potomac (*see* mile 48.4). The emperor assured the emissaries of his peaceful intentions, but politely refused their invitation to come to Williamsburg to speak to the governor.

The old iron bridge with its stone abutments was built in 1876 at E. V. White's request so that traffic could reach his ferry across the canal. With the canal out of operation, Whites Ferry Road now crosses at towpath level, just beyond the old bridge. The foundations on the berm side of the canal belonged to a granary for canal shipments, perhaps one of the warehouses that White owned until selling his interest in 1886. (White also owned warehouses at Sycamore Landing and Edwards Ferry, miles 27.2 and 30.9.)

***Whites Ferry.*** This is the only active ferry of the scores that once teemed along the Potomac. At first it was known as "Conrad's Ferry," which was in operation as early as 1817, when it was mentioned in Benjamin Latrobe's correspondence describing the Marble Quarry (*see* mile 38.2). Lieutenant Colonel E. V. White, who had

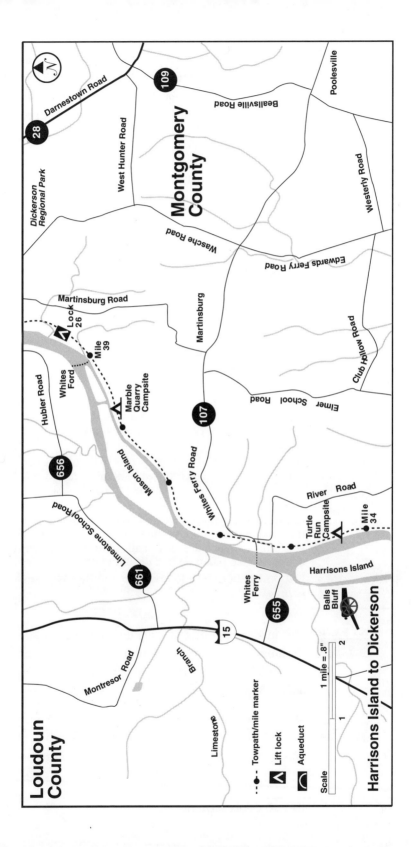

**Loudoun County**

**Montgomery County**

28

109

Darnestown Road

Dickerson Regional Park

West Hunter Road

Beallsville Road

Poolesville

Westerly Road

Wasche Road

Edwards Ferry Road

Martinsburg Road

Lock 26

Mile 39

Whites Ford

Marble Quarry Campsite

Martinsburg

Club Hollow Road

Hubler Road

Mason Island

656

Whites Ferry Road

107

Elmer School Road

River Road

Turtle Run Campsite

Mile 34

Limestone School Road

661

Whites Ferry

655

Harrisons Island

Balls Bluff

Montresor Road

Branch

Limestone

1 mile = .8"

2

- - - •  Towpath/mile marker

Lift lock

Aqueduct

Scale

1

**Harrisons Island to Dickerson**

a farm just upstream and served under Confederate General Jubal Early, purchased the ferry after the Civil War, hence the name of the ferry landing. The ferry boat is named the *General Jubal Early* in honor of White's old commander.

The ferry still serves as a good way to cross over to Leesburg by car or bicycle. The ferry operates year-round, with a small store that offers sandwiches, ice cream, and beverages on a seasonal basis. The store also rents canoes and will arrange trips with drop-offs upstream at Monocacy (2–3 hour trip), Point of Rocks (day trip), and Harpers Ferry (overnight). Call (301) 349-5200 for information.

If you go down to the water here and look downstream, you'll see the upstream end of **Harrisons Island.** Opposite Harrisons Island, on the Virginia side of the river, is the site of the battle of Balls Bluff.

---

### Leesburg Detour

**MILE 0.0**  Cross the Potomac on Whites Ferry (50¢ for bicyclists). Follow Whites Ferry Road to a T-intersection with Route 15.

**MILE 1.3**  Left on Route 15. The first quarter mile is a rather harrowing, busy stretch of two-lane highway with a gravel shoulder. If you have wide enough tires, stay on the shoulder.

**MILE 2.3**  Continue straight on Business 15 to Leesburg, rather than taking the turnoff for the Route 15 bypass (unless you want to take a detour to Balls Bluff by following the bypass 0.6 of a mile to Balls Bluff Road).

**MILE 4.2**  Left on Leesburg Pike to Days Inn and Best Western (1 mile).

---

**MILE 38**  This marker appears to be significantly out of place. Heading downstream, it's only 0.7 of a mile to mile marker 37; heading upstream, it's roughly 1.3 miles to marker 39.

**MILE 38.2**  *Marble Quarry Campsite.* Old maps show a "Marble Quarry" along the Maryland side of the river here. The quarry predated the C&O Canal and was said to run

# Lieutenant Colonel Elijah White

The only surviving reminder of this Confederate officer is the ferry that bears his name, but during the Civil War he was nearly as well known in the Piedmont Valley as the famous Partisan Ranger, John Singleton Mosby. "Lige" White was born in Poolesville in 1832, but as a young man he bought farmland on the other side of the Potomac in Loudoun County.

White began his military career as a lowly private in 1861, first gaining official notice for his actions in the battle of Balls Bluff, where his familiarity with the terrain helped the Confederates capture more than 250 Union soldiers. A year later, when the Army of Northern Virginia was ready to march into Maryland, White was temporarily assigned to Stonewall Jackson's command to advise him on the area. It was probably at this time that White suggested that Jackson's corps follow the road through his farm to a ford across the Potomac. Whites Ford would be used many times by the Confederate army, and was judged to be the most suitable crossing place between Washington and Harpers Ferry for heavy equipment.

Over the next two years, White continued a war of harassment against Union forces in Maryland, occasionally dashing across the river at Conrads Ferry to raid Poolesville or Point of Rocks and then returning by way of Whites Ford. His actions attracted the favorable notice of many Confederate commanders, including Robert E. Lee and J. E. B. Stuart. While White's battalion, known as "the Comanches," was based in Loudoun County for most of the war, they were often called to more distant places. They fought at Gettysburg under General Richard Ewell, accompanied Jubal Early on his winter raid into western Virginia in early 1864, and followed Lee's command south to the surrender at Appomattox.

After the war was over, White managed to become a successful businessman, founding a "country store" in Leesburg in 1865 and restoring ferry service across the Potomac in 1871. Over the years he built or acquired warehouses along the canal at Sycamore Landing, Edwards Ferry, and Whites Ferry. He also served as pastor to several Baptist churches in Loudoun County, which makes one wonder why, of all the famous generals he served, he named his ferryboat after Jubal Early, who was notorious for hard drinking and a most impious vocabulary. White sold the canal warehouses and the ferry business to a partner in 1886, concentrating on his business interests in Leesburg and founding the Peoples National Bank. He died in 1907 at the age of 74, survived by his second wife and five children (see miles 35.5, 38.7, and 173.5).

E. V. White as a Confederate colonel. He later bought Conrads Ferry, better known today as Whites Ferry. *Photo courtesy Montgomery County Historical Society.*

along the river for over a mile, perhaps including the area now occupied by the canal.

The stone that was quarried here was known as "Potomac marble," but it was quite different from the veined marble that was quarried in Tennessee and Georgia. Potomac marble was a "limestone breccia" or "pudding-stone" composed of angular pebbles cemented together in a limestone matrix. (Smoother, waterworn pebbles would have been described as a "conglomerate" rather than breccia.)

After the British burned the fledgling city of Washington in 1814, architect **Benjamin Latrobe** traveled up the Potomac to find suitable marble for the two-story columns in the House of Representatives chamber (now Statuary Hall) and the Senate chamber. Previously, stone from Aquia Creek had been used in the Capitol, and the use of the breccia became one of many controversies that swirled around Latrobe—ultimately, President James Monroe himself inspected the quarry. The C&O Canal had not yet been built, so the blocks of stone had to be boated down the river, using the Patowmack Company's skirting canals at Seneca, Great Falls, and Little Falls. In 1817, Latrobe wrote: "In this undertaking, every species of difficulty has been encountered, in opening the quarry, in collecting laborers, quarriers and marble masons, in providing dwellings, shops and tools, and in organizing a great undertaking on the banks of a river where no habitation before existed." Two of Latrobe's sons played major roles in the construction of the Baltimore and Ohio Railroad: John H. B. Latrobe as a company lawyer and Benjamin H. Latrobe, Jr. as an architect (*see* mile 60.7).

Civil War accounts and maps place **Whites Ford** here, just above the tip of Oxleys Island (a historical marker has been placed another third of a mile farther up). The ford takes its name from Elijah White, the same Confederate officer who later operated Whites Ferry (mile 35.5). White owned farmland on the Virginia side of the Potomac, and hence was well acquainted with this "obscure ford" when he was temporarily assigned to Stonewall Jackson's command in 1862. Jackson's men had to level the river banks to make the ford passable for their wagons and cannon and threw a makeshift bridge over Lock 26, just upstream, to haul them across the canal.

No longer so obscure, Whites Ford became known as the only suitable crossing point below Harpers Ferry for heavy equipment. Having no pontoons, the Confederate army used the ford frequently, but the Union army avoided it because they considered the river bottom too rough for heavier wagons and artillery.

Other notable crossings at this spot included J. E. B. Stuart's narrow escape back into Virginia in October 1862, as he completed his ride around the Union army after the battle at Antietam (*see also* McCoys Ferry, mile 110.2). The last major crossing of the ford was by Confederate General Jubal Early (July 14, 1864), who had advanced up the Shenandoah Valley, crossed at Botelors Ford (*see* mile 71.4), and marched to the outskirts of the city of Washington before retreating back to Virginia at this spot.

*Lock 26 (Woods Lock).* This lock is one of the subtle pleasures of the lower canal, an unexpected clearing along the densely forested trail. A stone-lined bypass flume with a concrete gate at its upper end circles around the stone foundations of the lockhouse. An enormous maple tree stands next to the lockhouse ruins on the little island created by the flume, perhaps old enough to have been here when the Confederate wagons rolled past on their way to Antietam. The lock itself is built of red sandstone boated upstream all the way from Seneca (16.7 miles on the river). Note the stone rubble lying in the channel just below the lock, showing where the lock was extended in the 1870s to accommodate two boats at a time.

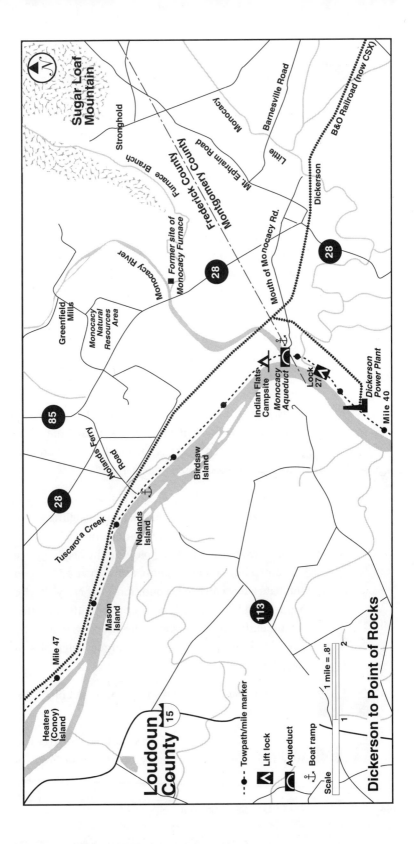

Sugar Loaf Mountain

Stronghold

Furnace Branch

Montgomery County
Frederick County

Mt. Ephraim Road

Little Monocacy

Barnesville Road

■ Former site of Monocacy Furnace

Monocacy River

Mouth of Monocacy Rd.

B&O Railroad (now CSX)

Dickerson

28

28

Greenfield Mills

Monocacy Natural Resources Area

Dickerson Power Plant

Indian Flats Campsite

Monocacy Aqueduct

Lock 27

Mile 40

85

Nolands Ferry Road

Birdsaw Island

28

Tuscarora Creek

Nolands Island

113

Mason Island

Mile 47

Heaters (Conoy) Island

Loudoun County 15

Towpath/mile marker

Lift lock

Aqueduct

Boat ramp

Scale

1 mile = .8"

1          2

**Dickerson to Point of Rocks**

**MILE 39.6** An earthen ramp leads to the parking lot for Dickerson Conservation area. The path down to the river at this spot is very popular for fishermen taking advantage of the lure of the warm water discharge from the power plant upstream, but watch out for the stinging nettles in summer.

**MILE 40.6** The *Dickerson Power Plant* was built in 1957–59 by PEPCO and is now owned by Mirant. The tallest and most recent of its three smokestacks (700 feet) is almost as prominent a landmark as Sugarloaf; it's even visible from Route 15 on the Virginia side of the river. Environmental regulations at the time of its construction (1978) required that the smokestack be tall enough to disperse the smoke over a wide region.

The power plant is a modern variation on the use of water and coal along the Potomac. The plant uses 150,000 tons of coal a day to generate electricity. The coal comes via railroad car from a spur of the CSX line. A "screen-house" on the Potomac takes in 300,000 gallons of water a minute, most of which is used to cool the steam pipes. The heated water is returned to the Potomac through a 900-foot discharge channel.

If you peer through the chain-link fence on the river side, you can see candy-striped kayak poles dangling above the concrete-lined discharge channel. In 1991, PEPCO contributed to the U.S. Olympic effort by helping place 75 "obstacles," some weighing as much as 17 tons, to simulate whitewater river conditions. The Navy's Taylor Model Boat Basin (near Carderock at mile 10.4) assisted in the design of the course. The course was used by kayakers training for the 1992 summer Olympics in Barcelona.

**MILE 41** Note: mile markers 40 and 41 appear to be only 0.8 of a mile apart.

**MILE 41.5** *Lock 27* was mostly built of red sandstone boated down-stream 5 miles from a quarry just south of Point of

Rocks, except for the coping, which was brought up from Seneca. The rubble remains of the extended portion of the lock lie along the upstream channel. A white-washed stone lock house still stands on the towpath side. A pivot bridge at this lock allowed local traffic to follow a road down to **Spinks Ferry** across the Potomac.

Confederate troops under General D. H. Hill, frustrated in their efforts to blow up the Monocacy Aqueduct at the outset of the Antietam campaign, turned their attention to disabling this lock (September 4 and 5, 1862). The damage from that raid may account for the lighter colored sandstone near the lock pockets. After the battle of Antietam, the canal company board dismissed the lockkeeper, Thomas Walters, for allegedly collaborating with the Confederates. Several of his neighbors petitioned the board of directors on his behalf, describing the lockkeeper's attempts to convince General Hill not to destroy his lock, a discussion that became so heated that "bystanders feared that Walters would be arrested." The company's records do not indicate whether or not the board was persuaded to change its decision.

Entering **Frederick County,** Maryland. Frederick County was a vast, sprawling county established in 1748. Like the city of Frederick, it was probably named for Frederick Calvert, the sixth Lord Baltimore, who had not yet reached majority at that time. The county was large enough to have upper, middle, and lower divisions, and in 1776 the Maryland Constitutional Convention created Montgomery County out of the lower division and Washington County out of the upper one (*see* miles 4.7 *and* 57.8).

At one time the jewel of the canal, the seven arches of the 560-foot **Monocacy Aqueduct** are now corseted with steel beams as it struggles against the current and shifting footing. Unlike the predominant sandstone and limestone structures along this part of the canal, the aqueduct was constructed of pink quartzite quarried from nearby Sugarloaf Mountain and brought down to the canal on a small railroad built for that purpose.

An occasional Civil War crossing point, **Haulings Ford** was said to be located at the mouth of the Monocacy. On September 4 and 5, 1862, Confederate General D. H. Hill's forces crossed here at the beginning of the Antietam campaign. To expedite the crossing into Maryland, Hill's men leveled the canal banks, wrecked the culvert for the Little Monocacy River (mile 42), drained the canal, and laid a corduroy path across the prism. Although they were unable to breach the majestic aqueduct, "for want of powder and tools," they did blow up a portion of Lock 27 downstream. On Lee's orders, a second attempt to demolish the aqueduct was made by Brigadier General John Walker on the night of September 9, but was unsuccessful. As Union forces approached, Walker's men had to hurry on, crossing back over the Potomac at Nolands Ferry on their way to Loudoun Heights to complete the encirclement of Harpers Ferry.

**MILE 42.4** *Indian Flats Campsite.*

The Monocacy Aqueduct in all its splendor. *Photo courtesy National Archives.*

This is the approximate location of **Cheeks Ford** (also known as Chicks Ford). It was occasionally used as a river crossing during the Civil War, most notably by Confederate soldiers crossing to Maryland at the outset of the Antietam campaign.

**MILE 43.6**

Culvert 71 for **Tuscarora Creek**. Tuscarora Creek runs along the canal for the next few miles, and once provided water for the canal through a feeder canal upstream (*see* mile 45.1). The creek takes its name from the fierce Tuscarora Indians, who had been driven from the Carolinas by English settlers in the early 1700s.

**MILE 44**

An access road crosses over the canal to the parking lot for **Nolands Ferry** picnic area and boat launch.

**MILE 44.6**

The sandstone abutments on each side of the canal were part of a bridge built in the 1850s to carry traffic over the canal. The canal had been in operation in this area since the 1830s, but the arrangement where farm produce was "ferried" across the canal was not working well, so a bridge was built.

The New Design water intake facility stands just beyond the access road for Nolands Ferry (the name comes from New Design Road, which provides access from Route 28). Unlike so many of the unappealing concrete public works projects along the canal, the stone exterior harks back to the old mills that used to populate the Potomac. This is no accident—the Park Service set some esthetic guidelines when East Alcoa built the facility in 1970–71 to provide water to an aluminum plant several miles inland. Though the facility was built by East Alcoa, Frederick County has operated it for most of its existence. It wasn't until fairly recently (1990) that the facility was upgraded to produce potable water, but it still provides around a million gallons a day to the aluminum plant. All told, the intake supplies around 3 to 4 million gallons of water a day to southern Frederick County. Thirsty as the county is, don't be surprised if another intake facility sprouts up further downstream in the next few years.

## Nolands Ferry

This was an important crossing point for settlers following the old Indian trail and wagon road along the Monocacy River from the Susquehanna Valley in Pennsylvania. Originally licensed by Ebenezer Floyd in 1742, ferry operations at this landing were taken over by Philip Noland around 1754. (Noland was the son-in-law of Francis Awbrey, who had licensed a very early Potomac ferry operation at the base of Conoy Island, two miles upstream, in 1735.) Noland competed successfully with Josiah Clapham's ferry at the mouth of the Monocacy (mile 42.2). On the Virginia side of the river, the route south through Leesburg was known as the Carolina Road, with German artisans sending their wares as far as Georgia. (The Carolina Road also became known as the Rogue's Road because of horse and cattle thieves.)

Many of the 5,000 or so British and German prisoners from Saratoga (1778) crossed at the ferry on their way to prison camps in Virginia. It was a difficult winter crossing, with the scows frequently trapped by ice floes and drifting as far as a mile below the ferry landing. If the river was high, the crossing could be perilous in any season: American General Anthony Wayne, crossing to join the Yorktown campaign in the much warmer month of May (1781), lost a scow with four men and cannon here.

This route became less popular as the city of Washington was built further downstream, and it gradually vanished from maps of the region. It was an occasional crossing point during the Civil War for small outfits such as Mosby's famous Partisan Rangers, who were based across the river in Loudoun County.

**MILE 45.1** *Tuscarora feeder canal.* The canal company used a feeder canal from Tuscarora Creek to water this stretch of the canal for a while, to supplement the water provided by Dam no. 3 up at Harpers Ferry. Built during the controversy with the railroad over the right-of-way at Point of Rocks, this feeder canal may originally have been an attempt to provide an alternate supply of water in case construction continued to be stalled short of the dam at Harpers Ferry. The Metropolitan branch of the B&O Railroad (completed in 1873) now blocks the feeder, but the ditch is visible on the other side of the railroad tracks along the canal berm, marked by a line of trees perpendicular to the canal and railroad.

**MILE 47.1** The private dock along the river is connected by a path across the canal and railroad tracks to ***Camp Kanawha,*** a group of private cabins owned by the Frederick

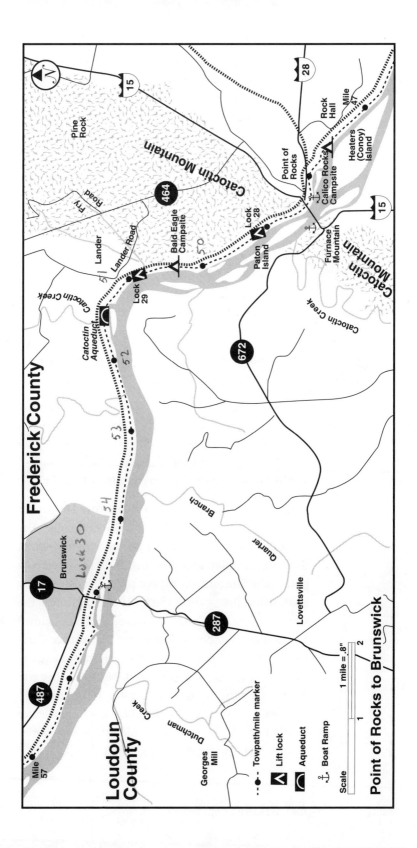

**Point of Rocks to Brunswick**

Scale

1 mile = .8"

Frederick County

Loudoun County

Catoctin Mountain

Pine Rock

Fry Road

Lander

Lander Road

Bald Eagle Campsite

Lock 28

Paton Island

Point of Rocks

Calico Rocks Campsite

Rock Hall

Mile 47

Heaters (Conoy) Island

Furnace Mountain

Catoctin Mountain

Catoctin Creek

Catoctin Aqueduct

Lock 29

Brunswick

Lock 30

Quarter Branch

Lovettsville

Georges Mill

Dutchman Creek

Mile 57

— — — Towpath/mile marker

Lift lock

Aqueduct

Boat Ramp

County Fish and Game Protective Association. The path leads between two rock outcroppings that are good examples of the "calico rocks" of the region—a composite of multicolored pebbles held together by a natural cement of limestone, referred to as "Potomac Marble." Benjamin Henry Latrobe, the famous architect, found this puddingstone "at the foot of the Catoctin" much to his liking but ultimately decided to use a quarry further downstream for the construction of the Capitol (*see* mile 38.2).

 **Kanawha Spring.** The unsightly chain-link fence is meant to protect visitors from falling into the cavity in the vicinity of the small dam that the Park Service built around Kanawha Spring in a failed attempt to divert water from the spring into the canal.

 **Calico Rocks Campsite.** Named for the composite rocks of this region; see discussion above.

**MILE 48.2** The towpath merges with a paved road along the canal. The road crosses over the canal on the piers of a former pivot bridge (later fixed in place, but at a higher elevation to provide 17-foot clearance for canal boats), and leads into the small town of *Point of Rocks.*

At this point, there's a brief vista of *Furnace Mountain* on the opposite shore, part of the Catoctin Ridge. The Potomac Furnace was located on the Virginia side of the Catoctin Ridge, and operated from the late 1700s until 1870. The furnace shipped some of its pig iron by boat, using the skirting canals at the falls until the advent of the C&O Canal. It also used the B&O Railroad for shipment. In the 1850s the Potomac Furnace Company built a narrow bridge across the Potomac to carry the iron to the canal and railroad, but the bridge was destroyed by the Confederate army at the beginning of the Civil War. Early in the Civil War, the Confederates dragged a cannon up Furnace Mountain and lobbed shells at the Union camp at Point of Rocks.

The town of **Point of Rocks** consists of little more than a three-block stretch of Clay Street (Route 28), running parallel to the canal and the railroad tracks. But it's worth the brief detour across the pivot bridge to see the Victorian train station. If you're on an extended trip, you may want to pick up some beverages or snacks at the country store.

## Baron von Graffenried at Conoy Island

The large island lying in the Potomac opposite the town of Point of Rocks, now known as Heaters Island, was identified as one of the "Conoy Islands" on old maps of the region. One of the Conoy tribes, the Piscataway Indians, had settled here in the early 1700s as they moved ever westward to avoid the encroaching English settlements in Maryland (*see* Harrisons Island, mile 34.3). An early visitor to the region above the falls, Baron Christoph von Graffenried found the Conoy to be relatively friendly to Europeans, just as they had been when Lord Calvert first settled along the Chesapeake Bay. Friendly relations with the Indians were very important to the baron, who had tried to found a colony of Swiss and German immigrants at New Bern, North Carolina. Most of that colony was wiped out by the Tuscarora Indians in 1712.

The baron, who had evidently charmed Queen Anne of England, held a royal grant for unspecified lands along the upper Potomac as well as in North Carolina. And he was quite delighted by these "enchanted islands in the Potomac River above the Falls," where he found a small Indian village called Canavest and a Frenchman from Canada named Martin Charetier, who had married an Indian woman. When the baron returned to Williamsburg, however, he discovered that his partners had already left for England without him.

Unlike most immigrants, the baron had a sizable inheritance to return to in Switzerland, and it was easy enough for him to abandon his projects in the New World. Ironically, the Tuscarora Indians who had destroyed New Bern were driven from North Carolina, joined the Iroquois Confederacy, and left their mark in the same region that the baron had planned to settle along the Potomac. We know them through the stream called the Tuscarora (mile 44), which testifies to the years when they undoubtedly wreaked great havoc on the unfortunate Piscataway as they traveled the warriors' trails that led up to the Iroquois strongholds near the Great Lakes.

**MILE 48.4** The road ends in a parking and boat launch area next to the piers for the bridge carrying Route 15 across the Potomac in the direction of Leesburg. The unpaved towpath resumes at this point.

If you go down to the boat ramp, you'll get a good view of *Heaters (Conoy) Island* just downstream.

The entrance to the first of the railroad tunnels through *Catoctin Ridge* can be seen on the other side of the canal. The canal bed is unusually narrow here, because the railroad added another line of track after the canal had closed. Blocks of stone, railroad ties, and even fairly sizable train parts can be found tumbled into the canal bed along this stretch.

**MILE 49** *Lock 28.* The lock was mostly built of hard white flint-stone from a quarry about 4 miles away in Virginia, with some granite brought in by the B&O Railroad from the Patapsco quarry, about 45 miles east. The cooperation of the railroad, unthinkable during the four-year court battle over the right-of-way, was made possible by the agreement for joint construction between Point of Rocks and Harpers Ferry.

**MILE 50** To the right, the B&O Railroad enters a tunnel through Catoctin Mountain. The tunnel was built only in 1868; before that time, the railroad ran between the canal and the cliffs. It was this narrow squeeze that occasioned the great court battle between the canal and the railroad in 1828–32.

**MILE 50.3** *Bald Eagle Campsite.* The uncomfortable proximity of the canal and the railroad makes this the noisiest campsite along the canal. However, it's a long way to the nearest campsite upstream (about 12.5 miles), so this is the most convenient stopping point on a four-day bicycle ride.

**MILE 50.9** *Lock 29 (Lander Lock).* Two-thirds of the stone for this lock was granite brought by railroad from Patapsco, the remainder being the white flintstone from across the river in Virginia. The brick lockhouse is still standing.

The towpath crosses Catoctin Creek on a "Bailey Bridge" provided by the U.S. Army Corps of Engineers in 1980. If you look below the bridge (upstream side), you can see the single remaining arch of the *Catoctin Aqueduct.*

**M I L E**
**51.5**

Work on the aqueduct, long delayed by the court case, began in 1832 but was almost immediately interrupted by the cholera epidemic that fall. Nevertheless, the aqueduct was finished by October 1833, when the canal was watered from Dam no. 3 at Harpers Ferry down to Seneca. As with many locks in this region, most of the stone was brought in by the B&O Railroad from the granite quarries of Patapsco, though some may have come from local quarries. The aqueduct was known as the Swayback Aqueduct as it became progressively more deformed because of its flawed design (an elliptical center arch bracketed by two smaller circular arches).

The elegant stone B&O railroad bridge or viaduct just upstream is also worth a longer look. It is a good example of the stone construction favored by Caspar Wever, who was the superintendent of construction for the railroad. Some of the B&O's other engineers favored less expensive wooden truss bridges, but more than 160 years later, Wever's decision has withstood the test of time and the ravages of several major floods. The Thomas Viaduct, another example of Wever's work for the railroad, has been designated a historic landmark in the city of Baltimore (*see* mile 58 for more about Wever). The contractor who completed the viaduct, however, is the true hero of this story. John Littlejohn found himself short of men because of the cholera outbreak, and short of funds because the B&O Railroad had delayed in specifying the route. Stricken with cholera and abandoned by his partners, he still managed to finish the job and was later commended by the railroad and awarded additional compensation.

**MILE 52.5** Exposed remains of a culvert are visible in the canal bed, giving a cutaway view of the barrel of the culvert. The reinforcing rods and concrete are evidently replacement work, but if you go down to the streambed, you'll find a traditional stone arch in very good condition.

 **MILE 53** The long railroad yards at Brunswick begin on the berm side of the canal. The B&O Railroad built these "classification yards" in the 1890s to replace its smaller yard in Martinsburg, West Virginia. These are reputed to be the largest yards owned by a single railroad in the United States, stretching for 7 miles.

 **MILE 53.8** Access gate; the towpath continues on a roadway for residents of the mobile homes between the towpath and the river.

 **MILE 54** Brunswick Recreation Area; a small river park operated by the town that includes picnic tables, shelters, soda machines, campsites, boat ramps, and boat rentals. The showers are of particular interest to hiker-bikers. Stop by the manager's office to get permission before using them.

 **MILE 54.5** Passing the Brunswick Waste Treatment Plant along the towpath.

**MILE 54.6** The curious cylindrical structure with an imitation rockface is a recent addition to the treatment plant.

**MILE 54.7** Until very recently, a semicircular **roundhouse** for the B&O Railroad was visible on the berm side of the canal. Sadly, this distinctive structure was razed during the winter of 1996.

## Brunswick, Maryland

Since 1890, Brunswick has been first and foremost a railroad town, but its varied history can be told by its many names. The town lies at a primeval crossroads, first known as Buffalo Wallow, where the valley between the Catoctin and the Blue Ridge meets the Potomac. It was also known as Eel Pot for the weirs that the Indians would build in the river to trap eel and fish. After the buffalo and the Indians had passed from the landscape, a man named John Hawkins began operating a ferry here in 1741, and this point on the Potomac became known as German Crossing. In 1753 Hawkins obtained a patent for land here. He named his tract Merry Peep-O-Day, purportedly referring to that first hopeful glint of sunlight over the eastern hills. Still later the town became known as Berlin, testifying further to the many German settlers passing down this valley corridor. Because of the confusion between Berlin and another town by that name on the eastern shore, the postal service named its local office Barry, rather than Berlin, in 1832.

The river crossing, at first a ford and then a ferry, was greatly eased by the construction of a covered wooden bridge that opened in 1857. Unfortunately, the bridge was torched just four years later by Confederate cavalry. The ferry had to suffice for the next two decades until a steel bridge was built in 1893. The bridge survived the catastrophic floods, even that of 1936, but was replaced in 1955 by the present concrete structure.

Life in the modest little town of Barry was completely changed in 1890 when the B&O Railroad decided to move its yard here from Martinsburg. The town was incorporated as Brunswick, reportedly at the suggestion of a B&O official, in recognition of the many immigrant workers from that German city. The railroad yard was a "classification yard," used for switching cars from different lines. Seven miles long, the Brunswick yard was said to be the longest yard owned by a single railroad. With the arrival of the railroad, Brunswick essentially became a "company town," as the B&O exercised its considerable leverage in the political and social life of the community. It encouraged its workers to participate in the YMCA that was established soon after the yards arrived, and contributed to other worth-while causes. Around the turn of the century, the B&O pushed through a temperance measure which simply meant that the town was soon ringed by saloons just beyond its limits.

The most distinctive railroad structure in Brunswick was the roundhouse, begun as an ironclad structure in 1891 and eventually converted to a brick building with 12 stalls in 1907. Extensions were added in 1917 and 1927.

The decline of the railroads has made the town a quiet little place, not quite as rough as Hancock nor as genteel as Williamsport. The glory days are enshrined in a small railroad museum, open seasonally and by appointment.

### AMENITIES

One hiker sums up the advice from a Brunswick resident: "Eight churches and 16 liquor stores—take your pick!" It's still a lot easier to find liquor than breakfast, but try the Silver Rail Diner on Maple Street, just above the railroad station. The best (and only) place to stay is the former YMCA, now the Sleepers Motel at Tracks End. It has a contract arrangement with MARC and AMTRAK, so it's clean, but the language you hear in the lobby may not be. The motel is about 2 miles outside of town, over rolling hills (take Route 17 to a right on Souder Road). The Brunswick Railroad Museum is open on weekends from April through mid-November, at 40 West Potomac Street, (301) 834-7100.

**MILE 55** The remains of **Lock 30** lie next to downtown Brunswick. The lockhouse is long since gone. The lock was originally built of red sandstone carried by boat from Seneca, along with some local stone "found scattered throughout the neighborhood" and some granite carried in by railroad from Patapsco, but there is much replacement stone in the present structure. The rubble on the upstream end shows where this lock was extended in the 1870s (*see* mile 30.9).

Overhead, a bridge carries Route 17 over the Potomac. This is the modern descendant of several earlier ferries and bridges at this point, including a wooden bridge that was burned by the Confederates early in the Civil War. An access road connects the town of Brunswick to the boat ramp and park.

A mill on the berm side of the canal drew water from the bypass flume for its operation.

**MILE 57.8** The river passes through a notch in a ridge just before the Blue Ridge, known as **South Mountain** in Maryland, and Short Hill Mountain in Virginia.

South Mountain is geographically and historically significant because of the battles fought in the mountain gaps just 10 miles north of here as Confederate forces tried to delay General McClellan's advance on Lee's army at Antietam (September 1862). The mountain also conveniently divides **Washington** and **Frederick counties.** Washington County was formed from Frederick County in 1776 and was named for the patriot leader, even though he had yet to meet with any significant military success (*see* miles 4.7 *and* 42).

**MILE 57.9** A trail leads down to the river, crossing the millrace that runs beside the canal. The millrace, leading from a former river dam just upstream, is one of the few traces of the industrial village of Weverton, the brainchild of Casper Wever. The trail leads to the formidable remains of the stone intake gates for a cotton mill that was operated on this site.

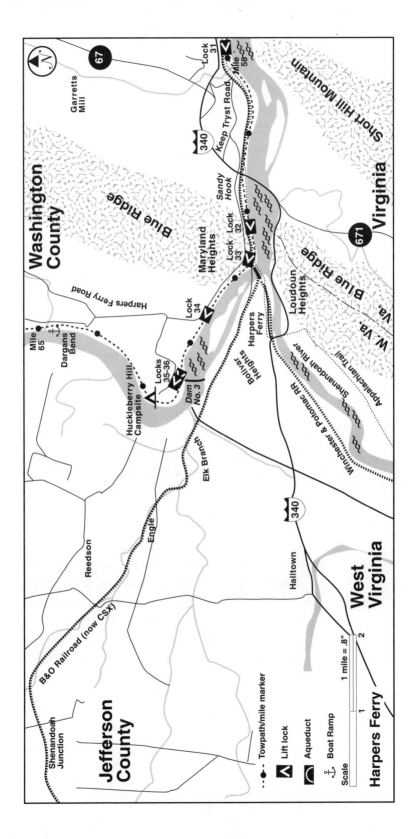

*Lock 31.* The lock was originally built of white flintstone and granite from nearby Virginia quarries, now touched up with some concrete replacement work. The culvert that runs under the upper end of the lock was unusual in that it was built for the tailrace of a mill that was built before the canal. The mill drew water from Israel Creek, a little further along, and later supplemented its intake with water from the canal.

This area is the site of the ghost town of **Weverton.** Years ago, the view across the lock would have included the Bingham Store next to the lockhouse, as well as a hotel, a train station, and a saloon on the other side of the railroad tracks.

**Caspar Wever,** an engineer who had worked on the National Road, was hired by the B&O Railroad in 1829 as superintendant of construction. Wever developed a reputation for rapid completion of his projects, massive cost overruns, and some very shady business practices (*see* mile 60.7). In the course of his work, which included the construction of several elegant viaducts for the railroad (*see* mile 51.5), Wever decided that this location just below Harpers Ferry would make an ideal site for an industrial community. The river level dropped 15 feet here, providing a ready supply of potential energy for a factory complex, and the railroad would soon arrive to carry away the manufactured goods. Wever bought property here and bitterly resisted the condemnation of a strip of his land for the C&O Canal, holding up the canal construction in the courts until he had extracted full compensation. Unfortunately, he was not as successful with his town plan, as he found few tenants willing to lease buildings and water at the rates he had established.

The most notable of the enterprises here was General Henderson's Steel and File Manufacturing Company, which supplied files to the armory at Harpers Ferry.

Wever died in the late 1840s, and his initial hopes for the town were never fulfilled. In the 1850s, legislation was introduced in Congress to establish a "national foundry" here, presumably taking advantage of the canal and iron from the Antietam Furnace. But that proposal died, as did the plans of a mysterious utopian commune that erected three buildings to serve as living quarters and a factory for their "secret" method of processing cotton. The commune buildings were used as barracks for Union forces as they concentrated around Harpers Ferry after the battle at Antietam. In 1877 the C&O Canal bought much of the industrial property near the river and razed it as a flood hazard. The community of Weverton persevered for many years, however, with its own post office, church, distillery, hotel, and, until the 1930s, a railroad station that served as transfer point for passengers, baggage, and mail from the B&O main line and another line to Hagerstown.

Marker for the *Appalachian Trail.* The trail follows South Mountain through Maryland to the Potomac, and merges with the towpath for the next few miles. To follow the Appalachian Trail south along the Blue Ridge Mountains, you can cross the river either on the highway bridge for Route 340 or on the pedestrian bridge at Harpers Ferry. Development of the Appalachian Trail began in 1923, and it now stretches 2,147 miles from Springer Mountain in Georgia to Mount Katahdin, Maine.

You can also follow the footpath down to the river at this point, to see the beginning of the Weverton millrace and the location of its dam. The enterprises at Weverton included a flour mill on the Virginia side of the Potomac (Wever owned the rights to the Potomac river bottom here), a sawmill at this spot, and later the General Henderson Steel and File Manufacturing Company.

**MILE 58.2** On the berm side, there's a nice view of a stream coming over the rocks and through the railroad culvert. This is Israel Creek, which drains the valley between Short Mountain and the Blue Ridge and passes under the canal through a large 20-foot culvert.

**MILE 59.5** Overhead, a bridge carries Highway 340 over to the Virginia side of the river on its way to Harpers Ferry. Just beyond, there is a path across the canal that leads to the small community of **Sandy Hook.** It's hard to imagine now, but this small strip of land at Sandy Hook served as the terminal yards for the B&O Railroad until the railroad was able to build west of Harpers Ferry in the late 1830s. This is your exit if you are headed to the American Youth Hostel or the Hillside Motel. Cross the railroad tracks and take a right on Harpers Ferry Road (be prepared for a steep hill).

# The Blue Ridge
# and the Great Valley

Once beyond the Shenandoah Falls and the Blue Ridge, the Potomac wends its way through the Great Valley of Maryland for approximately 65 river miles, finally reentering the mountains just beyond the town of Hancock. South of the Potomac, this broad valley was known by its river as the Shenandoah Valley. In Pennsylvania, it is known as the Cumberland Valley (not to be confused with the valley around the city of Cumberland). The plentiful game in these woods and meadows sustained the Iroquois south along the many warriors' trails, when they traveled as far as 600 miles to do battle with the Catawba and the Cherokee. Similarly, in the 1700s, German and Scotch-Irish settlers were drawn here from Pennsylvania by the promise of rich farmland for relatively modest rent.

The distinguishing characteristic of the valley during the era of canal construction was the plentiful supply of limestone in this region, which not only provided the cut blocks of stone for locks, culverts, and aqueducts, but was also ground up and burned down to powder for fertilizer, cement, and plaster. The limestone also tends to be dissolved by acidic groundwater, creating sinkholes and caves in the cliffs along the canal.

During the Civil War, the Shenandoah Valley in Virginia was always a separate theater of war from that portion of Northern Virginia that lay between Richmond and Washington. The Valley campaigns of Stonewall Jackson, Jubal Early, and Union General Philip Sheridan provided a contrapuntal theme to the major battles between Lee's Army of Northern Virginia and the Union Army of the Potomac. When Lee moved north in the Antietam and Gettysburg campaigns, he was inevitably drawn to the Great Valley, which gave him easy access to Pennsylvania, but was also screened by the Blue Ridge and South Mountains. Here we will pass the historic river crossings at Botelors Ford and Falling Waters, as well as the battlefield at Antietam.

---

**Lock 32,** originally built of limestone from upriver quarries, with some granite from Virginia quarries. A "Long Wall" along the canal embankment up to the next lock protected the embankment from the recurring flood damage in this area. Three sluices, or skirting canals, to bypass the rapids and falls in this area were built by the Patowmack Company in the 1780s. The sluices began just below this lock and ran intermittently along the next 2 miles, to a point above Dam no. 3.

MILE
60.2

The canal company had originally planned to build Dam no. 3 at this location, but ran into numerous difficulties. The armory at Harpers Ferry resisted this plan, and John Hall, operating the Hall Rifle Works, complained in a letter that the dam would raise the water level in the area 2 feet, reducing the "head" of water that drove his factory's waterwheels. Eventually the canal company agreed to tap into the water supply created by the Armory Dam above Harpers Ferry, and that became Dam no. 3.

The raised stone embankment at the end of the "Long Wall" also marks the approximate location of the **Shenandoah River Lock,** built in 1833. As with the river lock at Edwards Ferry, this lock did not turn out to be very useful. As a part of the agreement resolving the right-of-way dispute between Point of Rocks and Harpers Ferry, the B&O Railroad was supposed to provide a "tracking path" as part of the bridge it was building over the river. The mules were to use the tracking path to tow the canal boats over to the town and the skirting canals along the Shenandoah River. The agreement was thwarted by problems with obtaining a right-of-way on the opposite side of the river—George Wager, the most prominent citizen of the town, had an interest in the B&O Railroad and would not accommodate the canal. In addition, the traffic along the Shenandoah River was soon absorbed by the Winchester and Potomac Railroad. The river lock was cannibalized for stone after the great flood of 1889.

The entrance to the B&O railroad tunnel is above and to the right, with two railroad bridges to Harpers Ferry overhead. Use the spiral staircase and pedestrian walkway along the downstream bridge to cross the river to the town of **Harpers Ferry.**

At this juncture of the two rivers, you can see the piers for the old B&O bridge across the Potomac and a wagon bridge across the Shenandoah River. Both bridges were wiped out by the great flood of 1936.

A succession of earlier bridges over both rivers were destroyed by periodic floods and attacks during the Civil War. The original B&O bridge was Caspar Wever's last project for the railroad. Wever let the contract to the highest of three bidders, Charles Wilson, who agreed to use more expensive but inferior stone from a quarry owned by Wever. (The low bidder was John Littlejohn, the extraordinary contractor who built the Catoctin Viaduct, mile 51.5.) The stone at the top of the bridge piers cracked just a few months after the bridge was completed in December 1836, and it had to be repaired at great expense. The railroad's architect, Benjamin H. Latrobe, Jr., attributed the calamity to Wever's dishonesty. However, his brother, the attorney John H. B. Latrobe, concluded that the railroad could not prove a case of fraud against Wever or the contractor. In Charles Wilson's case, the contractor had made no effort to conceal the bridge's defects from the company's agents and had in fact told others that he hoped to get paid as soon as possible, because the bridge would not hold up.

This first B&O bridge, which was used by John Brown's men to cross the river in 1859, was destroyed by Confederate soldiers in 1861. Replacements that were erected during the war suffered frequent attacks. After the war, Wendell Bollmann erected one of his classic iron truss bridges for the railroad (*see* mile 99.5), where the original bridge once stood. In 1894, when the railroad first tunneled through Maryland Heights, it built a second bridge just upstream from the Bollmann Bridge. The flood of 1936 left only the newer bridge standing.

Built by
Henry Latrobe

**Lock 33,** which was not only an important place of exchange between the canal and Harpers Ferry, but may have played a role in John Brown's raid on the armory across the river. Brown had sent John Cook to Harpers Ferry in 1858, a year before the raid, to reconnoiter the area. Cook married a local woman during his stay, and she indicated in an interview long after the raid that Cook had made a living for a while by tending one of

A rare view of the Harpers Ferry Bridge before its destruction during the Civil War. Designed by Benjamin Latrobe and Lewis Wernwag, the bridge suffered because of Caspar Wever's suspect contracting practices. This first bridge was covered with a wooden roof, and the track had to make a sharp right turn on the Maryland side to avoid the cliffs. Not until the 1890s did the B&O tunnel through Maryland Heights. *Photo courtesy National Park Service.*

the canal locks across the river from the town. This lock and Lock 32 are the likely candidates, because of their proximity to the road.

This lock was mostly built of granite from a quarry in Virginia. The stone was hauled 1.5 miles by wagons that had to cross both the Shenandoah and Potomac rivers. The lock was finished in September 1833, and the lockhouse was probably built on the river side of the canal a few years later. (The shed shown over the bypass flume in later photographs was probably associated with the loading dock along the flume.) Note the arched culvert for the bypass flume, seen from the downstream side.

The building on the other side of Harpers Ferry Road, at the base of Maryland Heights, is variously identified as

A canal boat leaves the lock at Harpers Ferry, headed downstream. *Photo courtesy National Park Service.*

Spencer's Store or the Elgin House, and is often confused with the remains of the infamous "Salty Dog" tavern of the post-canal era. Maryland Heights is a towering and craggy cliff of Harper's shale that gives a splendid view of the junction of the rivers.

## Harpers Ferry, West Virginia

Harpers Ferry is a small town handsomely but not strategically situated at the juncture of the Potomac and Shenandoah rivers. Thomas Jefferson summarized the landscape splendidly in his *Notes on the State of Virginia*:

The passage of the Patowmac through the Blue ridge is perhaps one of the most stupendous scenes in nature. On your right comes up the Shenandoah, having ranged along the foot of the mountain an hundred miles to seek a vent. On your left approaches the Patowmac, in quest of a passage also. In the moment of their junction they rush together against the mountain, rend in asunder, and pass off to the sea. . . . This scene is worth a voyage across the Atlantic.

On a pleasant day, the wildness of the rivers is not so dramatic as Jefferson describes. His memory of the scene may well have come from a visit when floodwaters were boiling and crashing through the rapids.

One has to wonder if Jefferson had yet to visit Great Falls when he penned these lines.

In 1733 a man named Peter Stephens settled at this river fork and established a trading post and started a ferry. The town takes its name from Robert Harper, who arrived in 1747 and took advantage of the rushing waters to open a mill. Harper also operated a ferry for farmers to transport their grain to the mill for grinding.

In the 1790s, George Washington, patron saint of the Potomac Valley, conceived the idea of a federal armory at this site, taking advantage of the natural waterpower and the nearby ironworks. The government purchased land here in 1796, and built an armory with its own canal and dam (to provide water power) around the turn of the century. The dam was later incorporated into the C&O Canal system as Dam no. 3. The once pristine gorge celebrated by Jefferson eventually became a smoky, polluted victim of the industrial revolution, with a gristmill, an iron foundry, a cotton mill, a pulp mill, Hall's rifle works, and an iron sheet-rolling mill, in addition to the government armory. The neighboring hills were stripped bare to feed the furnaces with charcoal (coal was not used until the 1840s).

In the late 1850s, the armory with its store of weapons attracted the attention of a militant abolitionist named John Brown. Brown and his men seized several buildings on the night of October 16, but they were captured two days later when U.S. Marines under the command of Robert E. Lee broke down the doors of the engine house. John Brown was hung six weeks later, but his largely symbolic act contributed to the growing distrust and eventual secession of the southern states.

While the location of the town between two major rivers was ideally suited to the production and transportation systems of that era, it was not a defensible position for the armory. Stonewall Jackson first thought that the narrow cut in the mountains could be defended like Thermopylae, but later changed his mind and said that he would rather take the town fifty times than defend it once. This point of view was convincingly proven by the Confederate army during the Antietam campaign (1862), when artillery units were able to rain shells on the town from all three directions: Loudoun Heights, Maryland Heights, and Bolivar Heights. The 12,000 Union soldiers who were penned in the town chose to surrender after a day's bombardment, a decision that allowed the Confederates just enough time to ransack the garrison's supplies and hike 14 miles to save Lee's army from annihilation at Antietam.

The town of Harpers Ferry never really recovered from the raids and hostile occupations of the Civil War. There was little point in rebuilding the armory after the war, since the federal government had found other ways to produce guns for its soldiers. With its industry reduced to historical artifacts and the riverbanks reforested, Harpers Ferry has regained some of the picturesque quality that originally inspired Thomas Jefferson. The natural splendor is complemented by some of the interesting remains scattered along the promontory, from John Brown's Fort to the old armory canal along the Potomac. In fact, the National Historical Park in Harpers Ferry includes two canals, the Armory Canal and one of the skirting canals built along the

Shenandoah. The Shenandoah canal has been closed off from the river so that it can be preserved as a wetland area, but the channel of the canal is still clearly visible between Virginius Island and the shore proper.

There's some good hiking across the river, with the Maryland Heights trail (about 2 hours, round trip) affording an unforgettable view of the town and the rivers.

**A M E N I T I E S**

The lower portion of the town is devoted to souvenir stores and sandwich shops that close in the late afternoon. There are many places to stay, several of them with excellent views of the river, but you have to make the steep ascent of High Street to get there. They tend to fill up quickly on the weekends, so be sure you have a reservation. The best restaurant in town is the Anvil, but to get to it, or even to a convenience store, for that matter, you have to follow High Street for a rugged mile to Bolivar.

On the opposite shore, you can see the Hilltop House looking down on the river. The channel for the old Armory Canal runs along the river at the foot of this rise, drawing its water from Dam no. 3 (*see* mile 62.3).

The trail on the other side of the road leads up to a spectacular view of the area from **Maryland Heights** (2-hour round trip). This was the view that Confederate soldiers had when they bombarded the town during its siege and capture in 1862. After running parallel to the canal, **Harpers Ferry Road** curls up into the hills on its way to Sharpsburg. John Brown's men followed this road down from the Kennedy farmhouse on their fateful raid in 1859. (The farmhouse is about 3 miles away on Chestnut Grove Road and is open to the public.)

**Lock 34.** As the canal enters the Great Valley, we find the first lock built largely of the distinctive gray limestone of this region. The limestone for Locks 34–36 was boated down from a quarry in (West) Virginia, about 5 miles upstream. There is a water pump here but no toilet.

The stone abutment jutting out into the river was the beginning of a replacement to the Armory Dam. Work on the replacement dam was begun in the fateful year of 1859, but it was never completed owing to the destruction of the armory during the Civil War.

**MILE 62.3** The towpath veers toward the river, separated from the canal by the inlet channel leading from the slackwater above Dam no. 3. *Lock 35* can be seen across the inlet channel, but can only be reached from Lock 36.

The jagged remains of *Dam no. 3 (Armory Dam)* are visible in the river. The first dam for the armory at Harpers Ferry was built here in 1799, but it was soon reported to be ineffective and "dilapidated." After two more tries and difficulty in supplying water to both the armory and the Patowmack Company's skirting canal during the dry season, the dam was rebuilt in the late 1820s using timber cribs filled with stone. The C&O canal company built a guard lock a few years later to use the water from this dam and began watering the canal from here all the way down to Seneca in the fall of 1833. The dam zigzagged across the river to take advantage of large rocks for support. The concrete facing on the upstream side is a later addition. The dam feeds water down the channel of the old Armory Canal to an abandoned electric power plant near the armory site.

**MILE 62.4** Remains of the *Guard Lock* for Dam no. 3, built of gray limestone. A portion of the lock has been filled in to allow the towpath to cross over, where it would originally have been open during the era of canal operations. This inlet lock not only brought water into the canal but was also a lift lock—the canal was at a lower level than the river here. The inlet lock was probably also used extensively as a river lock for shipments of iron ore from Elk Run on the West Virginia side of the Potomac (the site of the Keep Triest Furnace). Iron ore from Elk Run and the nearby ore banks on the Maryland side of the river was boated up to the Antietam Ironworks. For a little while, there was also a return traffic through this lock—pig iron was shipped back to Harpers Ferry from Antietam during the mid-1850s.

The brick shell of an old lockhouse stands between the inlet lock and Lock 36.

**Lock 36,** built of gray limestone. The steep hill on the berm side of the lock leads up to **Fort Duncan,** built by the Army of the Potomac during the Civil War to protect Harpers Ferry. The strategic need for the defenses had become apparent in September 1862, when Confederate General A. P. Hill captured Harpers Ferry during the Antietam campaign. The fort was begun in 1862 under Union General McClellan, and had 16 cannon. Fort Duncan served its purpose well in 1864, diverting Confederate forces under Jubal Early as they crossed South Mountain on the way to the city of Washington.

MILE
62.5

To reach **Lock 35,** take a short detour from the towpath, following the canal downstream 0.1 of a mile. The lock is built of gray limestone, and is flanked by a drydock for repairing canal boats. Boats were floated into the drydock, stop planks were inserted in the lower end, the drydock was drained through wickets in the sidewalls, and the boat ended up resting on the yokes across the bottom of the dock.

**Huckleberry Hill Campsite.** If you are coming downstream, you may want to stop here—it's a long way to the next downstream campsite (Bald Eagle Island, 12.5 miles).

MILE
62.9

**Dargans Bend** recreation area includes a boat ramp, as well as picnic tables and toilets. If you are coming down the river in a canoe, this is the most convenient place to get off before you hit the dam ruins and rapids above Harpers Ferry.

MILE
64.9

**Shinhan limestone kilns.** On the berm side of the canal, you can see brick-lined arches in a concrete facing. Thomas Hahn identifies O. J. Shinhan as the owner of the kilns, operating through the 1960s. Given the recent time period, it is likely that the limestone was burned for plaster or fertilizer rather than for cement. (Portland cement displaced natural limestone cement just after the turn of the century.) The adjacent shack

MILE
65.2

was a part of the mining operation, first owned by the Potomac Refining Company, that mined manganese until the discovery of the limestone deposits. Further evidence of the mining operation can be seen just upstream in the ruined cliffs of the old quarry.

 **MILE 66** The Potomac tumbles through **Hooks Falls** (also known as House Falls). This is sometimes indicated as the location of one of the Patowmack Company's skirting canals, but there is no true canal here. Instead, canoeists can still enjoy the use of a 150-foot sluice scooped out of the limestone bottom along the Virginia shore. **Cow Ring Sluice** was originally dug by John Semple around 1769 so that his boats could carry iron ore upstream from the Keep Triest Furnace to the Frederick Forge (later, the Antietam Ironworks). The Patowmack Company took over the sluice as one of its river improvements (*see* miles 5, 62.4, *and* 69.5).

 **MILE 66.9** **Lock 37 (Mountain Lock),** built of blue-gray limestone from a Maryland quarry about half a mile away. The brick lockhouse and the parking lot are accessible from Limekiln Road.

 **MILE 67.1** An access ramp across the canal bed connects to Limekiln Road.

 **MILE 68.3** Limekiln Road runs along the hill on the other side of the canal—a popular local dumping ground, judging from the old refrigerators and other discards.

 **MILE 68.5** The canal company's 1857 "Rates of Toll" lists this as the "Road Culvert at **Brien's Ferry,** Sharpless Landing." John Brien and John McPherson Brien owned the Antietam Ironworks just up the creek from the aqueduct (*see* mile 69.5). The canal company had to agree to provide access to the river from the ironworks.

 **MILE 69.4** **Antietam Creek Aqueduct.** Completed in 1834, this three-arch aqueduct of blue-gray limestone is in the best condition of any of the larger, multiple-arched aqueducts. Antietam Creek runs south from Pennsylvania,

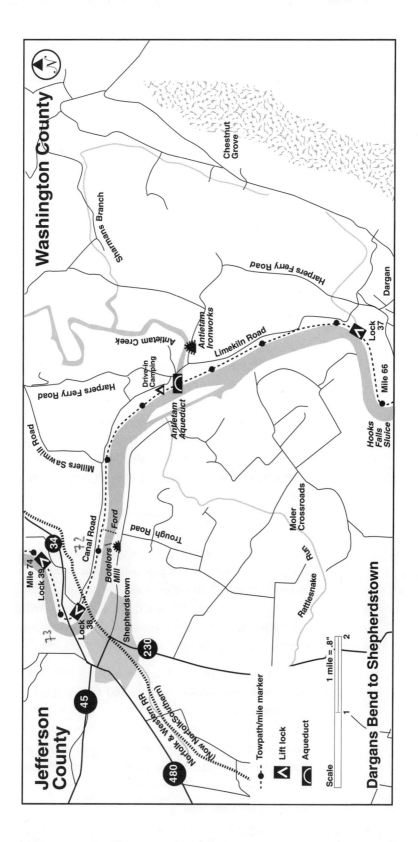

Dargans Bend to Shepherdstown

passing the little town of Sharpsburg, 3 miles upstream. The battle near Sharpsburg on September 17, 1862, produced the highest casualties of any single day of the Civil War; it is said that the Antietam "ran red with blood" that day. **Brien's Basin** lay on the downstream end of the aqueduct, where canal boats could load pig iron from the Antietam Ironworks.

**MILE**
**69.5**

Canal Road on the right leads away from the river toward the remnants of **Antietam Village**, and Harpers Ferry Road. Israel Friend bought land here in 1727, taking the unorthodox move of securing his property rights from Indians in the area rather than from Lord Baltimore. Friend was probably interested in starting a furnace, but he ended up building one in Virginia instead. Friend sold the Antietam tract, known as "the Indian deed," to John Semple, who had also begun work on the Keep Triest Furnace just above Harpers Ferry. However, Semple had to cede the property to a group of businessmen (David Ross, Samuel Beall, Joseph Chapline, and Richard Henderson) who had acquired all the land along the Maryland banks of the Potomac from here down to Maryland Heights (*see* mile 62.4). Semple was to provide pig iron to Ross & Company, who built the Frederick Forge at this site, but the terms of the agreement led to a legal dispute that briefly involved George Washington as a mediator. Despite these difficulties, the Frederick Forge persevered and became known as the Antietam Ironworks, producing some of the parts of James Rumsey's historic steamboat (*see* mile 72.7). (The Antietam Ironworks should not be confused with the Antietam Forge, which operated during the same period further up the creek near Hagerstown.)

John Brien and John McPherson Brien acquired the **Antietam Ironworks** in 1806, and it stayed open, with some interruptions and changes in ownership, until 1858. A man named Daniel Ahl purchased the ironworks after the Civil War and added a brick furnace stack in the 1870s, but the operation never really became profitable again and was closed for the last time in 1886. At its peak, the ironworks kept more than two hundred workers busy at its various enterprises: a blast furnace, a nail factory, a forge, a sawmill, a rolling mill, and a flour mill. Canal records show that a great deal of its iron ore came upstream by boat from the ore banks above Harpers Ferry (*see* mile 62.4), and that a substantial amount of the resulting pig iron was shipped down from Antietam to Harpers Ferry and to Georgetown.

The only remains of the industrial complex at Antietam lie just beyond the stone bridge at Antietam Creek, consisting of several kilns that produced lime for use as fertilizer.

### Antietam Ironworks Detour

**M I L E  0.0**  Cross canal bed and follow Canal Road away from river.

**M I L E  0.2**  Right on Harpers Ferry Road.

**M I L E  0.3**  Cross Antietam Creek on one-lane stone bridge; take left turn to follow road upstream along creek.

**M I L E  0.4**  Limekiln ruins.

### Antietam Battlefield Detour

**M I L E  0.0**  Cross canal bed and follow Canal Road away from river.

**M I L E  0.2**  Left on Harpers Ferry Road (ascend a steep hill).

**M I L E  2.2**  Pass lower portion of Antietam Battlefield.

**M I L E  3.2**  Harpers Ferry Road enters Sharpsburg and becomes South Mechanic Street. Take a right on Main Street (Route 34).

**M I L E  3.3**  Take a left on Sharpsburg Pike (Route 65).

**M I L E  3.8**  Antietam Battlefield Visitor's Center.

**M I L E  4.8**  Left on Taylor's Landing Road.

**M I L E  5.8**  Rejoin Chesapeake and Ohio Canal.

*Antietam Creek Drive-in Campground.* The drive-in campgrounds have the same amenities as the hiker-biker campsites (picnic table, water pump, portable toilets), but tend to attract the more casual weekend camper who wants to have a portable stereo system and a cooler of beverages close at hand. To each his own taste, but don't expect a wilderness experience here.

 **MILE 70.7** During the canal years, a small community grew up around **Miller's Basin,** which included Miller's Sawmill. Like Snyders Landing and Taylors Landing (miles 76.8 and 81), this served as a place of exchange for finished goods brought by canal boats and local produce.

You can take another route to Antietam by following Millers Sawmill Road up a steep hill, followed by rolling hills, to intersect Harpers Ferry Road (in 1.7 miles) near the lower portion of the battlefield.

**MILE 71.4** *Packhorse Ford/Botelers Ford.* One of the most traveled fords on the Potomac, as evidenced by its many names: Packhorse Ford, Wagon Road Ford, Shepherdstown Ford, Botelers Ford, and the somewhat redundant Blacksfords Ford. The shallow crossing was first used by Indians and then by the settlers coming down the Great Valley. As wheeled traffic increased, the old packhorse ford became part of the "Philadelphia Waggon Road," shown on Jefferson and Fry's map of the mid-Atlantic region (1755). Later, when Botelor built his mill just upstream, it became known as Botelors Ford.

The Confederate army made frequent use of the ford to maneuver up and down the Shenandoah Valley. The better part of the Confederate army used the ford during the invasion of Pennsylvania (the Gettysburg campaign), and Jubal Early crossed here to begin his raid on Washington in 1864. But by far the most famous crossing was made after the battle of Antietam (September 17, 1862). While a skeleton force kept campfires going along the Confederate lines near Sharpsburg, the main body of Lee's army began massing here on the night of the eighteenth to cross back to West Virginia. It was an eerie scene, with the dark bluffs of Shepherdstown looming behind a long string of cannon, wagons, and wading men whose progress was illuminated by torches at each side of the ford. As the last division crossed in the morning's light, they were surprised to see their commanding general, Robert E. Lee, sitting on horseback in midstream, anxiously ushering them on.

The line of rapids in the river are the remains of an old dam that fed water to the millrace for **Botelor's Mill,** also known as **Potomac Mill.** The mill, whose ruins stand on the West Virginia side of the Potomac, was originally a flour mill and later produced cement that was used in canal construction. The mill and the bridge to Shepherdstown were destroyed during the Civil War, although the mill was rebuilt and resumed operation after the war. This is a popular fishing area, and the water is usually shallow enough that you can comfortably wade across the river in the summer to take a look at the kilns and mill ruins on the West Virginia side. The massive timbers that are still embedded in the river bottom indicate that this was a carefully constructed crib dam.

**MILE**
**71.7**

The **Norfolk and Western Railroad** bridge crosses the river valley high overhead on an iron trestle. The Norfolk and Western was the successor to the **Shenandoah Valley Railroad,** completed from Roanoke to

**MILE**
**72.4**

Botelor's Mill and the timber dam that supplied water to the mill were rebuilt after the Civil War, as shown in this photograph. *Photo courtesy National Park Service.*

Hagerstown in 1881. (At Hagerstown the railroad connected to Pennsylvania traffic through an interchange with the Cumberland Valley Railroad; *see* mile 97.3.) The Norfolk and Western has since been subsumed into the Norfolk Southern system.

Shepherdstown's monument to steamboat pioneer James Rumsey is visible above the cliffs on the far side of the river.

The ruined stone piers standing in the river belonged to the former Shenandoah Valley Railroad bridge (1880).

***Shepherdstown River Lock.*** Built of gray limestone, this was one of the three river locks that were designed to draw traffic from the Virginia side of the river, and the only one of the three to do much business (*see* miles 30.7 *and* 60.6).

A series of stone piers leads across the river to the foot of the Shepherdstown bluffs. These are the remains of the **Potomac Bridge,** a covered bridge built by the Virginia and Maryland Bridge Company soon after the completion of the canal. When the Confederates decided to abandon Harpers Ferry in June 1861, they sent a regiment to Shepherdstown to burn the bridge. One of the soldiers was Henry Kyd Douglas, who had grown up on Ferry Hill Plantation next to the bridge. In his memoirs he described his emotions as he stood on the West Virginia side of the Potomac, "when, in the glare of the burning timbers, I saw the glowing windows in my home on the hill beyond the river and knew my father was a stockholder in the property that I was helping to destroy, I knew that war had begun. I knew I was severing all connection between me and my family and understood the sensation of one who, sitting aloft on the limb of a tree, cuts it off between himself and the trunk, and awaits results."

Two years earlier, Douglas had had another strange experience as he crossed this bridge on a rainy day. He saw a man ahead of him struggling to get his two-horse wagon up the hill. The man was a recluse, known to everyone as Isaac Smith, who lived on a farm just beyond the Antietam Ironworks. He said that he was carrying miner's tools; Douglas graciously volunteered to help and went up Ferry Hill to get his father's carriage horses. With Douglas's assistance, Isaac Smith was able to pull his wagon up the muddy road to Sharpsburg, where he could take Harpers Ferry Road home. It was not until a few months later that Douglas and his neighbors learned that Isaac Smith was really John Brown, and that the wagon had been loaded with pikes that he had picked up at the B&O Railroad Station across the river.

The Potomac Bridge was rebuilt after the war, destroyed by the great flood of 1889, and rebuilt again as an iron truss bridge, with a toll house on the West Virginia side of the river. The 1936 flood washed that bridge away, and until the Rumsey Bridge was finished in 1939 a ferry was the only way to cross the river to Shepherdstown.

A walk down to the water here gives you a nice view of the riverbend and the Shepherdstown bluffs. On December 3, 1787, twenty years before Robert Fulton unveiled the *Clermont,* James Rumsey demonstrated a working model of a steamboat along this stretch of the Potomac River. This early winter demonstration drew a crowd of skeptical townspeople and a notable veteran of the Revolutionary War, General Horatio Gates. Without the traditional sail or oars, no one was convinced that the eccentric inventor's "canoe powered by a teakettle" would ever leave the dock. But when it was finally launched from the Shepherdstown side of the river, Gates cried "she moves, by God, she moves!" and the crowd cheered as the boat steamed upriver for about half a mile and then passed downstream of the town before returning to the landing. On December 11, a second test of this futuristic craft (which used jet propulsion rather than paddles) achieved a speed of four miles an hour.

**Lock 38,** a handsome lock with an arched culvert on the berm side for the bypass flume. The limestone for these structures came from a quarry on the other side of the river. The buildings on the other side of the canal are now maintained by the National Park Service. They were formerly part of the Ferry Hill Plantation, and this little community was called Bridgeport.

The *James Rumsey Bridge* carries Route 34 overhead. The bridge is the most recent crossing at this point on the Potomac; Thomas Swearingen began operating a ferry here in 1755, just in time for Braddock and Washington to cross to rejoin the British regiments for their fateful march west through the mountains. The ford downstream and the ferry were used by the Continental Army during the Revolutionary War, as British and German prisoners were being marched from Virginia to prisons at Frederick and Fort Frederick.

*Ferry Hill Plantation.* Sometime during or after the War of 1812, John Blackford built his home at the top of the neighboring hill and tended to various enterprises that included orchards, livestock, and poultry. The plantation included a windmill, a cider press, a limekiln, and a blacksmith shop. The land and house were sold to the National Park Service in 1974 and now serve as the headquarters for the C&O Canal National Historical Park.

Like so many other local entrepreneurs, Blackford took exception to the plans for the canal. Blackford had taken over operation of the river ferry in 1816, and he charged in an unsuccessful legal suit that the river lock at Shepherdstown would take business away from the ferry. The ferry was replaced by a covered bridge in the 1850s. Ferry Hill plantation passed on through Blackford's daughter to her son Henry Kyd Douglas, who became an aide to Stonewall Jackson during the Civil War and lived to write a notable memoir, *I Rode with Stonewall.*

Despite the hill climb, it's a good idea to take a detour into Shepherdstown—this is the only convenient place to get solid food between Harpers Ferry and Williamsport. Or you can detour to the Antietam Battlefield by heading away from the river on Route 34. It's about 3.4 miles into Sharpsburg, and another mile out to the Battlefield Visitor's Center on Route 65 (north).

## Shepherdstown Detour

**MILE 0.0** Cross canal lock on wooden footbridge and follow paved road up the hill to Route 34.

**MILE 0.2** Turn left on Route 34. (The Park Headquarters is on the other side of the road at this intersection, but it has no visitor's center.)

**MILE 0.4** Cross over Potomac River on Rumsey Bridge.

**MILE 1.0** Intersection with German Street—turn left for historic buildings, Tony's Pizza, and the Yellow Bank Restaurant. Turn right for convenience store.

## Shepherdstown, West Virginia

Shepherdstown is a small town with no visible means of support other than Shepherd College (town population 1,800; college enrollment 3,500). Thomas Shepherd obtained a grant of land here in 1734 and built a gristmill a few years later. In 1762, at the conclusion of the French and Indian War, the town was first formed as Mecklenburg, the name (derived either from the German Duchy of Mecklenburg or Queen Charlotte of Mecklenburg) attesting to Shepherd's interest in selling lots to the German immigrants settling in the area. Later the town name was changed to Shepherd's Town, and still later to the present Shepherdstown.

James Rumsey, the inventor and engineer who worked on the Great Falls canal for the old Patowmack Company, lived here in the late 1700s. Although he had the respect of George Washington, Thomas Jefferson, and Benjamin Franklin, his failure to develop a commercially viable steamboat doomed him to obscurity outside this town. In 1787 he demonstrated his working steamboat in the river along Shepherdstown, 20 years before Fulton's *Clermont*.

If you take the walking tour described in the town brochure, you'll find some surprising points of interest tucked away along these brick sidewalks. Surviving historic architecture includes the old market houses, Shepherd's gristmill, Wynkoop's Tavern, and the Great Western Hotel. The Opera House, built in 1909, still shows movies. The "ingenious Mr. Rumsey" is honored by both a monument and a small museum that displays a working half-size replica of his steamboat.

The Civil War visited this town, as well as all the others on the Potomac—these old houses were filled with three thousand wounded men after the battle at Antietam. A half mile down German Street, the ruins of Botelor's Mill stand near the ford where the Confederate army retreated after the battle. Shepherdstown even had its own battle a few days later, when Confederate forces under A. P. Hill drove Union forces back across the river from the Shepherdstown bluffs.

Shepherdstown also serves as the Washington Bullets' training camp—apparently the management likes the town because it is far away from the distractions and bright lights of the city. The players are reportedly less enthusiastic about the small-town environment, but most visitors seem to enjoy Shepherdstown's relaxed atmosphere and quaint architecture.

### A M E N I T I E S

Shepherdstown is one of the best places near the canal to stop and eat, whether it's something quick at the bakery or Tony's Pizza, or a full dinner at the Yellow Bank Restaurant. You can also stock up for the towpath at the local Sheetz. (The Sheetz chain of attractive modern convenience stores is a real boon to canal travelers—the staff is uniformly pleasant and can fix a mean sandwich to go.) Like Harpers Ferry, there are many places to stay, mostly bed and breakfasts, which are relatively expensive and very popular on weekends.

**MILE 73.2** The gray cliffs on the berm side are popular with rock climbers.

**MILE 74** *Lock 39,* built of bluish limestone from a quarry about a mile away on the (West) Virginia side of the Potomac.

**MILE 74.3** A path leads down to a metal tower with a "High Voltage" warning sign. This is a modest pumping station that was built in 1968 to supply water to the town of Sharpsburg. The station provides around 100,000 gallons of water a day, but may soon be replaced by another intake facility or several wells, because of problems with the current intake filling with silt.

**MILE 75.4** *Killiansburg Cave Campsite.* Named for the historic cave/overhang just upstream.

**MILE 75.6** Several caves are visible in the rock face on the other side of the canal, sometimes referred to as the first of the Snyders Landing Caves or the Sharpsburg Shelter

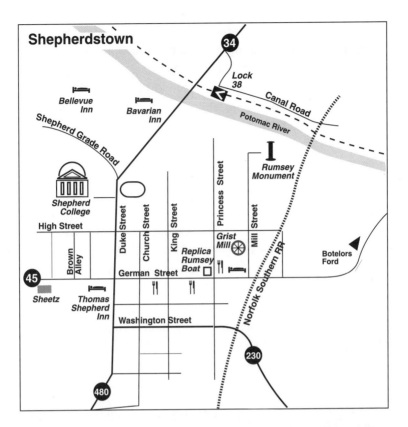

Caves. Some spelunking is possible, but be sure you have an experienced guide.

**_Killiansburg Cave._** This "cave" is actually just a large overhang at the top of the steep slope on the berm side of the canal. Some of the townspeople of Sharpsburg are said to have sheltered here during the battle of Antietam. If you want to take a closer look, be forewarned: the overhang itself is on private property.

**MILE**
**75.7**

The concrete piers and steps next to canal are the remains of an old footbridge, another of the expedients that the canal company had to provide to permit local access to the river. The use of concrete indicates that the footbridge was built after 1906; if it was built during the last years of the canal, it would have to have been high enough to permit canal boats to pass.

**MILE**
**76.7**

**MILE 76.8**

***Snyders Landing.*** This area was originally known as Sharpsburg Landing, but the current name comes from the Snyder's Coal and Grain warehouse that was on the berm side of the canal here. There's an access road down to a boat ramp, with parking on the berm side of the canal. Snyders Landing Road leads back to Route 34.

**MILE 77.2**

Snyders Landing Cave 2 in cliffs on the berm side.

**MILE 79.4**

***Lock 40*** was built of blue-gray limestone from a quarry about a half mile away on the (West) Virginia side of the Potomac. This lock was reported to have been severely damaged during one of Jubal Early's raids in July 1864. The Antietam Aqueduct also sustained some damage, and the Confederates burned about sixty canal boats for good measure. Attacks on private property were becoming more frequent in the later stages of the war, as the Union army had taken to burning the homes of suspected Confederate guerillas in the Shenandoah Valley.

**MILE 79.7**

***Horseshoe Bend Campsite.*** As the name suggests, the Potomac takes a sharp turn here. Just upstream was one of the areas that collected a great deal of waterborne detritus during the 1996 flood, including masses of fallen timber and even a shack or two.

**MILE 81**

***Taylors Landing.*** The 1857 "Rate of Tolls" lists this as the site of "Harris' Warehouse, at Mercerville." Mercerville took its name from the canal company's organizer and first president, Charles Fenton Mercer, but the name didn't stick. This is the third of the small canal communities that we've passed in the last 10 miles.

An access road leads down to a boat ramp on the Potomac. The Reels and Wheels store on the other side of the canal is a rather recent addition to this stretch of towpath. Open seasonally, it offers sodas and snacks and some basic bicycling accessories.

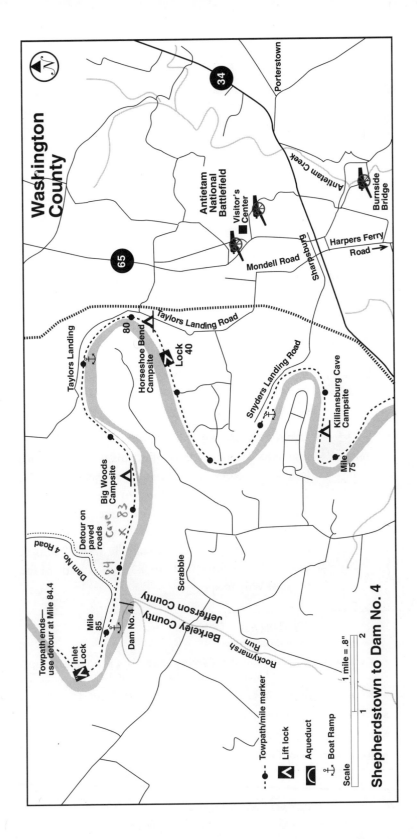

Washington County

Porterstown

34

Antietam Creek

Burnside Bridge

Antietam National Battlefield

Visitor's Center

65

Mondell Road

Sharpsburg

Harpers Ferry Road →

Taylors Landing Road

Taylors Landing

80

Horseshoe Bend Campsite

Lock 40

Snyders Landing Road

Killiansburg Cave Campsite

Mile 75

Big Woods Campsite

Detour on paved roads

Cave ✕ 83

84

Dam No. 4 Road

Mile 85

Inlet Lock

Towpath ends— use detour at Mile 84.4

Dam No. 4

Scrabble

Berkeley County

Jefferson County

Rockymarsh Run

Scale

Towpath/mile marker

Lift lock

Aqueduct

Boat Ramp

1 mile = .8"

1        2

**Shepherdstown to Dam No. 4**

## Antietam Detour

Taylors Landing Road will take you a hilly 1.2 miles to Sharpsburg Pike and the Ground Squirrel Holler Bed and Breakfast. Take a right on Sharpsburg Pike and follow for 2 miles to reach the Antietam Battlefield Visitor's Center.

**MILE 81.6** A nice culvert graces the upstream end of the landing, for the burbling waters of Marsh Run. The canal company's "Rate of Tolls" (1857) lists this as the site of *Middlekauff's Basin.*

**MILE 81.9** If you walk down along the embankment you'll find some log cribbing with water from a natural spring draining into the Potomac from underneath the cribbing.

**MILE 82.7** *Big Woods Campsite.* The water pump is rather inconveniently located a fifth of a mile downstream.

**MILE 83.3** *Dam no. 4 Cave,* also known as "Bear Cave." This is a fairly large cave that opens directly into the canal bed, usually with a stream coming out of its entrance.

**MILE 84.4** Sign for *Big Slackwater detour.* The towpath is still usable for another 2 miles, but this is the best place to start the detour, without having to double back. The detour affords a distant view of South Mountain downstream. If you like, you can save about 8 miles of bicycling by simply continuing on Dam no. 4 Road (instead of taking the left turn at mile 3.5 on Dellinger Road) to a left turn on Route 63, which leads to the town of Williamsport.

## Big Slackwater Detour
*(from downstream)*

**MILE 0.0** Cross canal bed and follow Dam no. 4 Road directly up steep hill for 0.1 of a mile. Continue on Dam no. 4 Road.

**MILE 2.5** At fork in road, veer left to follow Dam no. 4 Road.

**MILE 3.5** Left on Dellinger Road.

**MILE 3.9** Left on Avis Mill Road.

**MILE 4.7** Rejoin towpath just beyond old mill.

At **Dam no. 4,** the trail winds around a **stop gate**  adjacent to the dam. This stop gate has a restored winch-house, which was used to raise and lower the beams that served as a gate. The trail continues along the rise, above the original towpath. The dam, originally a "rock rubble" dam with timber cribs, had to be rebuilt several times after severe flood damage and was eventually converted to a masonry "high-rock" dam. The dam is approximately 800 feet across and 20 feet high.

**Potomac Edison Power Plant.** In 1909 the Martins-burg Power Company built a power plant on the West Virginia side of the dam and leased water rights from the C&O canal for a minimum annual payment of $500. These early electrical power plants were the natural suc-cessors to the water-powered mills along the Potomac.

The plant now belongs to Potomac Edison, and still produces a modest amount of electricity, about enough to run one-third of Shepherdstown. The plant is small but has at least two exotic details worth noting. The power plant still uses African sisal rope as the "drive" between its waterwheels and generators. (Rope drives were once common, but as of 1971 this was the last plant still using them.) The plant also uses wooden bearings that are carved from South American guaiacum trees.

A modern bridge leads over the canal to a boat landing.

The Big Slackwater parking lot lies between the canal and the river (not to be confused with the Park's Dam no. 4 Parking Lot just up the road). This is a popular boat launch area, accounting for some heavy late afternoon traffic on the Dam no. 4 Road detour.

A **guard lock,** built of blue-gray limestone, allowed  canal boats to enter and exit the river. This region is known as "Big Slackwater," a peaceful stretch of river behind the dam that always had enough water for canal boats to navigate. The guard lock also lifted the boats, as the canal was actually below river level here.

MILE 84.6

MILE 84.9

MILE 85.6

MILE 85.8

The canal ends, but the towpath continues, as the mules towed the boats along the riverbank for the next 2 miles.

 **MILE 86.7** This is the end of the line for bike riding. If you were a mule, you would have had to keep going, but then, the riverbank wasn't crumbling and the towpath wasn't as overgrown back when the canal was in operation.

---

### Big Slackwater Detour
*(from upstream)*

**MILE 0.0** Turn left off of the towpath, pass the old mill and head up Avis Mill Road.

**MILE 0.8** Turn right on Dellinger Road (T intersection).

**MILE 1.2** Turn right on Dam no. 4 Road.

**MILE 2.2** Veer right to stay on Dam no. 4 Road.

**MILE 4.7** After descending a steep hill, take the footpath across the dry canal bed and rejoin the towpath.

---

 **MILE 88.1** The detour ends at **McMahon's Mill,** and the towpath becomes usable again at this point, although the canal has not yet reappeared. The mill has been known by various names over the years, including Charles Mill, Cedar Grove Mill, Shaffer's Old Flouring Mills, and Avis Mill, which causes some confusion as the road name does not always keep up with the mill's name. The mill is a wooden structure that the Park Service has restored to passable condition, but nothing has come of the plans to open it to the public.

Cross the small concrete walkway over Downey Branch. The trail is a bit irregular here—there are many boat landings along the water for the next half mile, with steps leading up to the cliffside cottages.

**MILE 88.3** A small stream runs across the towpath here, coming from a cave in the neighboring cliffs (Howell Cave). For the next quarter mile, you can see a variety of small caves and overhangs in the cliffs.

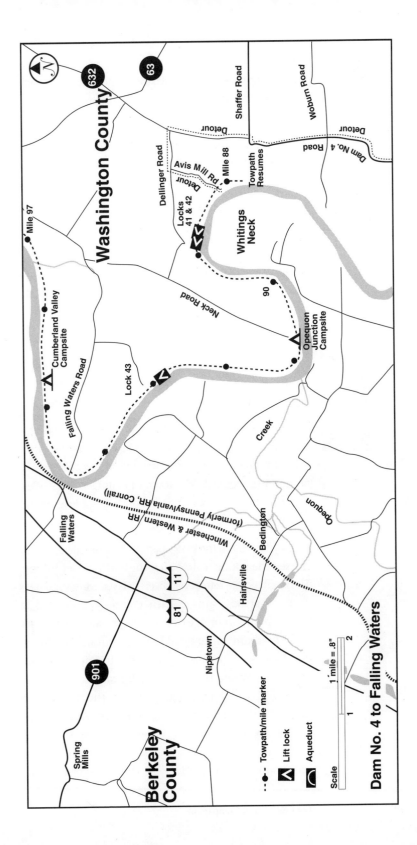

Washington County

Berkeley County

632

63

901

81

11

Spring Mills

Nipetown

Hainsville

Falling Waters

Bedington

Opequon

Creek

Winchester & Western RR
(formerly Pennsylvania RR, Conrail)

Mile 97

Cumberland Valley
Campsite

Falling Waters Road

Lock 43

90

Neck Road

Opequon
Junction
Campsite

Whitings
Neck

Locks
41 & 42

Towpath
Resumes

Mile 88

Detour

Avis Mill Rd.

Dellinger Road

Detour

Shaffer Road

Woburn Road

Detour

Dam No. 4 Road

Detour

Scale

1 mile = .8"

1          2

Dam No. 4 to Falling Waters

••• Towpath/mile marker

◤ Lift lock

◠ Aqueduct

**MILE 88.9** Canal boats entered and exited the slackwater area through ***Lock 41,*** which was originally built of blue-gray limestone from nearby quarries, with much concrete replacement.

**MILE 89** ***Lock 42,*** of similar construction. The two lift locks were built close together here to restore the canal quickly to the preferred 16-foot height above the river.

**MILE 90.8** ***Opequon Junction Campsite.*** The campsite takes its name from the Opequon River, which feeds into the Potomac on the West Virginia side.

In the mid-1800s, Foreman's Ferry operated across the Potomac between the mouth of the Opequon and the canal, at mile 91 just upstream.

**MILE 92.9** ***Lock 43,*** built of blue-gray limestone, with a lockhouse of whitewashed brick.

**MILE 93.5** For the better part of a mile, the "towpath" runs along a gravel access road beside a colony of river cottages.

**MILE 94.4** A historical marker for ***Falling Waters*** stands beside the stone abutments for a former bridge over the canal. If you follow the road over to the river at this point, you'll be standing opposite the town of Falling Waters, West Virginia, which took its name from a cascading stream near the Potomac.

In early July 1863, the better part of the Confederate army crossed the Potomac here after the battle of Gettysburg. The Confederate retreat had been delayed for several days during a steady rain, as their engineers struggled to build a pontoon bridge over the high waters. The work crews used timber that had been torn from abandoned buildings in Williamsport and floated downstream, and they covered the planks with branches to muffle the sounds of the crossing. Finally, as the floodwaters subsided, the two corps that had been guarding the southern perimeter around Williamsport (under A. P. Hill and James Longstreet) crossed at Falling Waters in the early morning hours of July 14. The third corps, under

Ewell's command, forded the river at Williamsport, upstream (*see* mile 99.6).

Robert E. Lee attended this night crossing with the same concern he had shown at Botelors Ford, nervously crossing the bridge back to the Maryland shore at one point to help sort out the confusion as the wagons bogged down and torches were extinguished in the heavy rains. The Confederates lost only two cannons in the crossing, mired in mud on the Maryland side, but there was a brief skirmish at the very end. Ironically, this rear-guard action involved Henry Heth's division, which had opened the fighting at Gettysburg. There were few Confederate casualties, but General Johnston Pettigrew was thrown from his horse and shot in the groin at close range as he and his men successfully fended off a suicidal charge by 40 Union cavalrymen. Pettigrew made it over the bridge but died three days later. Only a few hundred stragglers were unaccounted for when the Confederates cut the bridge from the West Virginia shore and let it drift downstream.

***Cumberland Valley Campsite.*** "Cumberland Valley" is another of the names for the "Great Valley" that stretches between Harpers Ferry and Hancock.

**MILE 95.2**

The canal is bracketed by the stone remains of a pier and abutments for the ***Cumberland Valley Railroad.*** The canal company hoped that it could augment its business by linking to the Cumberland Valley Railroad, which eventually ran from Harrisburg, Pennsylvania, to Winchester, Virginia. The Cumberland Valley line was initially built in Pennsylvania, and did not reach Hagerstown until the connecting Franklin Railroad was built in 1841. The railroad line was used to supply the Union army in the Civil War, and was greatly damaged by Confederate forces during the Gettysburg campaign (1863) and the Chambersburg raid (1864). After the war, the Cumberland Valley crossed the Potomac, tapping into the coal trade from Cumberland by

**MILE 97.3**

extending its line from Hagerstown to connect with the B&O at Martinsburg. By 1889 subsidiaries to the Cumberland Valley system had reached Winchester, Virginia. The Cumberland Valley was eventually subsumed by the Pennsylvania Railroad system in 1919, although the latter had held a controlling interest for many years. The newer bridge just beyond the ruins was built as a replacement for this line, owned in succession by the Pennsylvania Railroad and Penn Central, before the cataclysmic bankruptcy that led to the formation of the Conrail system in 1976. In the 1980s, Conrail sold the Hagerstown-Winchester line to the Winchester Western Railroad.

The Cumberland Valley Railroad occupies a peculiar niche in transportation history, having been the first railroad to experiment with sleeper cars (from Chambersburg to Harrisburg, 1837–48).

**MILE 98.5** The double highway bridge overhead carrries Interstate 81 into West Virginia. The interstate is now the major thoroughfare from Pennsylvania through the Shenandoah Valley, replacing the old wagon roads that the first settlers used.

**MILE 99.1** *Lock 44,* completed in 1834, was built of gray and white limestone. The whitewashed frame lockhouse on the other side of the towpath is being converted into an exhibit area.

Earthen ramp over to Main Street, Williamsport. The **R. Paul Smith Power Station** (owned by Potomac Edison) lies between the canal and the river. The first generating unit began operating at this site in 1923. Like the Dickerson Power Plant at mile 40, this is a coal-fired steam-electric plant, using water from the Potomac and coal brought in by truck (originally by railroad).

The stone wharf on the berm side of the canal marks the location of the Steffey and Findlay Warehouse; the Darby Flour Mill stood just upstream from the warehouse.

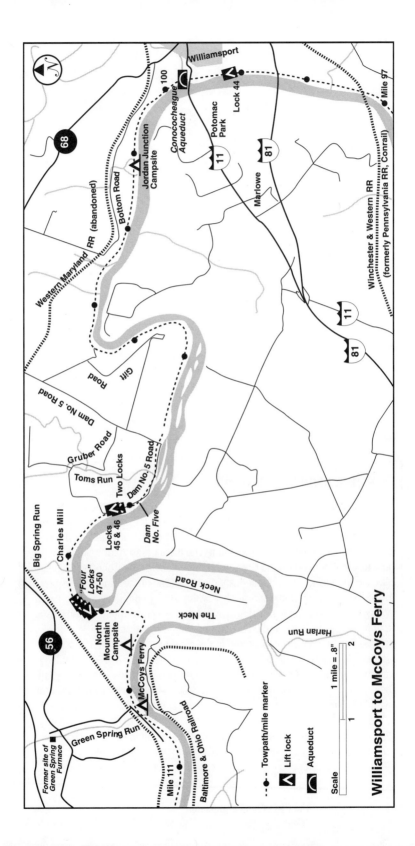

# Williamsport to McCoys Ferry

Williamsport

Lock 44

100

Conococheague Aqueduct

Jordan Junction Campsite

Bottom Road

Potomac Park

Marlowe

11

81

11

81

68

Western Maryland RR (abandoned)

Gift Road

Dam No. 5 Road

Gruber Road

Toms Run

Two Locks

Dam No. 5 Road

"Four Locks" 47-50

Locks 45 & 46

Dam No. Five

Charles Mill

Big Spring Run

Neck Road

The Neck

Harlan Run

56

North Mountain Campsite

McCoys Ferry

Green Spring Run

Mile 111

Former site of Green Spring Furnace

Baltimore & Ohio Railroad

Winchester & Western RR (formerly Pennsylvania RR, Conrail)

Mile 97

Scale    1 mile = .8"

1        2

Towpath/mile marker

Lift lock

Aqueduct

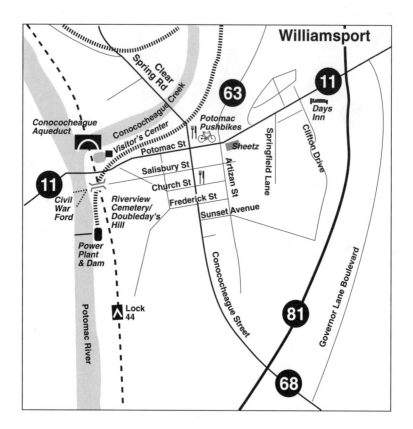

## Williamsport, Maryland

A canal town in the purest sense, Williamsport was never tainted to any significant degree by association with rival forms of transportation. The turnpike passed north of here on its way west, and the railroads came and went without leaving much of an impression. The town's reason for being is the juncture of Conococheague Creek with the Potomac. The Conococheague, like the Monocacy in the Frederick Valley, was one of the canoe routes used by Indians traveling north and south. For the settlers coming down the Great Valley, it was a Potomac crossing, and for the farmers in the region, it was a trading place for goods and grain shipped on the Potomac.

The first land officially patented in the area was "Jack's Bottom," a royal grant of 175 acres to one Jeremiah Jack, who settled here in 1740. Not long afterwards, Thomas Cresap settled along the Conococheague for a few years before moving on to Oldtown (*see* mile 166.7). Town apocrypha credits Cresap with building the stone house over the spring at nearby Springfield Farms. By 1755 Evans Watkins was operating a ferry at this crossing, though he lived on the Virginia side of the river, at Maidstone-on-the-Potomac, near one of the Ohio Company's storehouses. A part of Braddock's army crossed over to Virginia at Maidstone to continue their journey to Fort Cumberland and the debacle in the western mountains. During the ensuing French and Indian War, there were several brutal attacks at Maidstone and "Conococheague," as it was known.

The town is named for General Otho Holland Williams (1749–94), and its distinctive broad streets, laid out in 1787, seemed to promise great things. General Williams was something of a war hero, having been captured at Fort Washington on the Hudson but exchanged to fight again at the battles of Monmouth, Camden, and Eutaw. These auspicious associations may have contributed to George Washington's visit in October 1790 on his journey to inspect possible sites for the new capital city. Disappointed in that bid, the town was able to find other amusements. Racing began in the late 1700s and continued into the canal days, with a racetrack between the canal and the Potomac, just downstream from the Conococheague. There was never a shortage of libations, as canal workers and race-goers could choose between the Blue Hen Tavern, the White Swan Tavern, the Golden Swan Tavern, and the Spread Eagle Tavern.

Williamsport's future hinges on several canal restoration projects, starting with its newly opened Park Service Visitor's Center. At this writing, the first steps are under way to refurbish Lock 44 and rewater the canal for boat rides similar to the ones offered at Georgetown and Great Falls. A more ambitious proposal to restore the Conococheague Aqueduct to navigable condition has yet to be approved.

### A M E N I T I E S

Potomac Pushbikes is a well-equipped bicycle store, but it closes at 3 p.m. on Saturdays and is not open on Sunday. The only place to stay in town is the Days Inn, up the hill on Potomac Street. The Days Inn also used to be the best place to eat, until they closed their restaurant. Your culinary options are limited to Jeanne's Diner, Tony's Pizza, the batter-fried offerings of the Williamsport Inn, and the American Legion Hall, which is about a mile down Conococheague Street. Also keep in mind that restaurants aren't permitted to sell alcoholic beverages—for that, you have to go to a liquor store or a bar.

The long hill along the berm side of the canal is the site of Riverview Cemetery and is sometimes referred to as **Battery Hill** or **Doubledays Hill.** If you take the time to visit the cemetery, you'll find not only the grave of Otho Williams but also several small cannon pointing out over the canal. According to town lore, Union troops under General Abner Doubleday occupied this hill in 1863 and played baseball in the fields below. However, this is another of the myths surrounding Doubleday, who was once credited with laying out the first baseball diamond in Cooperstown before the war.

**MILE 99.4**

In fact, Doubleday's battery was briefly stationed here when he was still a major early in the war. Doubleday and his men were part of the Union garrison that surrendered at Fort Sumter on April 14, 1861. Two months later he and his men were part of the Union forces maneuvering on the upper Potomac. Major General Richard Patterson reported on June 19, 1861, that Doubleday's battery was in place at Williamsport, guarding the river ford. But the soldiers began moving downstream in the direction of Harpers Ferry soon afterward.

**M I L E**
**99.5**
***Bollman Bridge.*** Wendell Bollman was a self-taught engineer who began his career at age 15 laying track for the B&O Railroad. He later became the railroad's foreman of bridges and designed the "Bollman truss," which had distinctive radiating struts. The design was used for as many as 100 bridges, including the post–Civil War bridge at Harpers Ferry, but heavier loads rendered it obsolete by the 1870s. This bridge was built in 1879 and does not have the Bollman truss.

An earlier bridge stood on these piers, carrying traffic to and from the "Good Ford" on the Potomac. During the battle of Antietam, Union General McClellan ordered Captain Charles Russell of the First Maryland Cavalry to destroy this bridge and the aqueduct to prevent a Confederate withdrawal. Russell's men caused minor damage to the aqueduct but did burn the bridge. This unpleasant duty capped an exciting week for Russell, a native son of Washington County, whose reconnaissance activities included slipping into Harpers Ferry during the siege and then back out again.

The Second Corps of the Army of Northern Virginia (commanded by General Richard Ewell) used the ford and the rebuilt bridge on June 15 and 16, 1863, as it marched to Gettysburg. After that climactic battle, Ewell's corps recrossed farther upstream (using the aqueduct) because the Potomac was too high below the mouth of the Conococheague.

The lift bridge just beyond the Bollman Bridge, built in 1923, raised this piece of railroad track leading to the

A canal boat passes through Williamsport. Note the small bridge at the lower right designed by Wendell Bollman. *Photo courtesy National Park Service.*

power plant. It may have been used once before the 1924 flood.

Overhead, a concrete bridge for Route 11 (built 1909) crosses the Potomac toward Martinsburg, West Virginia.

***Cushwa loading basin.*** The old Cushwa warehouse on the other side of this basin has been restored as a Visitor's Center for the C&O Canal. A Park Service study dates the warehouse to around 1800, and suggests that it was built on the site of an earlier tobacco warehouse. Victor Cushwa began his business career in the mid-1850s by assuming half-ownership of the company of Charles Embrey & Son, which dealt in coal, cement, and plaster. By 1880 he had acquired full ownership and renamed the company Victor Cushwa. The company also dealt in some grain and fertilizer, but its main business was selling the coal brought by the canal from Cumberland.

**MILE 99.6**

***Conococheague Creek*** was another canoe route used by Indians traveling up and down the Great Valley. In the 1740s Evan Watkins secured permission from the Virginia Assembly for a ferry across the Potomac at Conococheague. Watkins lived on the (West) Virginia side of the river at Maidstone-on-the-Potomac. The

A canal boat floats in Conococheague Creek after breaking through the side of the aqueduct in 1920 *Photo courtesy National Park Service.*

Ohio Company built a storehouse at Maidstone in the early 1750s as a way station on its route to the west. This is where Braddock's 48th Regiment crossed the Potomac to continue its march to Fort Cumberland by following the trail through western Virginia (1755). (Contrary to many accounts, however, Braddock and Washington took a different route and crossed at Swearingen's Ferry near present-day Shepherdstown.) After the massacre of Braddock's expeditionary force, Washington ordered the construction of a large fort at Maidstone, garrisoned by 133 men.

***Conococheague Aqueduct,*** a three-arch, 210-foot aqueduct. A portion of the parapet on the berm side was knocked out by a canal boat heading up to Cumberland in the early morning of April 20, 1920. The water in the aqueduct poured through the hole, carrying the boat with it. (The captain's son, walking with the mules, was able to cut the towline just in time to keep the mules from being dragged along with the boat.) The boat lay in the creek long after the canal had closed, until it was finally carried away in the great flood of 1936.

The canal company repaired the aqueduct by boarding up the break. After the canal ceased operating, the boards rotted away and the rest of the parapet collapsed. There is a proposal afoot to restore the aqueduct to working condition by rebuilding the parapet wall.

During the Confederate retreat from Gettysburg, General Richard Ewell's corps forded the Potomac just above the aqueduct. General Robert E. Rodes described the scene in his official report:

My division waded the river just above the aqueduct over the mouth of the Conococheague; the operation was a perilous one. It was dark, raining, and excessively muddy. The men had to wade through the aqueduct, down the steep bank of soft and slippery mud, in which numbers lost their shoes and down which many fell. The water was cold, deep, and rising: the lights on either side of the river were dim, just affording enough light to mark the places of entrance and exit; the cartridge boxes of the men had to be placed around their necks; some small men had to be carried by their comrades; the water was up to the armpits of a full-sized man.

Clearly, this was no place for heavy guns—Ewell sent his artillery down to the pontoon bridge at Falling Waters (*see* mile 94.4).

***Jordan Junction Campsite.*** The closest campsite to Williamsport, but also one of the most odiferous along the canal, getting its "atmosphere" from the tannery way back along the Conococheague.

**MILE 101.2**

The gap in the cliffs on the berm side is closed by a stone wall; the Pinesburg quarry lies on the other side. This limestone quarry, run by Martin Marietta since the 1960s, was once known as the "High Rock" quarry and may have supplied some stone to the canal works. A boom on the berm side was used to load canal boats.

**MILE 102.2**

The row of concrete piers across the river used to support a spur (1909–36) of the Western Maryland Railroad that carried limestone from the Nessle quarry in West Virginia back to Williamsport. At the time, both the Nessle and Pinesburg quarries were owned by U.S. Steel, which shipped the stone by railroad to Pittsburgh. The Nessle quarry and bridge were washed out by the 1936 flood.

**MILE 104.9**

Cross the canal bed and take a right for a short detour (0.1 of a mile) to the bridge over Little Conococheague

**MILE 106.2**

Creek. Look upstream, you can see a stone dam providing a substantial head of water that was once used by a mill at this location. The mill was listed as **Middlekauff's Mill** on the canal's 1857 toll list. Thomas Hahn states that the mill predated the canal and was also known at various times as Colton's Mill and Charles Mill.

The "hill at Middlekauff's Dam" was the site of the canal's worst labor riot in January 1834. A party of men from County Cork (southern Ireland) were working on Dam no. 5 just upstream, and had engaged in a heated rivalry with the "Fardowners" from Longford who were working in the vicinity of Dam no. 4 below Williamsport. On January 16, some of the men from Cork had assaulted the Longford men, beating one of them to death. Eight days later, some 600 or 700 of the Longford men armed themselves with guns and clubs and marched up the canal to this spot. They found about 300 of the men from Cork waiting on this hill. As one might suspect, given their numbers, the men of Longford quickly routed the Corkonians and pursued them through the woods. Witnesses counted "five men in the agonies of death, who had been shot through the head," and observed other dead and wounded strewn about the vicinity. State militia and federal troops were sent to quell the riot, and the leaders of the two factions eventually met in a "peace conference" and signed a treaty pledging an end to attacks on other canal workers (*see* miles 108.8 *and* 155.2).

**MILE 106.6** The path follows a concrete embankment (built after the 1996 floods) up to **Dam no. 5** and a guard lock. (This is also a lift lock, though it is not one of the numbered lift locks.) The **guard lock** is now dammed up. When the canal was in operation, the boats would travel another fifth of a mile up the inlet channel, and then pass out into the river, as the mules continued along the towpath. The boats reentered the canal about 0.6 of a mile upstream. A brick lockhouse sits on the hillside above the canal, next to a parking area adjacent to Dam no. 5 Road.

Dam no. 5 is one of the canal's two "high rock" dams, approximately 700 feet across and 20 feet high. The current masonry dam was completed in 1860; this proved more impervious to flood damage than the original construction of timber cribs dating to the early 1830s. The Potomac Edison power plant on the other side of the river was completed in 1918 and is still operational (*see also* mile 84.6).

Stonewall Jackson's men shelled the dam several times on December 7, 1861, hoping to disrupt canal traffic. They returned later in the month (December 17–21), and several men waded into the freezing waters in an attempt to cut a breech in the dam. But the canal's solid stonework proved to be much harder to sabotage than the Baltimore and Ohio's railroad track and trestle bridges, as it would again at the Monocacy Aqueduct a year later (*see* mile 42.2).

The towpath is paved with concrete where it rounds several cliffs here. The decision to widen the trail here meant that the cliffs had to be blasted, which upset many preservationists. This cliffbend gives you a nice view of a broad expanse of river slackwater, with Fairview Mountain visible in the distance. This is the first glimpse of the Appalachian ridges that loom to the west.

Mile marker 107 stands just beyond the concrete apron, a little out of place. It is more than a mile from mile marker 106, and only 0.75 of a mile to mile marker 108.

*Lock 45,* built of blue-gray limestone, is both an inlet lock and a lift lock that let boats enter and exit the canal. The canal resumes at this point, with the towpath on the berm side of the canal.

*Lock 46,* built of blue-gray limestone. The keeper who lived in the whitewashed brick lockhouse served both locks.

The stone-faced incline on the river side of the lock and the arch structure on its berm side are the abutments for a mule crossover bridge (the arch let the bypass flume run underneath the bridge). The towpath had to run along the riverbank beside the slackwater area; where the canal resumed, the mules had to switch over to the other side. Crossover bridges were required at the beginning and end of the slackwaters, here and at Dam no. 4, but this one was more permanent than the wooden bridge that was used back at mile 88.8.

**MILE 107.6** The two stone abutments were part of a spillway for excess water.

**MILE 108.2** An interpretive display marks the stone ruins of *Charles Mill,* a mill for both grain and plaster on Big Spring Run. The mill used a 20-foot overshot waterwheel. (There were actually several mills in this area that were known as Charles Mill at one time or another, including one a little further up Big Spring Run, and the mills at miles 88.1 and 106.2.) The mill was in operation before the canal, perhaps as early as 1790, but it closed after the canal was devastated by the 1924 flood.

**MILE 108.8** These are the *Four Locks* that allowed the canal to cut quickly across *Prathers Neck* rather than following the riverbend. These locks were built between 1836 and 1839 of blue-gray limestone from nearby Prather's Quarry.

Locks 47-50

It is somewhat remarkable that the locks are here today, since the canal workers themselves threatened to blow them up in 1838. The two contractors in this section, David Lyles and Daniel Cahoon, had fallen deeply into debt that spring, and Lyles had fled to Washington. The destitute workers insisted on full payment of their back wages, rather than the piddling 25¢ on the dollar proposed by the canal company. The workers seized 140 casks of construction gunpowder and assured the company that they would undo their work if it was not paid for. One local observer warned the company that "if they cannot feed their families, they *will* feed their revenge." Ironically, the state militia initially refused to

Mrs. Cowan picking berries next to Charles Mill, with a typical pleasure craft in the background. *Photo courtesy National Park Service.*

respond to the crisis, because they too were owed wages for their most recent sortie on behalf of the canal company. In the end, though, the gunpowder was confiscated, and the canal company worked out an arrangement with the contractors that compensated the workers (*see also* miles 106.2 *and* 155.2).

**Lock 47.** If you walk around to the other side of the lock's bypass flume, you'll find the remains of a drydock used for canal boat repairs.

**Lock 48.** In 1875–76 a store was built over the bypass flume for this lock. The store became known as the Smith and Brother Store, dealing in dry goods, hats, caps, boots, shoes, and "everything usually kept in a first-class country store." Sometime in the 1880s it became the Snyder-Fernsner Store, which stocked everything from black powder and kerosene to candy and coffee and had some of the best hams in the area.

A road culvert under the lock leads to the Four Locks recreation area along the river (picnic tables, portable toilets). The road culvert was originally built by the canal company to accommodate the residents whose "neck" was about to be cut off by the canal.

**MILE 108.9**

**Lock 49.** For $10 a year (later $36) the canal company agreed in 1863 to let Denton Jacques build a feed and supply store and warehouse over the bypass flume. The warehouse was used to store hay, oats, and a feed grinder through the early 1900s.

Note the brick lockhouse on the opposite side of the berm road. This was the only lockhouse officially designated for the four locks, but the lockkeeping responsibilities were shared among the residences of this small canal community.

**MILE 109**

**Lock 50.** There was a lockhouse, since gone, on the other side of the berm road, as well as another feed store for the bypass flume. While the numerous sheds for tools and supplies for this very busy section of the canal have been demolished, the barn for wintering mules (200 feet upstream on the berm side) has been reconstructed by the Park Service. A small wooden wait house for the lockkeeper still stands on the upstream berm side of the lock. The concrete structure on the towpath side is a root cellar for storing fruit, potatoes, and vegetables.

Note that mile marker 109 is displaced about 0.3 of a mile further upstream.

**MILE 109.2**

Completing its transit across the Neck, the canal rejoins the Potomac, but at a much higher level.

**MILE 109.6**

**North Mountain Campsite.** North Mountain is the name of the adjacent ridge on the opposite side of the river; on the Maryland side, it is known as Fairview Mountain.

**MILE 109.7**

The elevation of the canal in this stretch creates some distinctive culverts, placed like small mouse holes at the foot of the tall embankment. Note the "stair stepping" of the stonework on the prominent wing walls to the culvert.

The stone walls of a *stop gate* are visible along the canal.

MILE
110.2

A historic marker commemorates **McCoys Ferry**, a ferry crossing that was the site of two notable events during the Civil War. On May 23, 1861, Confederates attempting to capture the ferry boat at McCoys Landing were driven off by the Clear Spring Guard.

Here on October 10, 1862, a month after the battle at Antietam, General J. E. B. Stuart crossed the Potomac to begin a raid that would end up circling the entire Union army. Stuart's cavalry rode to Chambersburg, ransacked the town, and escaped to the south, crossing the Potomac at Whites Ford (*see* mile 38.7).

A road culvert under the canal provides access to the McCoys Ferry Recreation Area.

Stuart's cavalry fords the Potomac and winds its way through the road culvert under the canal at McCoys Ferry. *Sketch courtesy National Park Service.*

**MILE 110.4** The canal passes over the culvert for ***Green Spring Run.*** This small stream provided the waterpower for one of the more significant, if short-lived, furnaces on the Potomac. The first ***Green Spring Furnace*** was constructed in 1765 by Launcelot Jacques and Thomas Johnson, but it only operated for ten years. Transportation was difficult. The pig iron was carried by wagon down to the river, where it was shipped over to Winchester via McCoys Ferry, or downstream to Georgetown on flat-bottomed boats. In the 1790s, Johnson and his three brothers invested in a furnace much more conveniently located along the Potomac at Point of Rocks (*see* mile 48.2). He and his brothers also owned the Catoctin Furnace, which has been preserved just north of Frederick, Maryland, on Route 15.

Thomas Johnson was a powerful figure in Maryland's political hierarchy and went on to become the first governor of the state in 1777. Both before and after the Revolutionary War, he assisted George Washington in getting Maryland's approval for the plan to improve navigation on the Potomac. Johnson also helped negotiate the historic Mount Vernon Compact, which regulated commerce on the Potomac, and was one of the first directors of the Patowmack Company.

The advent of the C&O Canal was probably a factor in the construction of a second furnace at Green Spring in 1848. The furnace was quite productive; canal records indicate that more than 900 tons of pig iron were shipped downstream from here to Georgetown in one year. The furnace survived the Civil War and operated until at least 1874. Given the time period, it is likely that the iron was used by Duvall's and Foxall's foundries (*see* miles 0.4 *and* 1.5).

**MILE 112.1** ***Fort Frederick State Park.*** A paved road across the canal leads uphill to this handsomely restored fort (0.3 mile). Snacks and drinks are available on a seasonal basis at the gift shop next to the fort. On selected

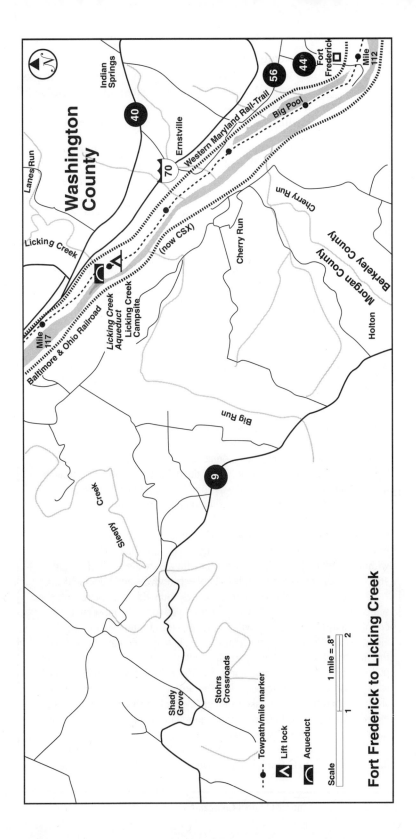

# Fort Frederick to Licking Creek

Washington County

Indian Springs

Lanes Run

Licking Creek

Mile 117

Baltimore & Ohio Railroad

Licking Creek
Aqueduct

Licking Creek
Campsite

Ernstville

Western Maryland Rail-Trail

(now CSX)

Big Pool

Fort
Frederick

Mile
112

Cherry Run

Morgan County

Berkeley County

Holton

Big Run

Sleepy

Creek

Stohrs
Crossroads

Shady
Grove

40

70

56

44

9

**Scale**

1 mile = .8"

1        2

— • — • —  Towpath/mile marker

▲  Lift lock

◖  Aqueduct

weekends, primitive gun lovers bring their muzzleloaders to the black powder firing range to test their marksmanship. You can take an alternate route to Hancock by going a half mile beyond the fort to the paved trail following the route of the old Western Maryland Railroad.

This modern road bridge over the canal somewhat obscures the stop lock, which had its own pivot bridge. Some of the stone for this lock was allegedly pirated from nearby Fort Frederick. If you follow the road downhill from the stop lock, it will lead to the Beaver Pond Hiking Trail (0.4 mile).

**_Big Pool_** begins here, a natural pool that made a convenient turning basin for canal boats.

## Fort Frederick

Built of stone, which was unusual for a frontier fort, this was Maryland Governor Horatio Sharpe's very expensive contribution to the defense of the western frontier during the French and Indian War. In the aftermath of Braddock's stunning defeat on the other side of the Appalachians, Washington had persuaded the colony of Virginia to build a string of rough timber forts along the Appalachians south of the Potomac. Thanks to the encroachments of Lord Fairfax and the colony of Pennsylvania, Maryland's western frontier was relatively small, so the governor concerned himself with defending only the tenuous supply route along the Potomac to Oldtown and Fort Cumberland. Work was begun on the fort shortly after the debacle of Braddock's army in the summer of 1755, and the fort was completed the following year.

Unfortunately, the chain of forts provided little protection from the "outrages" along the frontier. The settlers could not take refuge indefinitely behind the walls of the fort. When they returned to their fields, they were easy prey for the Indian war parties, who often ambushed their victims within earshot of the garrison. By the time they were alerted to the latest attack, the soldiers could do little but collect survivors and bury the dead.

Ultimately, it was the self-defense tactics and wilderness patrols of settlers like Cresap (*see* mile 166.7) that proved to be the most effective countermeasure. But Cresap was hardly oblivious to the new fort that lay along his supply route to the Great Valley. He may even have helped select the site, because the fort was partially built on a piece of land that he had purchased in the 1740s and named "Sky Thorn." The Maryland militiamen who garrisoned the fort respected the old frontiersman (who had been derisively dubbed "the Rattlesnake Colonel" by the British during Braddock's expedition) and brought Cresap's buckskin-clad riflemen to the fort to help train the new recruits in wilderness fighting.

The new fort also gave the impetus for a public works project that must have been much to Cresap's liking. In December 1758, the Rattlesnake

Colonel himself served on a committee in the Maryland Assembly that eventually recommended improvements to the primitive road that connected Fort Frederick to Fort Cumberland. The original road was truly wretched—so bad that General Braddock decided that it was unusable for his regiments in 1755, forcing them to cross back over to Virginia at Williamsport. Cresap's committee reported that "the distance by that Road from one Fort to another is Eighty miles, and . . . the wagons which go from one Fort to the other are obliged to pass the Patowmac River twice . . . for one third of the year they can't pass without boats to set them over the river." The committee believed that a road could be cleared entirely on the Maryland side of the Potomac, reducing the distance shortening the route by 18 miles. The road would "lessen the expense of carrying Provisions and warlike stores from Fort Frederick to Fort Cumberland, and will induce many people to travel and carry on a trade in and through the province, to and from the back country." Best of all, the estimate was a mere 250 pounds (a fraction of Fort Frederick's cost).

Even while the fort was being built, Governor Sharpe felt it necessary to respond to criticism from members of the Maryland Assembly that the stone construction was unnecessarily expensive. He noted in a letter to Lord Calvert that a party of French and Indians had used fire in a recent successful attack on Fort Granville on the Juniata River in Pennsylvania: "As I apprehended that the French would e'er long teach their Indian Allies to approach & set fire to our Stoccado or Wooden forts I thought it proper to build Fort Frederick of Stone, which Step I beleive [sic] even our Assembly will now approve of." While Sharpe's concern is more than understandable, the assembly members may have been right in the instance of Fort Frederick. Timber forts could not protect the surrounding countryside, but they were adequate to protect the garrison from occasional attacks, since the restless Indian warriors traveling many miles through the Appalachians had little inclination to lay siege to a fortification. (Later, during Pontiac's Rebellion, several forts far to the west of the Ohio River were overwhelmed, but nothing of the sort happened along the Potomac.) Whatever the reason, the fort was never directly involved in any Indian attack, and served mainly as a staging area and a safe haven for travelers. It was visited by George Washington on two occasions.

The rest of Fort Frederick's history continues in a similarly nonviolent theme. The fort saw no military action during the Revolutionary War. The British tried to organize Indian uprisings on the frontier, but by that time the frontier had moved west, and those battles were fought far from the Potomac. In fact, the upper Potomac was so far removed from combat that Fort Frederick became a prisoner-of-war camp, housing many of the German mercenaries captured at the Battle of Saratoga. For a while, the prisoners were allowed to work for neighboring farmers, which must have greatly alleviated the problem of feeding them. By the end of the war the existence of these indentured soldiers had been forgotten, and many of them simply mixed in with the Dutch and German settlers of the region rather than returning to the barracks and prisons of the continent.

The fort passed through several owners, the most interesting being Nathan Williams, who purchased it in 1857. Williams was a freedman whose grandmother, a slave, had taken refuge in the fort during Pontiac's Rebellion (1763). A Union garrison occupied the fort in the early years of the Civil War, and then it was returned to civilian hands until the state of Maryland repurchased it in 1922. The process of restoration continued over many years, with the Civilian Conservation Corps contributing some of the labor in the 1930s. The barracks are a modern (1975) interpretation, but the overall results have been well worth waiting for. Because so much of the original stonework survives, this is probably the most authentic American fort that dates to the French and Indian War. Seen from this broader historical perspective, Governor Sharpe's big-budget defense policy may not have been so wasteful, after all.

 **MILE 113°** The masonry abutments and concrete "dragon's teeth" are the remains of a spillway that let out excess water along the side of the canal.

 **MILE 113.7** The upstream end of Big Pool.

The elegantly restored stone walls of Fort Frederick are a unique survival of the French and Indian War—most frontier forts were built of timber. *Aerial photo by C. M. High and Mark Terry.*

The railroad bridge was part of a connecting line between the Western Maryland Railroad and the B&O Railroad stop at Cherry Run, West Virginia. This connection was built in 1892 and allowed the Western Maryland to bring some of the B&O's trans-Appalachian traffic over to the Philadelphia and Reading Railroad, serving the ports and terminals of the eastern seaboard. The B&O and Reading ended this agreement in 1902, and the Western Maryland built its own extension west of here along the canal route to Cumberland (1903–06).

**MILE**
**113.9**

The stone walls here are the remains of another stop lock.

**MILE**
**114**

**Licking Creek Campsite.**

**MILE**
**116**

**Licking Creek Aqueduct.** Constructed between 1836 and 1838, this is a single-arch aqueduct of limestone. The parapet on the upstream side of the aqueduct has washed away. Most of the cement for the aqueduct

**MILE**
**116.1**

The aqueduct at Licking Creek, touted by the canal company as the longest single arch of its kind. *Photo courtesy National Park Service.*

was brought down from Hook's cement mill, just across the river from Hancock. (Some cement had to be brought up from Botelor's Mill at Shepherdstown, and from George Shafer's new mill at Round Top; *see* miles 71.7 *and* 127.4.) The aqueduct was first used in 1839, as the canal was watered from Dam no. 6 down to Dam no. 5.

In an 1839 report, the canal company described this 90-foot span as "one of the longest, if not the longest aqueduct arch which has been constructed in the United States." Of course it pales in comparison to the 297-foot arch of the Cabin John aqueduct. Suffice it to say that this is the longest of the canal's six single-arch aqueducts, which are scattered through the mountain valleys between this spot and Cumberland.

 The parking lot on the berm side of the canal is accessible from Interstate 70 South (adjacent to the Indian Springs exit ramp).

 One of several spots along this stretch where the waste weir is placed on the berm side of the canal. This is an unusual arrangement because it made more sense to drain the water on the river side of the canal. Here the waste weir is built over a culvert so that the water could run under the canal and out to the river (*see also* miles 119.8 *and* 122.2).

 Another example of a waste weir on the berm side of the canal.

# The Endless Mountains

The surroundings take on a markedly different character after Hancock, as the Appalachian Mountains close in around the Potomac. The Indians called these the "endless mountains." When the colonists began moving into the Great Valley, the Iroquois and other northern tribes complained that their traditional passage to the south, or warriors' trail, could not be moved any further west because of the rough terrain and scarcity of game. The modern traveler will find no shortage of deer and groundhogs along the way, but one can certainly appreciate the difficulty of scrambling through these woodlands in search of provender. Agriculture in these mountain valleys changes from grain to apple orchards, and many people hunt to add meat to their table.

The mountain ridges above Hancock posed a series of staggering obstacles to those traveling west by horse and wagon. The first ridges near Point of Rocks and Harpers Ferry are around 900 to 1,200 feet in elevation. Here, at the other end of the Great Valley, the river passes through ridges that range from 1,500 to 2,500 feet in elevation, and the ridges follow one after another. Following the river channel, however, the canal rises only about 200 feet from Hancock to Cumberland.

The canal builders discovered that these mountains provided very poor quality building stone, in comparison with the limestone of the Great Valley and the sandstone used below that. Nevertheless, they were able to drive a tunnel through the ridge at Paw Paw and cobble together locks through the last 50 miles to complete the canal in 1850.

The great armies of the Civil War did not venture into these mountains, but there were almost continual skirmishes, raids, and troop movements in western Virginia and along the Maryland border. Stonewall Jackson and later Jubal Early visited this region on occasion, while Confederate cavalry under Generals John Imboden and Thomas Rosser were more common guests, usually pursued by William Averell, George Crook, and later George Custer. The partisan rangers led by John McNeill and his son were also extremely active, though they never became as famous as Mosby's Rangers in Loudoun County.

Ultimately, the narrow valleys here were not suited to vast agricultural or industrial enterprises. In many ways, the upper river valley suffered the same fate as the canal—industrial opportunities were limited by the declining importance of the river as a source of manufacturing power and as a transportation route. Instead, we've been left with nearly 60 miles of ridges, riverbends, and peaceful wilderness.

**MILE 120** The stone walls are the sides of a former *stop lock* just downstream from Little Pool.

**MILE 120.2** A wooden footbridge leads over the canal as it opens out at Little Pool. This path leads up across the Western Maryland trackbed to a parking lot off Interstate 70 South.

**MILE 120.7** *Little Pool Campsite.*

**MILE 120.9** The canal company's 1857 "Rates of Toll" charmingly refers to this spot as the *"Basin opposite Mrs. Bevans."*

**MILE 122.2** Yet another example of a waste weir on the berm side of the canal with a culvert to carry the water under the canal bed.

**MILE 122.7** *Lock 51,* built of gray limestone. The ruins of a stone lockhouse, built of limestone and red shale, stand on the river side of the towpath.

**MILE 122.9** *Lock 52.* This lock is nearly close enough to the aqueduct to have been built as one structure, as was the case at Seneca (mile 22).

**MILE 123** *Tonoloway Creek Aqueduct,* which was constructed between 1835 and 1839 of limestone quarried upstream on Tonoloway Creek. The cement came from Captain Hook's mill across the river from Hancock, and, in times of shortage, from Botelor's Mill at Shepherdstown. Some cement was also brought in from Baltimore to coat the trunk of the aqueduct.

**MILE 124.1** An iron truss bridge leads across the canal to a large parking area and the intersection of Main and Church Streets in downtown *Hancock,* where you can connect with the paved Western Maryland Rail-Trail over to Fort Frederick (mile 112.1). The peculiar concrete and metal tower on the other side of the towpath is a U.S. Geological Survey Stream Flow Measuring Station. The town has episodically tried to rewater the canal for the next half mile upstream from the earthen dam in the canal bed, but without much effect.

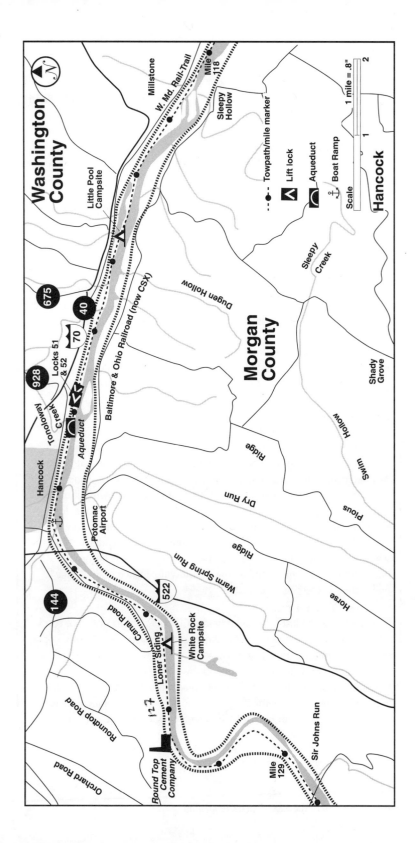

# Hancock, Maryland

The elongated town of Hancock is nestled on a narrow strip of lowland that runs along the Potomac, at the foot of the Appalachian Mountains. The road west ran through here long before there was a canal, and the road is still here even though the canal is gone. Hancock became an important stagecoach stop along the way when the National Road was built west of Cumberland, and it continues to have a profitable relationship with modern truck traffic headed east and west, although its cramped confines have made it a distant second choice to the diesel plazas of Breezewood, Pennsylvania.

The first European arrivals were hunters and trappers who built a cluster of huts here in the 1730s known as the Northbend Crossing Settlement. (This is in fact the northernmost bend in the Potomac River, coming within 2 miles of the Pennsylvania border.) In 1749 a man named Joseph Hancock settled here, and for lack of a more obvious candidate, it has been assumed that the town takes its name from him. The town itself was not incorporated until a century later, in 1853, three years after the northern stretch of the canal was opened all the way to Cumberland. By the time the canal made it to Hancock in 1839, the painted signs hanging over the doorways on Main Street already showed the influence of the passenger trade from the highway. Early taverns and hotels included the Sign of the Cross Keys, Sign of the Ship, Sign of the Green Tree Tavern, Sign of the Seven Stars Inn, the Bee Hive, and the Union Hotel.

Hancock must have been a coarse, jostling town when wagons and stagecoaches were rolling through, and it still has a roughneck reputation. As a member of the local constabulary once told me, it "has enough crime for a town four times as big." It's also a maverick town full of curiosities, from the liquor store that sells Native American collector's series decanters to the exotic trophy heads on the walls of the Town Tavern. I especially recommend sticking your head in Hendershot's, where you'll find such unexpected hunting necessities as hornet's nests hanging from the ceiling and a cow's skull with "Justice of the Peace" emblazoned across its forehead.

### AMENITIES

Hancock is the last large town before Cumberland, so stock up. Food and supplies can be procured at a Sheetz on the main drag. A cornucopia of small restaurants are strung along Main Street. Starting with the venerable Park-N-Dine and moving northwest, you'll find Tony's Mexican-Italian restaurant, the ever-popular Weaver's, and finally Fox's Pizza, Pizza Hut, and Hardee's. The Comfort Inn and the Hancock Motel are located at the north end of Main Street, just beyond the overpass for Route 522.

The towpath crosses an access road to the *Little Tonoloway Recreation Area* between the canal and river. This day-use recreation area has picnic tables and a boat launch.

**M I L E**
**124.4**

The culvert for *Little Tonoloway Creek,* with its 36-foot span, is almost large and elegant enough to be an aqueduct. *Fort Stoddert on the Tonoloways* was probably located not too far upstream from here. This was a small frontier fort built shortly after Braddock's defeat in the summer of 1755 and garrisoned by 15 men under the command of Lieutenant Stoddert. A member of the Maryland militia gave a dolorous account of the road to Fort Stoddert in the winter of 1756: 5 miles east of the fort they found the smouldering remains of a farmer's house and the carcasses of nine or ten cattle, 3 miles east of the fort they found the body of a settler named Hynes, who had been scalped and mutilated, and in the last mile they passed another burned house, surrounded by several dead hogs and sheep. Fort Stoddert was abandoned in August 1756 when Fort Frederick was ready for service (mile 112.1).

The modern highway bridge for Route 522 crosses high overhead, on its way to nearby Berkeley Springs, West Virginia.

**M I L E**
**124.7**

The *White Rock Campsite* is named for the rock outcrop visible on the other side of the Potomac just downstream.

**M I L E**
**126.4**

The glowering fold in the rock strata on the other side of the canal bed is known as the *Devil's Eyebrow.* This is one of the more distinctive exposed folds along the berm side of the canal, though there are several more of these anticlines ahead. (Eyebrow-shaped folds are *anticlines,* while U-shaped folds are *synclines.*)

**M I L E**
**127.2**

A row of eight stone arches are perched in the rock face on the berm side of canal. These were limestone kilns that were part of the cement mill.

**M I L E**
**127.4**

The Round Top Cement Mill after it was moved up from the river to the berm side of the canal. *Photo courtesy National Park Service.*

A smokestack and brick walls still stand at this spot, the remains of the **Round Top Cement Mill.** The cement mill originally stood next to the Potomac River, but was later relocated to the berm side of the canal where the present ruins are found.

In 1838 the canal company gave George Shafer permission to build a cement mill at the foot of Round Top Hill, renting him the property and the waterpower for the mill. The limestone was quarried in five tunnels in the hillside. The mill produced 200,000 bushels of cement over the next 25 years. Once the Round Top Mill began operation, it was able to supply much of the cement used in the final 60 miles of canal construction. (Botelor's Mill near Shepherdstown supplied most of the limestone cement for the lower portions of the canal; *see* mile 71.7.)

Shafer sold the mill in 1863 to Robert Bridges and Charles William Henderson, who renamed it the Round Top Hydraulic Cement Company. A 16-foot-diameter overshot waterwheel operated four pairs of grindstones, each 5 feet in diameter. There were eight supporting cement kilns, each fired by coal, which was shipped by canal boat. The mill employed up to 100 workers, who packed the cement in 300-pound barrels and 50- and 100-pound sacks. The mill produced 2,200 barrels of hydraulic cement a week, and by the 1880s had become one of Washington County's most prominent businesses. Round Top Cement, cleverly marketed as "Setter" brand with a setter's silhouette on the bag, found its way into such high-profile projects as the Washington Monument, the Cabin John Bridge, and the U.S. Capitol. It was then shipped by canal boat or pulled across the Potomac River on an overhead cable to be shipped by the B&O Railroad. The Round Top Hydraulic Cement Company closed in 1909, put out of business by superior Portland cement.

This spot affords a good view of the river bending to the south to pass **Tonoloway Ridge,** which looms directly upstream. This is the first of the Appalachian ridges to encroach on the river, though a relatively minor one, at an elevation of 900 feet.

Thomas Hahn, in his *Towpath Guide,* identifies the foundation at this spot as the remains of a water pumping station for sand glass mining operations. In 1894 a visitor taking a canal excursion boat noted that sand glass was being mined just across the river in West Virginia to be shipped to Pittsburgh. There are also extensive deposits of silica along Tonoloway Ridge, so it is also possible, given the location, that sand glass was shipped by the canal from here to the glassworks in Cumberland.

**MILE 128**

The **Leopards Mill Campsite** is named for an old cement mill located about a mile upstream.

**MILE 130**

**Lock 53,** built of limestone. Only the foundation for the lockhouse is left on the other side of the lock.

Interesting culvert with timbered floor.

**MILE 130.1**

**MILE 130.8** A wooden footbridge leads across the canal to the berm road. The canal company's 1857 "Rate of Tolls" lists this as the location of **Leopard's Mill,** a predecessor of the cement mill at Round Top (*see* mile 127.4). George Shafer started the mill in 1835, two years before the limestone deposits at Round Top were identified. Shafer leased the mill site at Round Top in 1838, but continued operating Leopard's Mill until 1841. The culvert at this point suggests that the mill was powered by a stream in the vicinity.

**MILE 132.7** Splendid vista of the towering ridge of **Great Cacapon** (over 1,800 feet elevation) downriver. There are many ridges yet to come, but this is the tallest one that the canal passes on its way to Cumberland.

**MILE 132.9** Another of the distinctive anticline rock folds is exposed on the cliffs next to the canal.

**MILE 133.7** **Cacapon Junction Campsite.** Named for the junction of the Cacapon River with the Potomac on the West Virginia side. This is one of the most scenic campsites on the canal, with a nice view of the two rivers and the stone arches of the B&O Railroad bridge across the mouth of the Cacapon. Stonewall Jackson's men burned the original bridge while shelling the town of Hancock on January 5, 1862.

The mouth of the Cacapon River was also the site of **Fort Dawson,** one of the string of frontier forts that Washington's soldiers built in the year after Braddock's defeat. These were frightening times, as Governor Horatio Sharpe of Maryland noted in a loosely punctuated letter in May 1756:

Capt. Mercier of the Virginia Regiment with a Detachment of 60 men from Fort Cumberland was fallen upon & defeated about a fortnight ago many Miles on this Side Fort Cumberland; the Captain, His Lieutenant & 15 men were killed & left to the Enemy the rest of the Detachment retired to a little Stoccado Fort near Cacapetion which runs into Potowmack. two of Capt Dagworthy's Company that were with the abovementioned Detachment were found

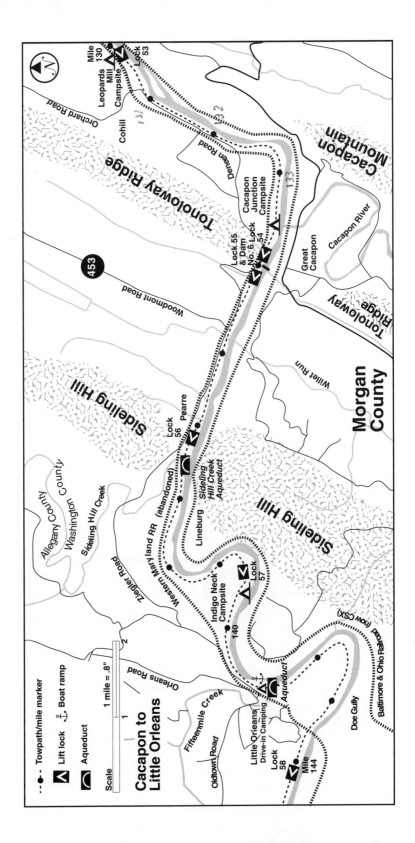

# Cacapon to
# Little Orleans

**Scale**  1 mile = .8"

Scale: 1 ———— 2

● - - - Towpath/mile marker

◄ Lift lock  ⚓ Boat ramp

**⊂** Aqueduct

Leopards Mill Campsite

Mile 130

Lock 53

Orchard Road

Cohill

Deneen Road

Cacapon Junction Campsite

Lock 55 & Dam No. 6, Lock 54

Great Cacapon

Cacapon River

Tonoloway Ridge

Cacapon Mountain

Tonoloway Ridge

453

Woodmont Road

Willet Run

Morgan County

Sideling Hill

Lock 56

Pearre

Sideling Hill Creek Aqueduct

Lineburg

Western Maryland RR (abandoned)

Allegany County

Washington County

Sideling Hill Creek

Ziegler Road

Sideling Hill

Lock 57

Indigo Neck Campsite

140

Baltimore & Ohio Railroad (now CSX)

Doe Gully

Orleans Road

Fifteenmile Creek

Oldtown Road

Little Orleans Drive-in Camping

Aqueduct

Lock 58

Mile 144

tied to Trees and their Bodies most horribly mangled, it is supposed that they were tied while living & put to the most cruel Death.

**MILE 134**

*Lock 54,* built of tan sandstone, with much replacement. Over the years since the canal was abandoned, the lock has been filled with earth. On the other side of the lock, only the stone foundations of the lockhouse remain. A feeder channel runs between the towpath and the river from here to the guard lock for Dam no. 6. The clearing on the berm side affords a good view of *Tonoloway Ridge,* rising up behind the lockhouse ruins. The river skirts the eastern slope of the ridge; here it cuts through it.

**MILE 134.2**

*Lock 55,* just upstream from Lock 54, lies next to *Guard Lock 6,* now filled with earth, and the ruins of *Dam no. 6,* extending into the Potomac River. The dam was first put into service in 1839, watering the canal down to Dam no. 5. This was the terminus of the canal until the upper section was completed to Cumberland in 1850.

Desperate for funds, the canal company worked out a brief arrangement with the B&O Railroad, which had already reached Cumberland. The B&O brought coal from Cumberland to a siding that it built on the other side of the river, and canal boats took the coal from there across the river and down the canal to Georgetown. (This transfer of coal made sense only because the B&O did not extend its line from Point of Rocks to Washington until after the Civil War.) It was an uncomfortable and unrewarding relationship for the canal company. The trade never amounted to more than 6,000 tons a year (1842–50), but it led to the railroad's helpful suggestion to the Maryland legislature that the canal no longer needed to be extended to Cumberland.

**MILE 134.5**

On the berm side, a narrow passage under the railroad trestle lets water in from Polly Pond on the other side, previously known as the Mouth of Long Hollow. The Western Maryland built the concrete dike here for its railroad embankment in the 1900s, leaving the narrow channel for water flow. There was just enough room for canal boats to use this passage to turn around in Polly Pond.

Just upstream along the towpath is a masonry spillway to discharge the overflow from Long Hollow.

Woodmont Road, which is perpendicular to the canal and Pearre Road, leads up to the **Woodmont Rod and Gun Club,** now managed by Maryland's Department of Natural Resources in conjunction with the Izaak Walton League. Hunting and hiking are permitted on the 2,000-acre property. For hunting information, contact the Wildlife Heritage Division (301-478-2525). Groups may arrange for use of the stone lodge; contact the Fort Frederick State Park (301-842-2155) for more information.

**M I L E**
**134.6**

The feeder channel from Dam no. 6 flows along the canal just below Pearre. A canal boat is just leaving Lock 54 to the far right. Note that the feeder canal entered the main canal at the lower level just beyond Lock 54. *Photo courtesy National Park Service.*

The club, one of several sportsmen's facilities along the Potomac, was founded in 1870 by a transplanted Virginian named Robert Lee Hill. Its membership included more than a few well-connected lawyers and businessmen from Baltimore and Pittsburgh. Six presidents have been guests over the years: James Garfield, Chester Arthur, Benjamin Harrison, Grover Cleveland, Herbert Hoover, and Franklin Roosevelt. Other famous visitors have included Babe Ruth, Justice William O. Douglas, and members of the Du Pont and Mellon families.

**M I L E**
**136.2**

*Lock 56 (Pearre).* A lockhouse stands by the towpath. The small public parking area next to the house is accessible from Pearre Road.

The towpath now passes by **Sideling Hill,** one of the major Appalachian ridges (1,500 feet). Sideling Hill and Town Hill are about 5 miles apart as the crow flies, but the canal winds 26 miles through the Paw Paw Bends before finally passing Town Hill at canal mile 160. (The Paw Paw Bends are about 5 miles longer if you're canoeing down the Potomac River, because the canal takes a shortcut through the Paw Paw Tunnel at mile 155.)

The original name, "Side Long Hill," is said to have appeared first on the famous map of the mid-Atlantic region made by Joshua Fry and Peter Jefferson in 1755. However, the name "Sidelong Hill Creek" appears as early as 1736, on the map that Winslow produced for the Fairfax survey. The creek was chosen as the dividing line when the Maryland Assembly created Allegany County out of Washington County on December 25, 1789. (Allegany thus became the westernmost county—Garrett County was not created until after the Civil War.)

**M I L E**
**136.6**

The **Sideling Hill Creek Aqueduct** has a single arch with a 70-foot span. It was built between 1837 and 1840 of limestone from a (West) Virginia quarry and some nearby sandstone. The cement for the aqueduct came from the Round Top Mill and Leopards Mill, just downstream (miles 127.4 and 130.8). The parapet on the berm side of the aqueduct was washed away by flooding. Steel beams hold the aqueduct together.

Sideling Hill Creek is the boundary between Washington County and Allegany County. After the spring and fall rains, when the water is high, the creek is a good venue for whitewater canoeing.

*Lock 57*, built of fairly good quality limestone. The stone foundations and the chimney are all that remain of the lockhouse along the towpath.

**MILE 139.4**

*Indigo Neck Campsite* lies along the southern side of Indigo Neck, and has a splendid view of Sideling Hill in West Virginia.

**MILE 139.5**

Another case of a misplaced mile marker, *Fifteenmile Creek Riverside Park* is actually more than a mile beyond milepost 140, but you won't find milepost 141 for another third of a mile. The two-building town of Little Orleans lies just on the other side of the road culvert under the Western Maryland track. This drive-in campsite tends to draw a rowdy, hard-drinking kind of

**MILE 140.9+**

## Little Orleans, Maryland

"Bill's place" is a bar and country store with a juke box and video games (nondigital), and it's the only place to get provisions on the canal for 30 miles. The historic building (see next page) that originally housed this establishment burned down in the fall of 2000, but the new building went up the very next spring.

Bill Schoenadel, a retired printer from the Cumberland-LaVale area, bought the grocery in 1969. The store and warehouse had been around since the first days of the canal, selling everything from sugar to nails to calico. The store originally sat right on the canal and had a boom to unload supplies from the boats. When the Western Maryland Railroad built its route west in the early 1900s, the store was moved back 100 yards from the canal to make room for the track.

The Orleans store also had a blacksmith's shop, which repaired wagons and shoed horses. This was a significant business because the old road from Fort Frederick to Fort Cumberland ran through Fifteenmile Creek, as this wilderness wayside was known (*see* mile 112.1, Fort Frederick). The road still leads down the hill, across the stream, and then winds its unpaved way through the mountains to Oldtown, just as it did in 1784 when George

Washington came through Fifteenmile Creek on his trip to his lands in the Ohio Valley. In the late 1700s this rough road was eclipsed by the Baltimore Pike (also known as the Bank Road), which took a more direct route through the mountains north of here.

These days the store is open when the owners are in the mood and the fish aren't biting. I've always been grateful to be riding a Schwinn bike when I stop here. It's probably not the kind of place that you want to bring your Asahi Twigsnapper or anything too exotic. The regulars are used to having bicyclists shoulder up to the bar but are still somewhat bemused by the Lycra-clad strangers in their midst. Every once in a while, though, you'll get some conversation, particularly if you're the only rider on the trail on a winter afternoon.

### AMENITIES

Look no further—if it's not under this roof, it's not in Little Orleans. You can pick up a sandwich, canned goods, or some batteries, but not much else. Beer, of course, is a staple, but you can't take it out of the establishment on Sundays.

The Little Orleans store in the 1890s before it was moved back from the canal to make room for the Western Maryland Railroad. *Photo courtesy Bill and Ethel Schoenadel.*

camper. I strongly recommend staying 2 miles downstream at the Indigo Neck campsite.

***Fifteenmile Creek Aqueduct,*** a small single-arch aqueduct, is in excellent condition. It was built between 1838 and 1850, using hard flintstone quarried at Sideling Hill on the (West) Virginia side of the river. Work was suspended in 1842 when the canal company ran out of funds. The aqueduct was completed in the final stage of construction and put into service in 1850.

If the water's high enough after a hard rain, you can take a rough canoe ride down *Fifteenmile Creek* from a put-in near Route 40.

Trestle for the **Western Maryland Railroad.** The railroad crossed the river here to take a more direct route through the Paw Paw Bends. It will recross the towpath several more times, as it takes a somewhat straighter course through the Paw Paw Bends.

**MILE**
**143.4**

## Trains along the Potomac

Despite the best efforts of the B&O Railroad to keep the narrow Potomac corridor to itself by taking over the canal after 1889, the Western Maryland was able to extend its line west from Hagerstown in 1906. For the most part, the Western Maryland extension follows along or near the canal berm to Cumberland, with the exception of the Paw Paw Bends, where it crosses back and forth over the river. This stretch of track was abandoned by the Western Maryland after the railroad was merged into the B&O and Chessie systems because it needlessly duplicates the B&O route. About 34 miles of the abandoned line were acquired by the National Park Service in the 1970s, but plans to convert it to a scenic bike trail have foundered because of local opposition.

The historic B&O track, originally constructed from Harpers Ferry to Cumberland in 1836–42 and frequently the target of Confederate raids during the Civil War, is still in use for both freight and Amtrak passenger service (the Capitol Limited) across the river. The long locomotive whistle and the rattling of railroad cars provide occasional accompaniment for travelers in this otherwise remote region.

**Lock 58.** This is the first of a series of "composite locks," which were partly built of wood. The canal company not only was in desperate financial straits by the time construction began above Orleans but also had trouble finding good-quality building stone in this stretch of the Potomac (*see* mile 153.3). The company decided to allow the contractors to use rubble stone for the sides of the locks in this stretch of the canal, protected by walls of kyanized wood. The wood quickly deteriorated, so the remains of the locks contain a great deal of replacement concrete.

**MILE**
**144**

The lack of stone and the remote location appear to have discouraged many contractors when bids were solicited for Locks 54–74 in 1836: the company received only one bid on Lock 58 (five to six bids was the norm). James Wherry was the lucky contractor, but he was unable to complete the work. This was probably the last lock that was readied for service when the canal opened in October 1850. (The stonework was completed before Locks 59 and 60 were finished, but at the last minute the contractor found that there were not enough bolts to hang the miter gates at this lock.)

A sign for the Green Ridge Hiking Trail indicates that the Pennsylvania state line is 17.2 hilly miles away. The **Green Ridge State Forest** lies directly adjacent to the canal for many stretches over the next 18 miles, but its full area occupies most of the region between Sideling Creek and Town Hill, north to Interstate 68. With 115 primitive campsites and more than 200 miles of dirt and gravel roads winding through, around, and over these Appalachian ridges, the forest is a quiet haven for serious hikers and mountain bikers with enough stamina to tackle the up-and-down terrain.

**MILE 144.5** *Devils Alley Campsite.* This campsite has a rather foreboding name, taken from a hollow another 2.5 miles upstream.

**MILE 146.5** *Lock 59.* Another composite lock, with some timbers still hanging on its walls. The stone foundations on the other side of the lock are the remains of the lockhouse.

**MILE 147.1** The trestle for the Western Maryland Railroad marks the second time that it crosses the Potomac in the Paw Paw Bends (*see* mile 143.4).

**MILE 147.4** An access road leads to Kasecamp Road, a small dirt road that winds through the riverbend and up to Oldtown Road. There aren't a lot of ways back to civilization in this stretch, but there are a few scattered residences along Oldtown Road.

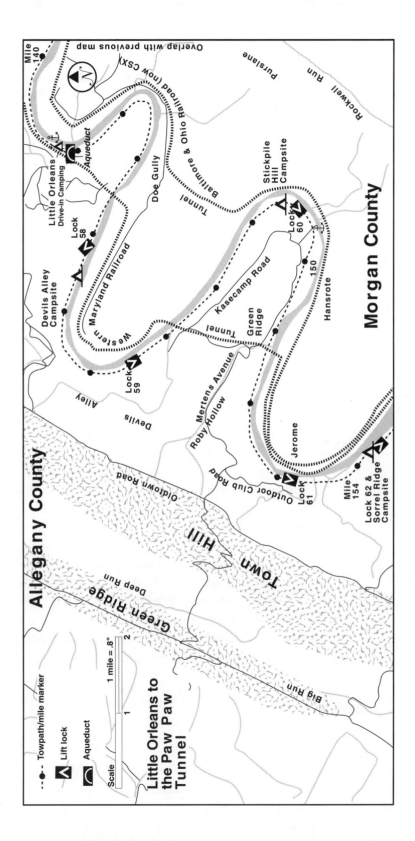

Little Orleans to the Paw Paw Tunnel

**MILE 49.3**

**Stickpile Hill Campsite.** Stickpile Hill is a minor ridge that juts out to the southeast, forcing the Potomac around yet another bend. In the early 1900s the Western Maryland Railroad drove the Stickpile Tunnel right through the hill rather than follow the river.

**MILE 49.6**

**Lock 60.** The concrete sides of this composite lock are now overgrown with ivy.

**MILE 50**

This access road from Kasecamp Road leads down to a riverside picnic area and boat ramp known as **Bonds Landing.**

**MILE 51.2**

A trestle carries the Western Maryland Railroad over the Paw Paw bends for a third time. The railroad will cross the Potomac three more times before Paw Paw, but we'll miss them because of the canal's shortcut through the Paw Paw Tunnel.

**MILE 53.1**

**Lock 61.** This former composite lock, now mostly concrete, has been dammed up with stone on its upstream end.

**MILE 53.3**

If you're in desperate need of egress, you can follow the small road up into **Twigg Hollow** to reach Outdoor Club Road. When work began on Locks 59–66 in August 1838, the contractor started quarrying stone in Twigg Hollow and brought it down to the locks on a small horse-drawn railway. The canal company was concerned about the poor quality of stone being used in these locks and began considering other alternatives, such as stone from Purslane Ridge (across the river) or Sideling Hill. The canal company's financial predicament in the 1840s postponed the dilemma. When the work was completed in the late 1840s, the contractors used 9 miles of horse-drawn railway to bring some of the stone for the locks down from Town Hill.

**MILE 53.8**

Good examples of exposed rock strata are visible along the berm cliffs in this area.

**MILE 54.1**

**Sorrel Ridge Campsite** and **Lock 62,** another composite lock with concrete replacing the original lock

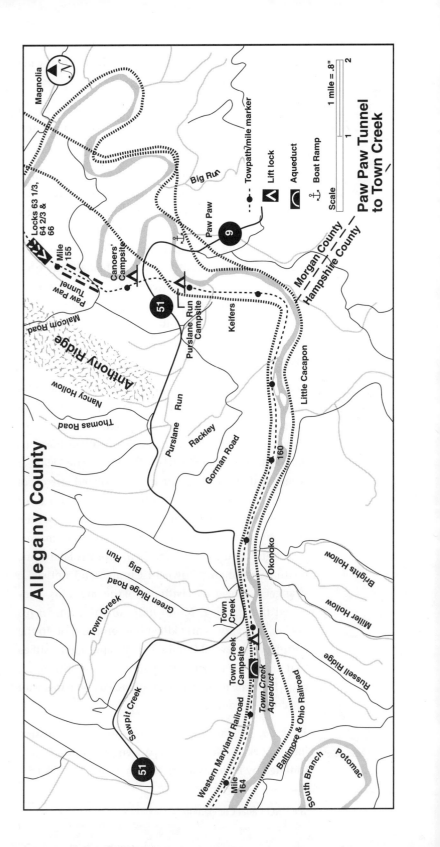

# Allegany County

Magnolia

Locks 63 1/3, 64 2/3 & 66

Paw Paw Tunnel

Mile 155

Canoers' Campsite

Malcom Road

Anthony Ridge

Nancy Hollow

Thomas Road

Purslane Run Campsite

Purslane Run

Rackley

Gorman Road

Keifers

Little Cacapon

Big Run

Paw Paw

Big Run

Green Ridge Road

Town Creek

Town Creek

Okonoko

Brights Hollow

Miller Hollow

Russell Ridge

Sawpit Creek

Western Maryland Railroad

Town Creek Campsite

Town Creek Aqueduct

160

Baltimore & Ohio Railroad

Mile 164

South Branch

Potomac

Morgan County

Hampshire County

**Scale**

- ●— Towpath/mile marker
- Lift lock
- Aqueduct
- Boat Ramp

1 mile = .8"

## Paw Paw Tunnel to Town Creek

pockets. The concrete foundation for the lockhouse lies next to the towpath.

**MILE 54.3** The semicircular stone walls beside the towpath were part of a relatively elaborate spillway to channel the waters away from a waste weir.

**MILE 154.5** *Lock 63⅓.* As the canal moves inland and rises to enter the Paw Paw Tunnel, we come to a series of three composite locks in quick succession. The canal company found it needed one less lock than it had planned, so it covered up the difference by numbering two locks with fractions. (Evidently contracts had already been let for the locks further upstream, and there was already too much paperwork in place for the canal company to renumber from this point on.) The lock pockets are formed of concrete; the rest of the lock is made of irregular reddish stone.

**MILE 54.6** *Lock 64⅔.* A similar composite lock, with timbers still hanging along its sides. In his homespun account of canal life, *I Drove Mules on the C&O Canal*, George "Hooper" Wolfe tells an unusual story about the murder of the lockkeeper at "Lock 64" in the late 1890s. It seems that the lockkeeper in this isolated stretch of the canal was well known to the passing boatmen for his collection of rare coins. The keeper's home burned down one night, and his body was found inside, marked with burns and the skull crushed. Months later some boatmen in Shanty Town in Cumberland noticed a stranger buying drinks with one of the rare coins. They seized the stranger, found more of the coins in his pocket, and very nearly killed him on the spot. In the ensuing trial, several Cumberland businessmen testified that they had also received some of the distinctive coins from the man, who was convicted and hanged for the crime of murder.

**MILE 154.7** *Lock 66.* The last lock before the tunnel; the missing lock is Lock 65. Newly hired park employees were often initiated by being asked to run an errand to Lock 65.

The path leading uphill to the left is the beginning of ***Tunnel Hill Trail***, which leads over the ridge and back down to the canal at the upstream portal of the tunnel. This 2-mile trail makes for an invigorating hike with good views of the river and the tunnel gorge, but it's not suitable for bicycling.

A boardwalk carries the towpath through the shale gorge approaching the tunnel. Old photographs indicate that this is pretty much the same construction as in the canal's heyday, when mules walked these planks. When you enter the tunnel, you'll find that the original railing is still in place, with grooves worn along its edge from the tow ropes.

The "North" portal of the ***Paw Paw Tunnel***, which is the downstream end. The orientation may be confusing, but you'll see on the Paw Paw Tunnel to Town Creek map that the canal stream is now flowing north as it leaves the tunnel.

A boat carrying sightseers pauses at the entrance to the Paw Paw Tunnel. *Photo courtesy National Park Service.*

The long "cut" leading to the tunnel was another difficult part of building the tunnel, which took 14 years. This is the "Slickenslide" area where water freezes in the steeply sloping layers of shale, breaking them off and sending them scudding down into the canal. Note the iron bars inserted in bored holes to help stabilize the surface.

It's best for bicyclists to dismount at this point, though the tunnel path can be ridden in low gear if you have a light. Proceed slowly and watch out for pedestrians.

## The Paw Paw Tunnel

The most difficult engineering challenge faced by construction crews, the Paw Paw Tunnel took 12 years to build, and almost bankrupted the canal company by itself. The purpose of the tunnel was to save 5 miles of canal construction along the Potomac by cutting across one of the "necks" of land formed by the Paw Paw bends. In retrospect, it might have been far easier to build those additional 5 miles, but the resulting tunnel is one of the most distinctive features of the canal.

The contractor working on the tunnel was Lee Montgomery, who had prior experience building a somewhat shorter tunnel (729 feet) on the Union Canal in Pennsylvania. Montgomery was described as a "Methodist parson-contractor" by one of the canal officials, but he was hardly the sort to turn the other cheek when the workers in the upper part of the canal turned violent. Work on the tunnel continued during the general strikes of 1836 because, Montgomery said, his force consisted largely of "picked men" who had outfitted themselves with guns and "Little Sticks." As for Montgomery, one official noted that "few men would probably use a 'Little Stick' more effectively than himself, though he would pray at the same time against being obliged to 'hold them uneasy.'"

Unfortunately, Montgomery eventually fell prey to the same discontent that was brewing elsewhere along the canal. Threatening notices were posted on his office door demanding that he fire certain supervisors. In the spring of 1837, he brought in some 40 miners from England, which angered the Irish workers. The Irish began a campaign of intimidation, and by next summer all but two of the English workers had left.

Because of their numbers, the men working the tunnel became one of the more volatile labor forces on the canal. On New Year's Day 1838, four hundred of the tunnel workers marched to Oldtown and raided several stores before militia from Cumberland broke up the mob. When the canal company couldn't pay its contractors the next month, Montgomery was forced into hiding until funds were delivered. The company tried to get rid of trouble-makers by blacklisting 127 men, but the number of disgruntled workers continued to grow along with the back wages that the company owed. The Irish laborers also resented the canal company's attempts to bring in other workers to reduce its labor costs. Matters came to a head on August 11, 1839, when a hundred men from the tunnel hiked down to Little Orleans and attacked a work camp full of German laborers. Many of the Germans were beaten, and one died after being thrown into a fire. A German priest who witnessed the attack said that if he had been superstitious, he would have believed the Irish to be "incarnate devils."

This last outbreak of violence provoked an equally violent backlash, as the militia arrested 30 rioters named by Father Guth, shooting 10 in the process and killing one. For good measure, the militia also ended up tearing down 30 to 50 workers' shanties and saloons, with no particular justification. On this occasion, the canal company went to extraordinary lengths to see that the rioters were prosecuted to the full extent of the law, even planting a spy among the workers to gather information that could be used against the accused. Fourteen of the accused workers were convicted of major charges, earning sentences ranging from 5 to 18 years. Only a year later, though, the governor pardoned the men, some of whom were shortly seen back on the canal. Ultimately, the only thing to stop the outbreaks of violence was the financial collapse of the canal company in 1841–42 (see miles 106.2 and 108.8).

Despite this violent history, Montgomery and his men had actually succeeded in driving a tunnel through the ridge by the early 1840s. It was not ready for use, though, until the final work was completed in 1850. As it stands now, the Paw Paw Tunnel is the most remarkable structure along the canal, three-fifths of a mile long and lined on the inside with 7 to 11 layers of brick, approximately 5,800,000 bricks in all. Some of the railings along the towpath are original construction, still bearing the grooves from years of tow ropes sliding along the top rails.

The tunnel proved to be a bottleneck in the busiest years of canal traffic, as there was no room for turning or passing. When they got to the tunnel mouth, canal boats would put out a white lantern at the bow and a red lantern on the stern, so that other boats would know which direction they were traveling. The boat coming downstream was supposed to yield the right of way, by backing out of the tunnel, if necessary. On one noted occasion, two boats traveling in opposite directions met in the middle of the tunnel, and neither captain would yield the right-of-way. The standoff continued for a couple of days, until canal workers started a fire upwind of the tunnel to smoke them out.

The south portal of the Paw Paw Tunnel opens out into a small picnic area.

The frame house at the end of the riverside field once belonged to the superintendent for this section of the canal. The field adjoins the Paw Paw Tunnel parking area, which is accessible from Route 51. This is identified as a "canoe staging area," with tent camping restricted to one night.

Route 51 crosses over the canal on its way across the river to Paw Paw, West Virginia. Route 51 is referred to on some maps as the "Uhl Highway," but the road signs in Maryland now refer to it by the more historic name of "Oldtown Road." Like the original Oldtown Road, which was cleared during the French and Indian War at the urging of Thomas Cresap, Route 51 follows the river to Oldtown and on to Cumberland.

## Paw Paw, West Virginia

The short (less than a mile) detour over to Paw Paw is justified by the charming view of this small Potomac crossroads ringed by low-lying hills, including the tunnel ridge just downstream. The first settlers arrived in the early 1800s, but the town wasn't incorporated until 1891. Soon after that, Henry W. Miller, Sr. arrived and began the apple-packing operation that became the town's most notable industry. Miller was an innovator, planting orchards on the mountaintops to avoid the early spring frost in the valleys. He did not retire until 1959, when he was 91 years old. When the company was sold to outside investors in 1977, it was reputed to be the tenth largest apple distributor in the country.

Riding into town between the aging yellow hulk of the Vesuvius Crucible factory and the vacant warehouse of the Consolidated Orchard Company is like entering a ghost town. The tannery is long gone. The B&O Railroad closed its station here in 1961. The Vesuvius Crucible buildings were converted into a shiitake mushroom venture for a few years, but that business failed.

Still, life goes on. The lives of the six hundred or so residents revolve around the hunting seasons, so the Almost Home Restaurant opens its doors before sunup in the fall. The passing stranger should be prepared for some peculiar moments, for instance, a gentleman seated at one of the diner's tables suddenly speaking up in a loud voice, addressing no one in particular: "Anyone been doing any black powder hunting round here?" Sociological interest aside, I've never visited the town without picking up at least one colorful expression. The work ethic in the town boils down to a simple question: "Been working hard, or are you just keeping at it?" If the answer is the former, then it stands to reason that you'd be "tarred."

### AMENITIES
There is a small but pleasant bed and breakfast, one restaurant, a general store, and a modern convenience store at the service station on the corner. I highly recommend the sandwich counter in the convenience store—one of their "halfsize" subs makes a full lunch for two.

The Western Maryland Railroad trestle crosses the canal overhead, back on the Maryland side of the river after its journey through the Paw Paw bends. The railroad has crossed the Potomac six times in the last 13 miles.

MILE
156.4

The **Purslane Run Campsite,** named for a major stream that drains this wooded plain between the Tunnel Ridge and Town Hill. The culvert for Purslane Run is another half mile upstream.

MILE
156.9

This is a combination spillway and waste weir similar to the one below the Paw Paw Tunnel (mile 154.3), with semicircular stone walls channeling the water flow into a single flume.

MILE
160.2°

**Lock 67,** a composite lock now almost entirely replaced by concrete. The lockhouse stood on the other side of the lock; only the foundations remain.

MILE
161.7

Another sign for the Green Ridge Circular Hiking Trail—now it's 19 miles from here to the Pennsylvania State Forest. This is the last point of contact along the canal for the **Green Ridge State Forest** (*see* mile 144).

The gravel parking lot on the berm side of the canal is accessible from Route 51 (Oldtown Road).

MILE
161.9

**Town Creek Campsite.** At this point, the canal and the Potomac have finally passed the twin barriers of **Green Ridge** (elevation 1,200 feet) and **Town Hill** (elevation 1,500 feet), after meandering some 26 miles down the Paw Paw bends from Sideling Hill (*see* mile 136.2).

MILE
162

**Town Creek Aqueduct** is a single span aqueduct built between 1837 and 1850. Work was suspended rather early at this aqueduct because of the disappearance of the contractor in 1840. Work would not resume until the late 1840s, when the aqueduct and the upper stretch of the canal were completed. The aqueduct was built mostly of a "bastard limestone" quarried at the mouth of the South Branch of the Potomac, with some sandstone and other stone from other quarries. Cement was first

MILE
162.4

boated down from Lynn's Mill in Cumberland, and in the late 1840s from the Round Top Mill near Hancock and Reynold's Mill in Cumberland. The parapet on the berm side of the aqueduct has collapsed.

**Town Creek** was considered to be a very reliable source of water. A man named Ash operated a saw and gristmill here in the 1820s and told the canal company that he usually had enough water to run his four waterwheels at least six hours a day. The assistant engineer, Ellwood Morris, proposed damming the creek to water the canal down to Dam no. 6, but the company decided this would be too expensive.

The canal has been dammed up at this point, and is watered up to Oldtown by local sport fishing groups.

**MILE 164.8** The old truss bridge overhead was for a road that led from Route 51 to the river ford and later ferry landing. This point is roughly opposite the forking of the Potomac between its North and South Branches (the canal follows the North Branch). Take a minute to walk down to the **Potomac Forks**—the view is not spectacular, but it is significant. If Thomas Cresap and Lord Baltimore had had their way, all of the land between the North and South Branches would be a part of Maryland, not West Virginia.

Lord Baltimore began to take an interest in the western boundary issue around 1753, when he began to suspect that the Fairfax Survey had encroached on his lands. Governor Sharpe of Maryland asked Cresap's opinion, and the frontiersman, who lived just a few miles from the forks, responded that the South Branch was indeed longer than the North Branch, which would have made it the source of the Potomac. Cresap's reconnaisance produced a rough map in 1754, but the issue was overshadowed by the ensuing French and Indian War. Cresap conducted a more detailed survey at Lord Baltimore's request in 1771–72, but the boundary question was soon obscured as Lord Baltimore lost

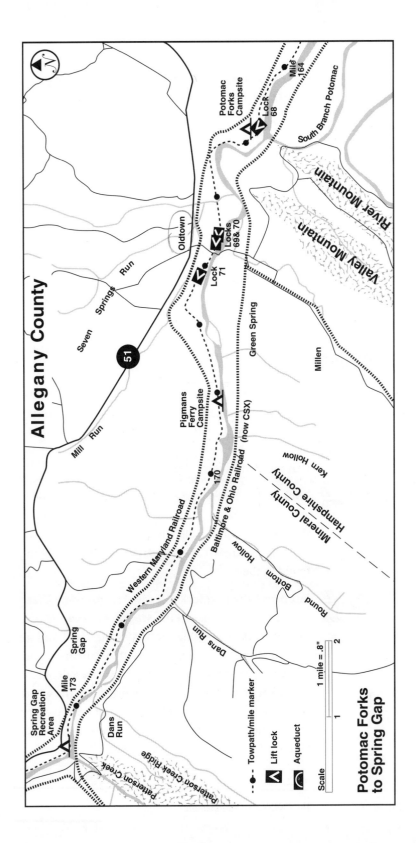

# Allegany County

**N**

## Potomac Forks to Spring Gap

Mile 164

Lock 68

Potomac Forks Campsite

South Branch Potomac

River Mountain

Valley Mountain

Locks 69 & 70

Oldtown

Lock 71

Seven Springs Run

Green Spring

Millen

**51**

Mill Run

Pigmans Ferry Campsite

170

Kern Hollow

Baltimore & Ohio Railroad (now CSX)

Mineral County

Hampshire County

Western Maryland Railroad

Round Bottom Hollow

Spring Gap

Mile 173

Dans Run

Spring Gap Recreation Area

Dans Run

Patterson Creek Ridge

Patterson Creek

### Scale

1 mile = .8"

1          2

● Towpath/mile marker

◀ Lift lock

⌂ Aqueduct

his entire colony in the Revolutionary War. The state of Maryland raised the point as late as 1910 in a Supreme Court case, but to no avail.

**Lock 68,** a composite lock, now mostly replaced by concrete. The lock channel has been boarded up, and the canal water flows around through the bypass flume. The whitewashed frame lockhouse is of later construction than the more spartan houses originally built for the keepers. The lockhouse and the lily pads in the canal make this one of the more distinctive and charming locks.

**Potomac Forks Campsite.** The sign for the campsite is along the towpath, but the water pump and toilet are on the berm side of the canal.

The canal takes a wide turn around cliffs of blue shale—a very attractive scene.

Glimpses of the fields around Oldtown and the low ridge beyond, most likely a welcome sight for the frontier travelers, who usually crossed into Maryland at the forks of the Potomac after following the mountainous trail through western Virginia.

**Lock 69,** the first of three locks in this half-mile stretch at Oldtown. These are the last three composite locks on the canal. The small hill between the Potomac and the canal here is known as **_Alum Hill,_** because of the alum found in the rocks.  *Battle fought here 8/2/64*

**M I L E  66.7**

Just before the next lock, the canal is crossed by Green Spring Road. A detour to the **Michael Cresap House** should be on your itinerary—cross the canal and go 0.1 mile to the T intersection with Main Street. The Cresap House faces on this intersection. Take a right turn and go 0.1 mile to get to a small country store. The school and a few houses are the only modern landmarks at the site of Thomas Cresap's little "fort," which was once Maryland's furthest western outpost.

In the direction of the Potomac, Green Spring Road leads down a **toll bridge.** This is referred to as a "low water" bridge, which is a polite way of saying that it is often submerged in times of flood. The bridge was built in 1937 under a federal law (no longer in effect) that permitted the purchase of the river bottom. It has been occasionally cited as the only privately owned interstate toll bridge in America. The bridge was officially closed by the state of Maryland in August 1995 because of structural deficiencies, but many people still use it to avoid going miles out of their way to the bridges at Paw Paw and Cumberland.

A notable skirmish took place on August 2, 1864, as Confederate cavalry fought their way back across the river after the raid that took them to Chambersburg, Hancock, and Cumberland. A small party of Union soldiers on Alum Hill tried to use the canal as a barrier, but the Confederates crossed the canal further upstream and drove the Yankees across the Potomac into West Virginia. It's 0.3 mile to the B&O tracks on the West Virginia side.

**Lock 70.** The white frame lockhouse alongside the towpath is in good condition but vacant. The geese and ducks are a familiar sight around this lock, through all four seasons.

## Oldtown, Maryland

In the immediate prehistory to English settlement, this was known as Shawnee Oldtown, an Indian village at one of the traditional river crossings used by hunters and warriors traveling the narrow valleys between the endless mountains. The site had been abandoned for several years when Thomas Cresap arrived here from the East to start a trading operation that soon began reaching west into the Ohio Valley. Cresap built a storehouse in the early 1740s, and his rustic dwelling sheltered all manner of travelers from George Washington to the legendary Pennsylvania trader George Croghan.

Braddock's regiments passed through here in 1755, following the rough trails that led through mountain gaps near Winchester, Virginia. Washington traveled this route many times, once referring to it as "the worst road ever trod by man or beast." So it must have been with some relief that Charles Lewis, a British captain, described Oldtown: "We arrived at two o'clock at a plantation of one Cresap's most delightfully situated on land that gave me great pleasure, 'twas a piece of low ground entirely surrounded by the mountains, the prospect romantic, high rocks on the sides of the mountains some hundred feet perpendicular to the Potomac."

The only remnant of Oldtown's frontier heritage is the house of Thomas Cresap's well-known son Michael. Michael and his father built the house in 1762 at the very end of the French and Indian War. The house had at least one convenience in the event of hostilities: a corner of the basement was open to a spring. The basement also served as a jail at one time, which explains the barred windows. The house is listed on the National Register of Historic Places and is privately maintained as a museum (entry by appointment only). Washington's diaries do not indicate exactly where he stayed when he stopped over in Oldtown, so the claim that "George Washington slept here" is purely conjectural; he may well have stayed here during his later visits, or he may have stayed at the elder Cresap's fortified house, which was closer to the river.

Most of the historic establishments in the town have long since been demolished. Thomas Cresap had a gristmill on the Potomac River crossing, and his grandson operated a mill on the small creek that now feeds the canal just above Green Spring Road. When the construction of the canal interfered with the gristmill, this younger Cresap took the C&O to court and forced the company to build a bridge across the canal to accommodate his operations. Mill Run was known as "Sawmill Run" in the early 1800s, so there is evidence of a timber operation long before the railroad arrived and the heyday of the Kulp brothers' lumber company.

Local history indicates that the need for libations was also of great commercial importance in this small river outpost. A saloon run by one J. W. Corder is reported to have been extant as early as 1800, long before the canal arrived. Later, a place called Ryan's Saloon is known to us because a party of workmen from the tunneling at Paw Paw came upriver and trashed it in 1839. Still later, old photographs from the canal days show "Lee Haines Pocomoke Rye Wines & Liquors" on the other side of the crossroads from the Cresap House.

The single road running through Oldtown was probably a descendant of Cresap's western road (see the description of Little Orleans at mile 140.9). The Western Maryland tracks also pass through here, but the train stop is gone and so are the trains, leaving a dwindling population that may soon be outnumbered by the ever-present swarm of geese and ducks that greet travelers year round at Lock 70.

### AMENITIES

A small country store on Oldtown's main street offers ice cream, sandwiches, and canned goods. The Cresap House is open by appointment only.

The lattice-truss bridge across the canal that led down to the river ford at Oldtown. *Photo courtesy National Park Service.*

**Lock 71.** This is the last of the composite locks, but in better condition than most. This lock was built mainly of stone, but the lock pockets have been replaced with concrete. Another white frame lockhouse stands along the towpath. **M I L E** **167**

A concrete waste weir frame on the berm side of the canal drains water into Mill Run, which runs parallel to the canal in this stretch. Old maps call this "Sawmill Run," but later-generation Cresaps also operated a gristmill in this vicinity. Contentious as ever, the Cresaps didn't take kindly to the intrusion of the canal and sued the canal company to require it to build a bridge so that farmers could get to the mill. In 1848 Luther Cresap compromised with the canal company, which agreed to reimburse him if he built a permanent bridge with its own flume to carry water from the mill over the canal.

A dam has been thrown across the canal at this spot, diverting Mill Run into the canal bed to water the canal down to Town Creek. **M I L E**

**MILE 67.5** The canal travels through an interesting cut through a ridge of shale. The towpath is often littered with sharp pieces of shale, which can pose a hazard to the passing bicycle tire.

**MILE 68** The towpath resumes its course along the river but at a higher elevation.

**MILE 68.7** As the canal moves inland again, it passes through mountain meadows and the first scattered evergreens appear.

**MILE 69.1** *Pigmans Ferry Campsite* is a small, fenced-off area along the border of a meadow. This would not be my choice for a campsite—there's not much shade for those stopping in summer and the cool waters of the Potomac are far off.

**MILE 70.8** The culvert at this spot was listed as *Kelly's Road Culvert* in the company's 1857 "Rates of Toll," and led to Pigmans Ferry across the Potomac.

**MILE 71.4** These stone and concrete "dragon's teeth" along the towpath are the remains of a masonry spillway, as at Big Pool and above Dam no. 6.

**MILE 72.5** The canal company's 1857 "Rates of Toll" lists this as the location of the *Basin at Alkyre's House.*

**MILE 73.3** *Spring Gap* drive-in recreation area, right off Route 51.

**MILE 73.5** The stone abutments on both sides of the canal are the remains of a road bridge that led down to the river crossing opposite the *Patterson Creek* valley in western Virginia. George Washington used the Patterson Creek crossing when he was just 16, as he accompanied a surveying expedition in 1748. The bridge over the canal was built in 1850 and burned by Confederate raiders on February 2, 1864, during General Jubal Early's winter foray into the mountains west of the Shenandoah Valley. Operating with Early on this mission were cavalry under the command of Elijah White and McNeill's

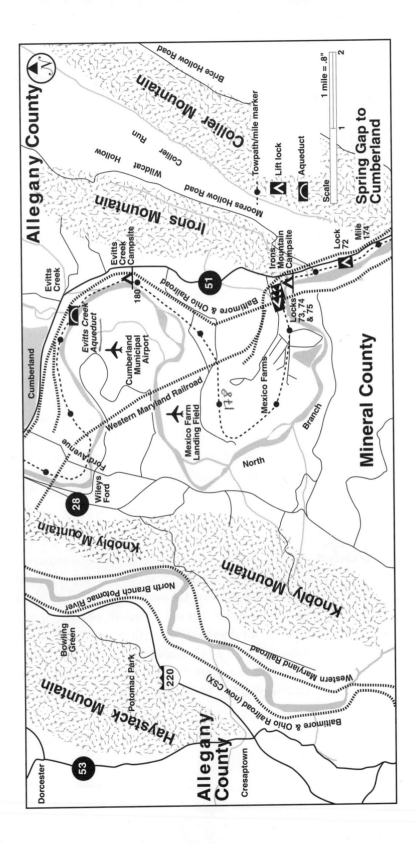

Partisan Rangers (*see* mile 35.5). Canal company records indicate that a fair amount of lumber was shipped from the Patterson Creek area to Cumberland.

The concrete foundation marks the location of the *steam pump* that supplied water to this section of the canal. Originally, the canal company had planned to build a seventh dam near Paw Paw to provide water to the levels down to Dam no. 6. By the time the company got around to finishing the upper portions of the canal, a steam pump seemed like a cheaper expedient. The first pump was installed just below Oldtown at the Potomac Forks. The pump operated for 20 years, but it was inefficient and unreliable during periods of drought. On several occasions, canal levels dropped so low that the boats were forced to carry less coal, costing the boat operators money.

In 1872 the canal company decided to build a new pumping station 10 miles upstream from the old pump, after the chief engineer, Charles Fisk, estimated that the river volume here was sufficient to fill the canal as far as Dam no. 6, 40 miles downstream. The steam pump was finished in the late 1870s, and consisted of a brick boiler room and a wooden engine room. The pump could raise 24 cubic feet of water per second.

*Lock 72.* The difference between the next 4 locks and the previous 13, which were composite wood and stone, is striking. The stone for Locks 72–75 is cleanly cut and regular in appearance. The canal company was delighted to find limestone that was "beautiful, of good quality, and in great abundance" on Evitts Creek near Cumberland, and used it in the last four locks on the canal as well as in the Evitts Creek Aqueduct. A white frame lockhouse stands on the towpath side.

This spot was known as **The Narrows,** where the canal squeezed between the river and Irons Mountain to enter the valley extending up to Cumberland.

***Lock 73*** and the ***Irons Mountain Campsite.*** The  campsite is named for the massive ridge that looms just downstream.

This railroad trestle was built for the B&O Railroad, as it  crossed back into Maryland for the first time since Harpers Ferry. The B&O agreed to use the Virginia side of the river west of Harpers Ferry partly to avoid conflict with the canal and partly as a compromise to get the Virginia legislature to extend its charter for completing the track west. In the 1836 compromise, the Virginia legislature stipulated that the railroad stay on the Virginia side of the Potomac until a point 6 miles below Cumberland. (The 6 miles were not measured along the river but "as the crow flies," which gave the railroad the maximum advantage.)

***North Branch*** drive-in recreation area and ***Lock 74.***

***Lock 75*** is the last lift lock on the canal, built with limestone from Evitts Creek (*see* mile 174.4). The lockhouse is particularly interesting, built of logs and wattling—a sign that we're approaching the frontier.

A path crosses the canal. The North Branch Sewage  Pumping Station lies along the towpath, the successor to the Pittsburgh Plate Glass operation. The Potomac is far to the south now, across a wide field. The towpath is shaded only by a narrow line of trees along the canal, so there are several good vistas of the surrounding mountains in the next 2 miles.

The open field in the direction of the river gives a good  view of the odd bumpy ridge aptly known as ***Knobly Mountain,*** which points straight to Cumberland. The Potomac curls around Knobly Mountain at Cumberland and heads in a southwesterly direction on the other side.

The canal company's 1857 "Rates of Toll" lists this as  the location for ***Van Metre's Ferry.***

Lock 75, the last lift lock on the canal, with its distinctive willow tree. It's still another 9 miles to Cumberland! *Photo courtesy National Park Service.*

**MILE 178**

A nice view of ***The Narrows*** at Cumberland from this spot. Westbound travelers followed Wills Creek through this mountain gap and headed through the Appalachians to the Ohio Valley.

**MILE 178.3**

The canal is intersected by Mexico Farms Road. The abutments at this intersection are the remains of yet another bridge for the Western Maryland Railroad, which continued to crisscross the canal and the river on the way to Cumberland.

The towpath now passes through a brief stretch virtually in the backyards of some homes in the residential area of **Mexico Farms;** sometimes the trail becomes a single track. The origin of the name Mexico Farms has never been convincingly explained; land records for the area indicate that the name predates even the Mexican-American War.

An airport was built in this area (Mexico Farms Landing Fields). The larger Cumberland Municipal Airport lies along Knobly Mountain, across the river in West Virginia.

**MILE 178.4**

The towpath crosses Canal Road.

**MILE 178.9**

The towpath crosses Brehm Road.

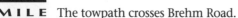

The canal company's 1857 "Rates of Toll" lists this as the location for **Kirkendall's Ferry.**

MILE
**179**

The canal rejoins the Potomac, leaving the residential area.

MILE
**179.3**

**Evitts Creek Campsite** is named for the creek and aqueduct just upstream. On the other side of the canal, you can see the trains in the Cumberland yards. The yards were originally built by the B&O Railroad and are now part of the CSX system.

MILE
**180**

**Evitts Creek Aqueduct.** The last of the 11 canal aqueducts, this single-arch structure was built between 1837 and 1850 of stone quarried along Evitts Creek and brought to the site by a 1.5-mile wooden railroad. The cement was supplied by Lynn's Mill in Cumberland, though recourse may have been had to the Round Top Mill in times of shortage. An 1839 canal company report described the stone as "a compact limestone or rather marble in some parts densely filled with marine shells . . . when polished, [it] presents a very interesting object, and is admirably adopted for ornamental work." Unfortunately, the contractor had to suspend work in 1841, just short of completion, because the canal company could no longer pay him. Finished in the late 1840s, the aqueduct was put into service when the upper section was finally watered in 1850.

MILE
**180.7**

The parapet on the berm side of the aqueduct is crumbling and boarded up. The stonework is in good condition, but reinforced by steel beams.

Several historic incidents have been recorded along Evitts Creek. In colonial days, Frazier's Plantation lay just upstream; Jane Frazier was carried west by Indians in 1755, escaping and making her way back a year later. Union forces turned back Confederate cavalry in the battle at Folck's Mill in August 1864, at the conclusion of the raid that burned Chambersburg, Pennsylvania. From here the Confederates retreated to Oldtown and crossed the river after another skirmish.

**MILE**

**181.2**

The canal runs along the CSX railroad yards (originally B&O Railroad track).

**MILE**
**181.7**

The canal company's 1857 "Rates of Toll" lists this as the location for ***Thistle's Ferry.***

**MILE**

**181.8**

The towpath passes the Cumberland Waste Water Treatment Plant and the adjacent Riverside Recreation Park. Candoc Lane runs along the berm side of the canal as it passes some of the residential backstreets of Cumberland. *Candoc* stood for the *"C and O Canal"* and was emblazoned on the canal company's pay boat.

**MILE**

**182.2**

A trestle for the Western Maryland Railroad crosses overhead as it cuts straight across this riverbend.

**MILE**
**82.6**

***Ford Avenue*** crosses the canal. The Ford Avenue bridge is near a crossing on the Potomac once known as ***Wileys Ford.*** The bridges over the canal and the Potomac are relatively recent improvements. After capturing Union generals George Crook and Benjamin Kelley on the night of February 21, 1865, McNeill and his partisan rangers rode down the towpath to the ford, where they crossed back into West Virginia.

**MILE**
**182.9**

Another trestle for the Western Maryland Railroad as it crosses back into West Virginia (*see* mile 182.2). The Western Maryland had to avoid the B&O railroad yards along the Maryland side of the Potomac, so the company dug a tunnel through Knobly Mountain and built its line along the Potomac on the western side of the mountain.

**MILE**
**83.4**

Referred to on various surveys as a "stop lock" or a "stop gate," this structure is different from any other because it has a middle pier. The surveys indicate that the far channel was to be closed off as a stop gate or waste weir, while water continued to flow through the channel nearer to the towpath. Note that the nearer passageway has lock pockets for miter gates—a unique feature for a stop lock.

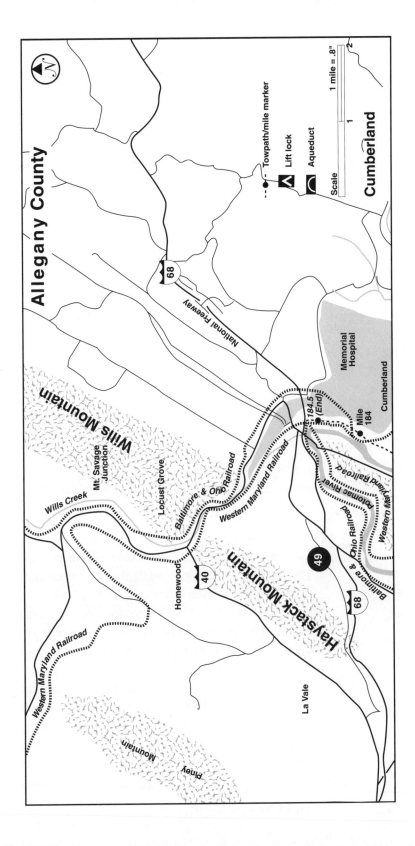

Allegany County

Wills Mountain

Haystack Mountain

Piney Mountain

Western Maryland Railroad

Wills Creek

Mt. Savage Junction

Locust Grove

Baltimore & Ohio Railroad

Western Maryland Railroad

Homewood

La Vale

Potomac River

Baltimore & Ohio Railroad

Western Maryland Railroad

National Freeway

Memorial Hospital

Cumberland

184.5 (End)

Mile 184

68

40

49

68

Scale

Towpath/mile marker
Lift lock
Aqueduct

1 mile = .8"

Cumberland

The building for the **Queen City Glassworks** (previously the Warren Glass Works) was located just beyond the berm side of the canal. Glassmaking became a significant industry in Cumberland in the 1880s, when the Warren Glass Works were founded at this location and the Cumberland Glass Works were founded at the end of North Mechanic Street. The source of the glass sand for these operations was Berkeley Springs, West Virginia (opposite Hancock, mile 124.7), and both glassworks were conveniently located adjacent to the canal and railroad. Unfortunately, the glassworks were vulnerable to frequent fires and a shortage of skilled artisans, so this industry tapered off after the early 1920s.

 A tall concrete spillway runs along the river side of the towpath; on turn-of-the-century maps, the original structure was marked as a combination "waste weir/overflow."

 This towpath rises to a higher level; downtown Cumberland is now visible in the distance, with its distinctive steeples and the Narrows beyond. The Potomac runs through a broad meadow along the canal. Looking downstream from here, you can see how the canal and river have been running parallel to Knobly Mountain since Wileys Ford (mile 182.6).

MILE 184 As the canal approached downtown Cumberland, it divided into two elongated basins. **Shrivers Basin** angled inland from this spot, while the Main Basin continued along the river. Many of the canal boats were built at Frederick Mertens's drydocks, on the canal berm just before Shrivers Basin. At the entrance to the basin, the Consolidation Coal Company built elevated tracks across the wharves, so that trains coming down from the mines could drop the coal directly into the holds of the canal boats. Clustered around the basin was a shantytown, mostly two-story wooden buildings with flat roofs, described by contemporaries as having a "western" look. A warren of saloons, pool parlors, and houses of even lesser repute provided suitable diversion

for canal workers wearied by their labors or simply whiling away the winter season.

***Canal Terminus.*** The towpath becomes a small path down the embankment into what was once the Main Basin. Twin locks stood here, side by side, just above Dam no. 8. One lock let water into the basins; the other let boats pass back and forth from the basin to the river. At one time, there was also a Little Basin that extended up to the site of the present railroad station, where the company had its own boatyard. But the Western Maryland built its station in 1913 and later placed its track over the canal locks. In 1957 Dam no. 8 was removed and the embankment around the locks was raised as part of a flood control project.

**M I L E**
**184.5**

The original vista has been completely obscured over the years by newer construction. Today it's a tangled crossroads: the Potomac pours over a spillway at the fork in the river, a decaying blackened bridge brings the Western Maryland Railroad into town from West Virginia, the highway bridge for Interstate 68 passes high overhead, and historic old Wills Creek is a con-crete-lined channel.

If you could turn the clock back to the 1750s, the scene would have been much simpler. After a long trip on packhorse trails through western Virginia and Maryland, you would finally have come to the river fork, with the notch in the mountain range ahead pointing

Coal was loaded directly into the canal boats from railroad cars on the tracks that ran across the mouth of Shrivers Basin in Cumberland. *Photo courtesy National Park Service.*

to the west and the Ohio country. At first there was nothing but a storehouse down by the creek, and then a fort perched up on the hill, surrounded by a timber palisade. As travelers began passing through to the Ohio country, there came inns and stores and houses and churches, and then a National Road. Finally, the Baltimore and Ohio Railroad arrived, soon to be followed by the canal.

The towpath comes to an end here, merging with a pedestrian path that leads down from the embankment to the plaza at the foot of the Western Maryland Railroad Station. The turn of the century has seen the beginning of a significant facelift for the canal terminus. In addition to a riverfront park following the canal downstream, plans call for rewatering the last 2 miles (beginning just below Ford Avenue at mile 182.6).

Across the basin, you'll see a full-size replica of a canal boat, recently moved up from the Lock 75 area along with the Cumberland Canal Days celebration (every May). While it gives a better idea of the design of a canal boat than the passenger barges at Georgetown and Great Falls, it's a far cry from the real thing. Sadly, not one of the hundreds of canal-era boats has survived intact, though the parts of several boats were found in this basin during archeological digs in the spring of 1999 and 2000.

## Cumberland, Maryland

For those traveling the towpath north, there is no more welcome and stirring sight than the distinctive spires of Cumberland rising in the distance at the foot of Haystack Mountain. Behind the town you can see the Narrows, where Wills Creek slips between Haystack and Wills Mountains, a notch in the mountains that leads still further to the west. The Potomac changes its course here and turns southwest, leaving travelers to make their way over the rest of the mountain ranges as best they can.

In 1750 the Ohio Company ordered the construction of a storehouse here at Wills Creek, which was named for an Indian chief who lived on the nearby mountain ridge. What had been envisioned as a way station for the Ohio Valley trade was soon turned into a fort during the French and Indian War. The storehouse and fort were simply known as Wills Creek until the British forces arrived in 1755 and General Braddock renamed the fort in honor of that same duke of Cumberland who had provided his marching orders. The name didn't catch on right away with the colonials—George Washington continued to refer to "Will's Creek" for many years. The fort fell into disuse after the French and Indian War, but enjoyed a brief moment of glory when George Washington returned there in 1794 at the head of a peacetime army assembled to put down the Whiskey Rebellion along the western frontier.

While the military fort was no longer necessary, Cumberland, lying at the northwestern end of the passage carved by the Potomac, continued to be an important staging area for travel across the Applachians. In the early 1800s, the National Road was begun at Cumberland to cross the mountains to the Ohio Valley and points further west. The importance of the town's geographical placement was futher confirmed in 1842 by the arrival of the B&O Railroad, in 1850 by the C&O Canal, and by the Western Maryland Railroad in 1906. The coalfields in the mountains surrounding this transportation hub turned into the town's major industry. However, as the canal and railroad gave way to the modern highways of the twentieth century, Cumberland's location lost much of its commercial importance.

In its heyday, though, Cumberland was the second largest town in Maryland, after Baltimore, and called itself the Queen City. The downtown area, which is now filled in, was dominated by the turning basin for the canal, wharves, the boatyards that built the canal boats, and a variety of establishments catering to the canal workers, such as Aunt Susan's Rising Sun Saloon and Louise's Den of Iniquity. During the Civil War, Cumberland was garrisoned by Union soldiers and was threatened in August 1864 by Confederate raiders who were driven off in the battle of Folck's Mill just south of town. One of the most dramatic Confederate feats along the Potomac was a raid in February 1865 that kidnapped two Union generals from their hotels in Cumberland, as memorialized by a plaque at the corner of Baltimore Street and Queen City Drive.

While Louise's saloon is gone, there are still a tolerable number of ways to amuse oneself while staying in Cumberland. Stop by the Allegany County Visitor's Bureau in the basement of the Western Maryland train station for directions and literature about the area. The walking tour around the area of old Fort Cumberland takes about 45 minutes; there's a separate brochure for a tour of the Victorian houses downtown. The Allegany County Historical Society gives tours of the History House at 218 Washington Street (301-777-8678). From April to November you can take a ride on the Western Maryland Scenic Railroad to Frostburg and back (1-800-TRAIN-50).

### AMENITIES

Cumberland is the most accommodating town north of Shepherdstown. The Mall adjacent to the historic railroad station has a handful of eateries and, on the other side of the Mall, you'll even find a McDonald's. Accommodations range from the Holiday Inn downtown to the Inn at Walnut Bottom on the other side of Wills Creek. There's an excellent restaurant at the inn, but it's closed on Sundays.

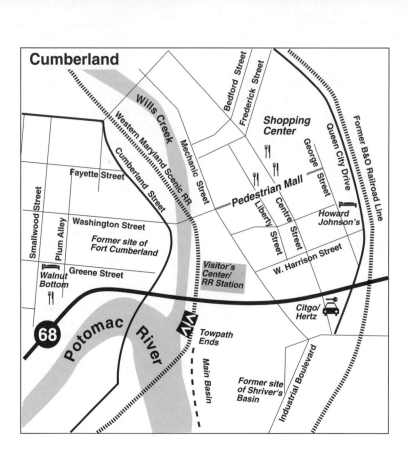

Cumberland

**MILE**
**184.6**

The old ***Western Maryland Railroad Station*** now houses visitor's centers for the National Park Service and Allegany County. The Western Maryland Railroad has not been entirely forgotten—a specialty shop offers railroad books and souvenirs, and the Western Maryland Scenic Railroad starts its run up to Frostburg from this station. The walking tour around the former site of Fort Cumberland begins just across from the station, on the other side of Wills Creek, and takes you by a restored log cabin that was purportedly used by George Washington during the French and Indian War. However, don't be misled by the historical marker— Washington received his first command before Fort Cumberland was built, and his frontier headquarters was in Winchester, Virginia.

Canal boats at Main Basin, with the spires of Cumberland looming in the background. *Photo courtesy National Park Service.*

## Further Routes West

The North Branch of the Potomac makes a sharp turn around Knobly Mountain here; its source lies 88 miles to the southwest at the Fairfax Stone. Travelers heading west generally left the river at this point and followed the trails through the Appalachians laid out by Cresap, Gist, and Nemacolin, and later enlarged by Washington and Braddock.

The original surveys for the canal in the 1820s gave a choice of two routes for the canal to cross the Appalachians, either continuing another 20 miles down the Potomac and then following the Savage River up into the mountains, or leaving the Potomac and following Wills Creek from here. (These were roughly the same options that Washington had weighed back in 1784 for the Patowmack Company.) A much more detailed later survey shows that the Wills Creek route was the more likely candidate in the 1870s. This would have taken the canal to a 4-mile summit tunnel through the eastern divide. On the other side of the divide, the canal would have followed Flaugherty Creek down to Casselman River, leading to the Youghiogheny, the Monongahela, and eventually the mighty Ohio. This is roughly the route the B&O Railroad used to build its branch line up to Pittsburgh.

But now there's another way to the west, following the Western Maryland Railroad and other railroads through the mountains to the Ohiopyle State Park and on to Pittsburgh. Except for the Scenic Railroad line to Frostburg, most of this track is abandoned and is being converted into a rail-trail. If plans to build the Maryland portion of the trail are carried out, we may be able to bike or hike all the way from Georgetown to Pittsburgh in a few years— a prospect which I'm sure would have made George Washington very happy.

# Resources

For the most up-to-date listings,
including address and phone number changes,
visit the **River & Canal Web Site** at:

www.press.jhu.edu/press/books/potomac-canal.html

## Canal Resources

**Recreation and Other
Associations**

**Appalachian Trail Headquarters**
P.O. Box 807
Harpers Ferry, WV 25425
(304) 535-6331

**New Columbia Audubon Society**
P.O. Box 15346
Washington, DC 20003
(202) 543-7433

**C&O Canal Association**
P.O. Box 366
Glen Echo, MD 20812

**Canoe Cruiser's Association**
4515 Evansdale Road
Dale City, VA 22193
(301) 656-2586

**Parks and History Association**
126 Raleigh Street, SE
Washington, DC 20032
(202) 472-3083

**Potomac Appalachian Trail Club**
118 Park Street, SE
Vienna, VA 22180
(703) 242-0315

**The Potomac Conservancy**
P.O. Box 2288
Merrifield, VA 22116
(703) 642-9880
web site: www.canal.com
e-mail: info@potomac.org

**Potomac Pedalers Touring Club**
6729 Curran Street
McLean, VA 22101
(202) 363-TOUR

**Ski Club of Washington DC**
5309 Lee Highway
Arlington, VA 22207
(703) 532-7776
(703) 536-TAPE

*+ Brunswick*

## Bicycle Tours and Bike Shops

**Allegany Adventures, Inc.**
14419 National Highway
LaVale, MD 21502
(301) 729-9708

**Bicycle Exchange/Georgetown**
3411 M Street, NW
Washington, DC 20007
(202) 337-8600

**Big Wheel Bikes**
1034 33rd Street, NW
Washington, DC 20007
(202) 337-0254

**Catoctin Bike Tours**
(800) BIKE CNO
(800) 868-7266

**C&O Bicycle**
9 S Pennsylvania Avenue
Hancock, MD 21750
1-800-678-BIKE

**Cycles and Things**
165 N Centre Street
Cumberland, MD 21502
(301) 722-5496

## C&O National Park & Adjacent Parks (History and Natural History Walks)

**Chesapeake and Ohio Canal National Historical Park**
P.O. Box 4
Sharpsburg, MD 21782
(301) 739-4200

**C&O Canal/Georgetown Visitor's Center**
(202) 653-5844 V/TDD

**C&O Canal/Great Falls Visitor's Center**
(301) 299-3613 V/TDD

**C&O Canal/Williamsport Visitor's Center**
(301) 582-0813

**C&O Canal/Hancock Visitor's Center**
(301) 678-5473 V/TDD

**C&O Canal/Cumberland Visitor's Center**
(Closed Mondays)
(301) 722-8226 V/TDD

**Antietam National Battlefield**
Box 158
Sharpsburg, MD 21782
(301) 432-5124

**Fort Frederick State Park**
(301) 842-2155

**Green Ridge State Forest**
Star Route, Box 50, Forest Court
Flintstone, MD 21530
(301) 478-3124

**Harpers Ferry National Historical Park**
Box 65
Harpers Ferry, WV 25425
(304) 535-6298

**Seneca Creek State Park**
(301) 924-2127

## *Kiosk* Newsletter

**Office of Public Affairs**
National Park Service
1100 Ohio Drive, SW
Washington, DC 20242

## Canoeing, Rafting, and Other Water Activities

**National Weather Service— Potomac River Levels**
(703) 260-0305

MILE 0 **Thompson's Boat Center**
(202) 333-9543

MILE 3 **Fletcher's Boathouse**
(202) 244-0461

MILE 7 **Potomac Outdoors**
(301) 515-7337
(877) KAYAKH20

MILE 16 **Swains Lock**
(301) 299-9006

MILE 22 **Outerquest**
(301) 258-1914
(800) 51-KAYAK

MILE 35 **Whites Ferry**
(301) 349-5200
MILE 59 **River and Trail
Outfitters/Sandy Hook**
(301) 834-9950
MILE 61 **River Riders**
(304) 535-2663
**Blue Ridge Outfitters**
(304) 725-3444
MILE 125 **Hancock Outfitters**
(301) 678-5050
MILE 140 **Bill's Boats/
Orleans Grocery**
(301) 478-2701
**Little Orleans
Campground**
(301) 478-2325

## Visitor's Information

**Frederick County, Maryland**
(800) 999-3613
**Washington County, Maryland**
(800) 228-STAY
**Allegany County, Maryland**
(301) 777-5905
**Western Maryland Gift Shop
(Railroad)**
(301) 724-1187
**Loudon County, Virginia**
(703) 771-2170
(800) 752-6118
**Jefferson County, West Virginia
(Harpers Ferry)**
(304) 535-2627
(800) 848-8687

# Transportation

*Since most bicyclists don't have the luxury of taking 7–8 days for a roundtrip ride on the canal, they've had to be quite resourceful in getting transportation to one end of the line or the other. Fortunately, there are more options than you think.*

*A train ride along the old B&O route has always been an intriguing way to see the Potomac Valley, and according to the latest information Amtrak now allows bikes; there is limited baggage space, though, so be sure to reserve tie-down space even if you don't need passenger reservations. The schedule is limited—an early-afternoon train to DC and a late-afternoon train to Cumberland.*

**Amtrak-Capitol Limited**
Union Station, DC to Cumberland, MD
(800) USA-RAIL
(800) 872-7245

*Even with the one-way drop-off charge, a rental car is an affordable option if the price is split between multiple riders. It's a very comfortable way to travel, with trunk space for the bikes being the main logistical concern.*

**Hertz Car Rental**
(800) 654-3131

**Hertz—Cumberland, MD**
(at the Citgo Station)
(301) 722-2522

**Hertz—Washington, DC**
901 11th Street, NW
(202) 628-6174

*Though it's not quite as convenient as a car and not quite as romantic as the train, some bike riders like to put their two-wheeler in a cardboard box and stow it in the cargo hold of a bus for the trip to or from Cumberland.*

**Greyhound**
DC to Hagerstown
to Cumberland
*(extra fee for bikes and they must be boxed)*
(800) 231-2222

**Greyhound Station**
Washington, DC
(202) 289-5120

**Greyhound Station**
Cumberland, MD
(301) 722-6226

# Hotels, Motels, and Inns

*These facilities are within 2 miles of the towpath unless otherwise specified.*

*The motor inns are typically your cheapest option, running from $22 to $50. A good B&B can run anywhere from $50 to $100. If you are having trouble finding a room, do not be afraid to ask the innkeeper if he or she knows of any alternatives—innkeepers are usually glad to help.*

**MILE 0 Georgetown/Rosslyn**
*Georgetown is a pricey venue, so you may want to consider lower cost options that are close to the Rock Creek bike trail (Windsor Park, Woodley Park, Doyle Normandy Inn). Rosslyn, on the other side of Key Bridge, is also a convenient alternative. For the truly budget minded, there's always the American Youth Hostel, which is about a mile away from the canal. If you're bringing bicycles, be sure to check on the policy for storing bikes—space is limited at many of these locations.*

**American Youth Hostel**
733 15th Street, NW
Washington, DC
(202) 783-6161

**Doyle Normandy Inn**
2118 Wyoming Avenue, NW
Washington, DC
(202) 483-1350
(800) 424-3729

**Windsor Park Hotel**
2116 Kalorama Road
Washington, DC
(202) 483-7700
(800) 424-3729

**Woodley Park Hotel**
2647 Woodley Road
Washington, DC
(202) 667-0218

**Quality Inn Iwo Jima**
1501 Arlington Boulevard
Rosslyn, VA
(703) 524-5000

**Key Bridge Marriott**
1401 North Lee Highway
Rosslyn, VA
(703) 524-6400

**Latham Hotel**
3000 M Street, NW
Washington, DC 20007
(202) 726-5000
(800) 528-4261

**Georgetown Dutch Inn**
1075 Thomas Jefferson Street, NW
Washington, DC 20007
(202) 337-0900

**Four Seasons Hotel**
2800 Pennsylvania Avenue, NW
Washington, DC 20007
(202) 342-0444
(800) 332-3442

## MILE 35 Leesburg, Virginia

*Leesburg is actually on the other side of the Potomac, and about a 5-mile ride, but it may come in handy if you want to stop nearer to Georgetown or plan to combine a canal ride with the W&OD trail (Alexandria to Purcellville via Leesburg). Cross at Whites Ferry and take a left on Route 15 to Leesburg—be careful on the brief stretch with only a gravel shoulder, or take advantage of the Norris House's shuttle service.*

**Days Inn**
721 East Market Street
(703) 777-6622

**Norris House Inn**
108 Loudoun Street, SW
(703) 777-1806

**Laurel Brigade Inn**
20 West Market Street
(703) 777-1010

## MILE 42.2 Barnesville/Boyd

*About 5 miles from the mouth of the Monocacy; check on availability of a shuttle.*

**Pleasant Springs B&B**
16112 Barnesville Road
Boyd, MD
(301) 972-3452

## MILE 55 Brunswick

*The Lockkeeper's Inn is a relatively new (November 1999) bed and breakfast very convenient to the canal in Brunswick. The Motel Sleepers caters to CSX and MARC employees; take Route 17 up the hill to a right turn on Souder Road (about two miles in all).*

**Lockkeeper's Inn**
11 South Maryland Avenue
Brunswick, MD 21716
(301) 834-6026

**Motel Sleepers & Tracks Inn**
620 Souder Road
(301) 834-9151

## MILE 55 Lovettsville, Virginia

*Approximately 4–5 miles from the C&O Canal, via the Route 17 bridge at Brunswick.*

**Victorian Farm B&B**
(540) 822-9120

**Georges Mill Inn**
11867 Georges Mill Road
Lovettsville, VA 20180
(540) 822-5224

## MILE 59 Sandy Hook

*Just beyond the Route 340 highway bridge, cross over to Harpers Ferry Road and turn right up a steep hill. The Youth Hostel will be on your right near the top of the hill. A quarter mile beyond the hostel, take a left on Keep Tryst Road to get to the Hillside Motel. Both places are inexpensive but do not usually accept advance reservations.*

**Harpers Ferry Youth Hostel**
Sandy Hook Road
(301) 834-7652

**Hillside Motel**
19105 Keep Tryst Road
(301) 834-8144

## MILE 60 Harpers Ferry, West Virginia

*If you're biking, be prepared to carry your bike up the spiral stairs to the pedestrian bridge to cross the river. Also be prepared to follow High Street up a steep hill. The Cliffside Inn is much further than the others but still within reasonable biking distance, and may have room on crowded fall weekends.*

**The Angler's Inn**
867 Washington Street
(304) 535-1239

**Briscoe House B&B**
828 Washington Street
(304) 535-2416

**Jackson Rose B&B**
1141 Washington Street
(304) 535-1528

**The Last Resort**
280 Clay Street
(304) 535-2812

**Hilltop House Hotel**
Ridge Street
(304) 535-2132

**Comfort Inn**
Route 340 and Union Street
(304) 535-6391
(800) 221-2222

**Between the Rivers B&B**
Ridge Street
(304) 535-2768

**Fillmore Street B&B**
Fillmore Street
(304) 535-2619
(301) 377-0070

**Ranson-Armory House B&B**
Washington Street
(304) 535-2142

**Harpers Ferry Guest House**
Washington Street
(304) 535-6955

**Cliffside Motor Inn**
Route 340
(304) 535-6302

**MILE 72 Shepherdstown, West Virginia**

*The accommodations in this quaint little town are charming but usually fairly expensive. The Bavarian Inn has the best river view.*

**The Bavarian Inn and Lodge**
Route 1, Box 30
(304) 876-2551

**The Little Inn**
(at Yellow Bank Restaurant)
(304) 876-2208

**Thomas Shepherd Inn**
Corner of German and
Duke Streets
(304) 876-3715

**Mecklenburg Inn**
(304) 876-2126

**MILE 72 Sharpsburg**

*These inns are about 4 miles from the towpath, but they're convenient if you want to take a detour to see the battlefield.*

**Inn at Antietam**
220 East Main Street
Sharpsburg, MD
(301) 432-6601

**Piper House**
Antietam National Battlefield
(301) 797-1862

**Jacob Rohrbach Inn**
138 West Main Street
(301) 432-5079

**MILE 80 Taylors Landing/ Antietam**

*About a mile from Taylors Landing on the towpath, and a mile from the Antietam Battlefield, this charming little B&B has its own herd of llamas and offers weekend hikes on the canal with the llamas carrying the provisions.*

**Ground Squirrel Holler B&B**
6736 Sharpsburg Pike
(301) 432-8288

**MILE 99 Williamsport**

*Situated on a hill about a mile from the canal, the management is quite used to cyclists and will usually try to provide a ground-floor room.*

**Red Roof Inn**
310 East Potomac Street
(301) 582-3500
(800) 733-7663

**MILE 107 Clear Spring**

*Approximately 4–5 miles from Dam no. 5 on the canal.*

**Breezee Hill Farm B&B**
(301) 842-2608

**Wildflowers B&B**
Cohill Road
(301) 842-1191

**MILE 124 Hancock**

**Econo Lodge**
118 Limestone Road
(301) 678-6101
(800) 553-2666

**Hancock Motel**
2 Blue Hill
Route 522
(301) 678-6108

**Cohill Manor**
5102 Western Pike
(301) 678-7573

**MILE 141 Little Orleans**
*There's nothing much right on the canal in this stretch, unless you're a member of the Potomac Appalachian Trail Club. But there are two places within convenient driving distance that will provide shuttle service. The Town Hill is 7 miles away with a spectacular view at 1,500 feet. Buck Valley Ranch is 10 miles from the C&O.*

**Town Hill Hotel**
(301) 478-2794

**Buck Valley Ranch**
Route 2, Box 1170
Warfordsburg, PA 17267-9667
(301) 678-5782
(800) 294-3759

**MILE 156 Paw Paw, West Virginia**
*This modest B&B in a private home is located on the West Virginia side of the Potomac, within 1 mile of the towpath.*

**Paw Paw Patch B&B**
Winchester Street
(304) 947-7496

**MILE 185 Cumberland**
*The Inn at Walnut Bottom is a professionally managed B&B with an excellent restaurant downstairs. The Holiday Inn is at the end of the downtown mall.*

**Holiday Inn/Downtown**
South George Street
(301) 724-8800
(800) 465-4329

**Inn at Walnut Bottom**
120 Greene Street
(301) 777-0003
(800) 286-9718

# Campsites and Stores

*Camping at the hiker-biker campsites is free, but the National Park Service now charges fees for the use of the drive-in campsites along the canal (Antietam, McCoys Ferry, Fifteenmile Creek, Paw Paw, and Spring Gap).*

**MILE 11 Marsden Tract**
*(camping by permit)*

**MILE 14 Great Falls**
*(seasonal concessions)*

**MILE 17 Swains Lock Campsite**
*(seasonal concessions)*

**MILE 26 Horsepen Branch Campsite**

**MILE 30 Chisel Branch Campsite**

**MILE 34 Turtle Run Campsite**

**MILE 35 Whites Ferry**
*(seasonal concessions)*

**MILE 38 Marble Quarry Campsite**

**MILE 42 Indian Flats Campsite**

**MILE 47 Calico Rocks Campsite**

**MILE 48 Point of Rocks**
*(country stores)*

MILE 50 **Bald Eagle Island Campsite**

MILE 54 **Brunswick Campground**

MILE 55 **Brunswick** (diner, small stores)

MILE 59 **Sandy Hook** (country store)

MILE 60 **Harpers Ferry** (cafes in lower town; restaurant and convenience stores in Bolivar)

MILE 62 **Huckleberry Hill Campsite**

MILE 69 **Antietam Creek Campsite** (drive-in)

MILE 72 **Shepherdstown** (grocery store, restaurants, laundromat)

MILE 75 **Killiansburg Cave Campsite**

MILE 81 **Taylors Landing** (small store with snacks, fishing gear, and bike rentals)

MILE 82 **Big Woods Campsite**

MILE 90 **Opequon Junction Campsite**

MILE 95 **Cumberland Valley Campsite**

MILE 99 **Williamsport** (convenience store, restaurants, bike shop)

MILE 101 **Jordan Junction Campsite**

MILE 109 **North Mountain Campsite**

MILE 110 **McCoys Ferry Campsite** (drive-in)

MILE 112 **Fort Frederick** (camping and snacks)

MILE 116 **Licking Creek Campsite**

MILE 120 **Little Pool Campsite**

MILE 124 **Hancock** (convenience store, restaurants, hardware store)

MILE 126 **White Rock Campsite**

MILE 130 **Leopards Mill Campsite**

MILE 133 **Cacapon Junction Campsite**

MILE 139 **Indigo Neck Campsite**

MILE 140 **Little Orleans** (country store, bar)

MILE 140 **Fifteenmile Creek Campsite** (drive-in)

MILE 144 **Devils Alley Campsite**

MILE 149 **Stickpile Hill Campsite**

MILE 154 **Sorrel Ridge Campsite**

MILE 156 **Paw Paw** (country store, convenience store, diner)

MILE 156 **Purslane Run Campsite**

MILE 162 **Town Creek Campsite**

MILE 164 **Potomac Forks Campsite**

MILE 166 **Oldtown** (country store)

MILE 169 **Pigmans Ferry Campsite**

MILE 173 **Spring Gap Campsite** (drive-in)

MILE 175 **Irons Mountain Campsite**

MILE 180 **Evitts Creek Campsite**

MILE 184 **Cumberland** (stores, restaurants)

# Sources and Suggested Further Reading

Material on the frontier in this book draws heavily from Washington's correspondence and diaries, J. Kenneth Bailey's study of the Ohio Company and his biography of Thomas Cresap, Governor Sharpe's correspondence, and various local histories of towns and forts.

The account of the Patowmack Company is based on Cora Bacon-Foster's detailed review of the company's meetings and transactions, *Early Chapters in the Development of the Patomac Route to the West*. The construction and operation of the C&O Canal is thoroughly covered in Walter Sanderlin's book, *The Great National Project* (still available in reprint from AMS Press in New York). I have also used various historical and structural reports kept at the Park headquarters near Sharpsburg, as well as canal company records, letters, and reports from the extensive collection at the National Archives. Peter Way's study *Common Labour* proved to be a fruitful analysis of worker unrest on the C&O and other American canals.

Material on the Civil War is taken from the *Official Records of the Union and Confederate Armies*, as well as first-person accounts in the *Confederate Veteran* and autobiographies. A very thorough account of Colonel E. V. White's adventures is provided by Charles and Marian Waters Jacobs in two issues of the Montgomery County Historical Society newsletter (November 1978 and February 1979).

Information on power plants and water intakes along the canal was supplied by the U.S. Army Corps of Engineers, Potomac Edison, PEPCO, and municipal waterworks. Information on the origin and operation of historic furnaces, mills, and forts was largely gleaned from articles and unpublished studies by local historians such as Eugene Scheel, Gerald Sword, John Frye, and Michael D. Thompson. A monograph on *Cement Mills along the Potomac River* by Thomas Hahn and Emory Kemp was also extremely helpful (Institute for the History of Technology and Industrial Technology, West Virginia University).

For purposes of comparison with other transportation systems, I have principally relied on John Stover's *History of the Baltimore and Ohio Railroad,* Merritt Ierley's *Travelling the National Road,* and Ronald Shaw's *Canals for a Nation.* In 1991 the Park Service also issued a very helpful book by Barry Mackintosh on the years of federal ownership: *C&O Canal: The Making of a Park.*

Most of the works that I have relied on are of more interest to the researcher than to the general public. Fortunately, there are also several excellent articles and books that I can suggest if you want to read further into the history of the region. The best description of the Patowmack Canal can be found in the handsomely illustrated article by Wilbur Garrett in the *National Geographic* of June 1987 (available in reprint from the park bookshop at Great Falls, Virginia). Two works in particular convey the flavor of the frontier period. Dale Van Every's book, *Forth to the Wilderness,* is a highly readable account of the struggle for the Forks of the Ohio and Pontiac's Rebellion. *For King and Country,* by Thomas Lewis, is an evocative if sometimes hypercritical study of George Washington's learning experiences during the French and Indian War.

There are so many excellent books on the Civil War that it's difficult to know where to begin. The book that is most closely related to the history of the Potomac is *Gray Ghosts and Rebel Raiders* by Virgil Carrington Jones. The author gives a vivid picture of the life of the partisan rangers and their Union adversaries along the Potomac and covers many of the events described in this book. For a general overview of the war, one can hardly go wrong by picking up Shelby Foote's absorbing three-volume history, *The Civil War.*

Closer to the canal and river is Frederic Gutheim's *The Potomac,* an elegant and insightful account of the history of the region. The most comprehensive information on the structural details of the canal and some local lore is available in Thomas Hahn's *Towpath Guide.* As guidebooks go, Dave Gilbert's *Hiker's Guide to Harper's Ferry* gives a marvelously illustrated tour of the industry and history of that town. James Dilts's marvelous account of the building of the B&O Railroad, *The Great Road,* contains much useful information on the rivalry with the canal. Finally, *Charles Fenton Mercer and the Trial of National Conservatism* by Douglas R. Egerton provided many interesting details on the remarkable life of the canal company's founder and first president.

Since the first edition of the *Companion,* I've come across two other very useful sources that provide detailed information about places and events in Montgomery County and its Virginia neighbor, Loudoun County: Charles T. Jacobs's *Civil War Guide to Montgomery County,* and John T. Phillips's *Historian's Guide to Loudoun County, Virginia.*

If your curiosity has been sufficiently piqued, you might visit the historical society or historic reading room in your area. They not only have many out-of-print books, but usually have collections of published and unpublished articles on people and places of local interest. I deeply appreciate the assistance I have received at the Lloyd House (Alexandria Public Library), the Virginia Room (Fairfax County Public Library), the Western Maryland Room (Hagerstown Free Library), the Thomas Balch Library (Leesburg), the Appalachian Collection (Allegany Community College), the Peabody Room and the Washingtoniana Collection (Martin Luther King, Jr., Public Library, Washington, D.C.), the Maryland Historical Society (Baltimore), the Montgomery County Historical Society (Rockville), and the Frederick County Historical Society (Frederick). These libraries and historical societies provide an invaluable service to researchers and to the community at large.

# Emergency Information

## Contacts for Medical Emergencies and Crimes

For emergencies and crimes in the Washington metropolitan area, call the United States Park Police: (202) 619-7300.

For emergencies outside the Washington area, call 911 or the 24-hour hotline for the National Capitol Region Communication Center (NCRCC): (866) 677-6677. The Park Service encourages you to use the NCRCC Hotline to report resource crimes, such as vandalism and arson, fish and wildlife poaching, dumping and water pollution, plant and tree cutting or theft, looting of archeological and historic resources, and public use violations (illegal campsites, off-road vehicles, etc.).

While infrequent cases of snakebite (copperheads) and occasional bear sightings do occur, the wildlife along the canal is generally docile. The greatest hazard is the river itself. Particularly around the falls, be aware of the dangers of rapids, invisible hydraulics, and fallen trees or obstructions where a boater or swimmer could be pinned by the river current. Also, many usually benign areas of the river can become dangerous during cold weather or when the river is running above normal levels.

Cell phones do not always work in remote areas, so try to get to high ground to make a call. Despite the natural surroundings, you are usually never far from a road and some houses. Check the maps in this book to locate your closest access point.

The NCRCC Hotline also serves several other parks in the area, including the Antietam National Battlefield, Catoctin Mountain Park, Monocacy National Battlefield, and Harpers Ferry National Park.

## Other Contacts

For non-emergency injuries, here are the hospitals beyond the Blue Ridge: Above Paw Paw, the nearest hospitals are in Cumberland (Memorial Hospital, 301-723-4000, and Sacred Heart, 301-723-4200). Between Paw Paw and Hancock, contact the War Memorial Hospital in Berkeley, West Virginia, (304-258-1234). Between Williamsport and Harpers Ferry contact either Washington County Hospital (301-790-8000) or Western Maryland Center (301-791-4400).

For other non-emergency situations, it is helpful to know that the Maryland Natural Resources Police are responsible for most of the islands in the Potomac and many of the parks that border the canal: 1-800-628-9944.